Young People's Voices in Physical Education and Youth Sport

How do children and young people experience and understand sport and physical activity, and what value do they attach to physical education and physical activity? This important new book attempts to engage more directly than ever before with the experiences of young people by placing the voices of the young people themselves at the centre of the discussion. As the need to listen to young people becomes increasingly enshrined in public policy and political debate, this book illuminates our understanding of an important aspect of the everyday lives of many young people.

With contributions from leading researchers and educationalists from around the world, the book draws on a diverse range of methodological and theoretical perspectives to demonstrate how we can better understand the unique perspectives of young people, how teachers and coaches can respond to and engage with the voices of young people, and how young people can be afforded opportunities to shape their education and leisure experiences. The book presents a fascinating range of case studies from around the world, including the experiences of African-American girls and masculine sporting identities in Australia, and addresses both theoretical and policy debates. *Young People's Voices in Physical Education and Youth Sport* is essential reading for any serious student or professional with an interest in physical education, youth sport, sports development, sports coaching, physical activity and health, education or youth work.

Mary O'Sullivan is Professor of Physical Education and Youth Sport and Dean of Education and Health Sciences at the University of Limerick, Ireland.

Ann MacPhail is Senior Lecturer in the Department of Physical Education and Sport Sciences at the University of Limerick, Ireland.

D0522492

International studies in physical education and youth sport

Series Editor: Richard Bailey
University of Birmingham, UK

Routledge's *International Studies in Physical Education and Youth Sport* series aims to stimulate discussion on the theory and practice of school physical education, youth sport, childhood physical activity and well-being. By drawing on international perspectives, both in terms of the background of the contributors and the selection of the subject matter, the series seeks to make a distinctive contribution to our understanding of issues that continue to attract attention from policy makers, academics and practitioners.

Also available in this series:

Young People's Voices in Physical Education and Youth Sport

Edited by Mary O'Sullivan and Ann MacPhail

YORK ST. JOHN
COLLEGE LIBRARY

Routledge
Taylor & Francis Group

LONDON AND NEW YORK

First published 2010
by Routledge
2 Park Square, Milton Park, Abingdon, Oxon OX14 4RN

Simultaneously published in the USA and Canada
by Routledge
270 Madison Avenue, New York, NY 10016

*Routledge is an imprint of the Taylor & Francis Group,
an informa business*

© 2010 selection and editorial material, Mary O'Sullivan and
Ann MacPhail; individual chapters, the contributors

Typeset in Times New Roman by Swales & Willis Ltd, Exeter, Devon
Printed and bound in Great Britain by CPI Antony Rowe,
Chippenham, Wiltshire

All rights reserved. No part of this book may be reprinted or
reproduced or utilized in any form or by any electronic,
mechanical, or other means, now known or hereafter
invented, including photocopying and recording, or in any
information storage or retrieval system, without permission in
writing from the publishers.

British Library Cataloguing in Publication Data
A catalogue record for this book is available from the British Library

Library of Congress Cataloging-in-Publication Data
Young people's voices in physical education and youth sport / edited by
Mary O'Sullivan and Ann Macphail. — 1st ed.
    p. cm.
    1. Physical education for children—Social aspects.
    2. Sports for children—Social aspects.
    I. O'Sullivan, Mary, 1955- II. Macphail, Ann.
    GV342.27.Y68 2010
    796.083—dc22
    2009050199

ISBN10: 0–415–48744–7 (hbk)
ISBN10: 0–415–48745–5 (pbk)
ISBN10: 0–203–88189–3 (ebk)

ISBN13: 978–0–415–48744–3 (hbk)
ISBN13: 978–0–415–48745–0 (pbk)
ISBN13: 978–0–203–88189–7 (ebk)

Contents

List of figures

Notes on contributors

Kathleen Armour is Professor of Education and Sport in the School of Education at Birmingham University, UK. Formerly, she held a Chair in the School of Sport, Exercise and Health Sciences at Loughborough University. Kathleen's main research interests are career-long professional learning for teachers and coaches, and its impact on young people's learning in physical education and sport.

Lisette Burrows is Associate Professor at the University of Otago's School of Physical Education in New Zealand. She draws on poststructural theoretical resources to examine how health imperatives are being recontextualized in and around homes and schools in the context of an avowed obesity 'epidemic'. She is also interested in the meanings children advance about their own and others' health and fitness, and, more generally, in the place and meaning of physical culture in the lives of young people. All of her work is informed by a recognition that physical and health education are normalized practices that derive from developmental, racialized, gendered and classed assumptions that do not necessarily serve all well.

David Carless, PhD, is Senior Research Fellow at Leeds Metropolitan University, UK. His research focuses on using a variety of narrative and arts-based approaches to explore identity, mental health and psychological well-being in and through physical activity and sport. His work has been published in journals such as *Qualitative Research in Psychology*, *Reflective Practice*, *Psychology of Sport and Exercise*, *International Journal of Men's Health*, *Qualitative Research in Sport and Exercise* and *Qualitative Inquiry*. He is co-author of *Physical Activity and Sport for Mental Health* (Wiley-Blackwell), which explores, through a narrative approach, the sport and exercise experiences of people with mental health problems.

Donetta Cothran received her PhD from the University of Maryland in 1996. She then joined the Department of Kinesiology at Indiana University, USA, where she lived happily ever after. Since her own student teaching days she has been intrigued by the questions: 'What in the world were they [students] thinking?' and the related 'Why did they do that?' Her research and practice focus on answering those questions for K-12 students, pre-service teachers and in-service teachers. Dr Cothran is the former co-editor of *Physical Activity Today* and serves on the editorial board of the *Journal of Teaching in Physical Education*. When not writing book chapters she enjoys travelling, gardening and the great outdoors.

Rebecca Duncombe has worked as a research associate within the Institute of Youth Sport at Loughborough University, UK, since March 2005. During this time, she has been responsible for the monitoring and evaluation of a number of projects, including two that use sport and physical activity as a 'vehicle' for re-engaging disaffected youth (BSkyB/YST Living for Sport and Deutsche Bank Moving Generations). Rebecca has also worked on a project that aims to facilitate high-quality teaching and learning in PE at a secondary school in the Midlands, UK. Prior to joining the university, Rebecca was employed as a primary school teacher where she was responsible for coordinating PE within the school.

Eimear Enright is an Irish Research Council for the Humanities and Social Sciences (IRCHSS) scholar and PhD student with the PE-PAYS Research Centre at the University of Limerick, Ireland. Her research interests include student voice and curricular innovation in physical education, youth sport and physical activity, gender, social class and physical education, and participatory methodologies.

Christopher Hickey is Associate Professor and Deputy Head in the School of Education at Deakin University, Australia. He has a strong research interest in the changing nature of youth experiences at the start of the twenty-first century, and the ways in which these experiences are governed by the self and others. Dr Hickey has undertaken extensive research around the behaviours and rationalizations of young males as members of peer groups, focusing on the links between identity formation and the place of sport, physical education and the media.

Jessica Lee is Lecturer in physical activity and health at Loughborough University, UK. Her main research interests lie in the sociocultural understandings of young people's engagements with physical activity and the broader notion of physical culture. Jessica conducted the research reported on in her chapter during her PhD candidacy at the University of Queensland, Australia.

Jonathan Long is Professor at the Carnegie Research Institute at Leeds Metropolitan University, UK. Apart from teaching on leisure and sport courses, he has been conducting research on behalf of external clients for over 30 years. His primary research interests are with issues of social justice and social change, which have resulted in him directing a suite of projects on the nature and extent of racism in sport, and also examining policy issues around social capital and social inclusion. He recently published a text on research methods and has been

on the editorial boards of several journals, most recently working with colleagues at Leeds Met and abroad to launch a policy journal through Routledge.

Ann MacPhail is Senior Lecturer in the Department of Physical Education and
Sport Sciences at the University of Limerick, Ireland. Ann's main teaching and
research interests revolve around physical education teacher education, young
people in sport, curriculum development in physical education, teaching, learning and assessment issues within school physical education, methodological
issues in working with young people, and ethnography.

Sarah Meegan is Lecturer in adapted physical activity and inclusive physical education with the School of Health and Human Performance, Dublin City
University, Ireland. Her research interests lie in physical activity access and promotion for people with disabilities and physical education provision for children
with disabilities. Sarah played a key role in setting up the first adapted physical
activity centre in Ireland, which provides physical activity programmes for people with disabilities.

Kimberly L. Oliver is Associate Professor in the Department of Human
Performance, Dance and Recreation at New Mexico State University, USA. She
is the director of the Physical Education Teacher Education Program and
teaches courses in PE pedagogy. Her line of inquiry focuses on helping adolescent girls learn to explore, critique and transform personal and cultural barriers
that limit their health and physical activity opportunities. She has one published
book with Peter Lang, *Bodily Knowledge: Learning about Equity and Justice
with Adolescent Girls*, and has published widely in the field of physical education and education in general.

Mary O'Sullivan is Professor of Physical Education and Youth Sport and current
Dean of the Faculty of Education and Health Sciences at the University of
Limerick, Ireland. She is also a Fellow of the American Academy of
Kinesiology and Physical Education (AAKPE). Mary's research interests are
teacher education and teacher professional development, and she is currently
working with the National Council for Curriculum and Assessment on the
national physical education curriculum for senior cycle physical education in
Ireland.

Clive C. Pope is Senior Lecturer and Chairperson in the Department of Sport and
Leisure Studies at the University of Waikato, New Zealand. Clive's teaching
focus is on sport pedagogy, particularly sport and young people at the under-
graduate and graduate level, and aspects of instruction in sport and leisure set-
tings. He has presented and published in England, North America, Europe and
Australia, and has given several invited keynote presentations in Aotearoa New
Zealand. Recently he was invited to present the 4th Lord Porritt Memorial
Lecture, and in 2006 presented the prestigious Philip Smithells Memorial
Lecture at International Council for Health, Physical Education and Recreation
(ICHPER) in Wellington. His research interests centre on sport and youth, youth

culture, sport and education and exploring the sport experience. Clive is interested in the promotion and development of qualitative research as a means of inquiry, particularly exploring the voices of youth. His most recent research has involved visual ethnography and photo-elicitation.

Rachel Sandford is Senior Research Associate in the Institute of Youth Sport, based within the School of Sport, Exercise and Health Sciences at Loughborough University, UK. Her doctoral research was concerned with issues relating to young people, embodied identity and physical culture, and she has also been involved with research projects focusing on the relationship between formal education and disordered eating. Her current research interests are built around an evaluation of physical activity programmes designed to re-engage disaffected youth, and include a focus on the processes of informal education and mentoring. She has published in refereed journals and books in the areas of sociology, physical education and health.

Heather Sykes is Associate Professor at the Ontario Institute for Studies in Education at the University of Toronto, Canada. Her research explores issues of embodied, psychic and social exclusion in education, physical education and sport. She teaches courses in queer theory, anti-homophobia education, curriculum studies and physical education teacher education. She has been co-editor of *Curriculum Inquiry*, is actively involved in the North American Society for Sport Sociology (NASSS), and has published her work in journals such as *Body and Society*, *Journal of Curriculum Studies* and *Sport, Education and Society*.

Addresses

Kathleen Armour
School of Education
University of Birmingham
Edgbaston
B15 2TT

Lisette Burrows
School of Physical Education
University of Otago
PO Box 56
Dunedin
New Zealand

Dr David Carless
Senior Research Fellow
Leeds Metropolitan
University
Fairfax Hall
Beckett Park Campus
Leeds LS6 3QS

Donetta Cothran
HPER 179
1025 East 7th St
Indiana University
Bloomington, IN 47405

Rebecca Duncombe
School of Sport, Exercise and
Health Sciences
Loughborough University
Loughborough
Leicestershire LE11 3TU

Eimear Enright
Physical Education and Sport
Sciences Department
University of Limerick
Limerick
Ireland

Professor Christopher Hickey
Deputy Head of School
Faculty of Arts & Education
Deakin University
Pigdons Road
Geelong
Victoria 3217

Jessica Lee PhD
Lecturer in Physical
Activity and Health
School of Sport and
Exercise Sciences
Loughborough University
Leicestershire LE11 3TU

Professor Jonathan Long
Carnegie Research Institute
Leeds Metropolitan
University
Cavendish Hall
Headingley Campus
Leeds LS6 3QS

Dr Sarah Meegan
Lecturer in Adapted Physical
Activity
School of Health and Human
Performance
Dublin City University
Dublin 9

Kimberly L. Oliver
Department of Human
Performance, Dance and
Recreation
PO Box 30001 MSC 3M
New Mexico State
University, Las Cruces,
NM 88003-3001 USA

Clive C. Pope PhD
Senior Lecturer
Chairperson
Department of Sport &
Leisure Studies
University of Waikato
Private Bag, 3105
Hamilton, 3240
New Zealand

Rachel Sandford
School of Sport, Exercise and
Health Sciences
Loughborough University
Loughborough
Leicestershire LE11 3TU

Heather Sykes
Ontario Institute for
Studies in Education
252 Bloor Street West
Toronto, ON M5S 1V6
Canada

Mary O'Sullivan
Professor and Dean
Education and Health
Sciences
University of Limerick
Limerick
Ireland

Ann MacPhail
Senior Lecturer
Department of Physical
Education & Sport Sciences
University of Limerick
Limerick
Ireland

1 Introduction

Re-visioning young people's voices in physical education and sport

Mary O'Sullivan and Ann MacPhail

The purpose of this book

The main purpose of this book is to focus on the voices and experiences of children and adolescents in various physical activity settings by exploring their understandings and experiences of physical education, physical activity and sport in their lives. It is anticipated that, by encouraging young people to share how different contexts contribute to their learning about, and involvement in, physical activity we may be in a better position to acknowledge and address how such contexts can most effectively work together to motivate young people to choose active lifestyles.

The intended readership is postgraduate students and academic researchers, while not dismissing that certain chapters will be valuable supplementary reading for undergraduate students interested in understanding what physical education and youth sport mean to contemporary young people in various places around the world.

The omission of '*listening to*' young people's voices from the title of the book is deliberate. We wish to avoid the notion that the authors who have contributed the chapters are interested only in 'consulting' young people, i.e. conversing with young people about what their experiences in physical education and youth sport are like from their perspective. Rather, with reference to Rudduck and McIntyre's (2007) use of 'participation', authors develop such consultation with a view to encourage young people's authentic involvement in opportunities for decision making, investment and participation around issues of direct interest to their lives – that is, lived experiences.

The chapters in this book convey the general consensus that teachers, facilitators, coaches and researchers strive to provide young people with authentic experiences in physical education and youth sport that meet their changing needs and interests, with the ultimate goal being to encourage more young people to be more physically active and to adopt a healthy lifestyle. The deconstruction of the term 'young people's voices' differs between the chapters due to the different populations, contexts and cultures the authors report, as does the deconstruction of healthy lifestyles. The degree of young people's voices and the extent to which they are consequently consulted vary according to the particular project and the needs and capacities of the young people involved. While all chapter authors appreciate the value of consulting young people and understanding their voices with respect to their experience in physical education and youth sport, examples are included that report how consulting with young people about their physical education and youth sport experiences has informed the development of effective and equitable practices. There are also examples of young people engaged as co-researchers and as researchers in shaping their own and others' experiences and policies around physical education and sport (see the chapters by Oliver, and Enright and O'Sullivan in this volume – Chapters 3 and 10, respectively).

The chapter authors present a diversity of theoretical traditions and methodological approaches that can be used to focus on young people's experiences in physical education, physical activity and sport. The different theoretical traditions addressed in the text include constructivism, feminism, poststructuralism, queer theory and typologies of student participation. The methodological approaches include the use of narratives, ethnography, visual methods and a variety of participatory action research strategies that critically engage students with sport and activity artefacts in their lives.

As editors we sought scholars across several countries who were researching different target populations of young people and/or different research methodologies about different aspects of sport, health, physical education or physical activity more generally. The authors discuss the findings from their research on different racial, ethnic, gender and socio-economic class groups, including urban and rural students in Australia (Lee), young people in New Zealand (Burrows, Pope), African-American and Mexican-American girls (Oliver), and Caucasian students in the United States (Cothran). Other voices shared include those from economically disadvantaged adolescent girls from an Irish secondary school (Enright and O'Sullivan), disengaged youths' involvement in sport and physical activity interventions in the UK (Sandford), boys' views of physical education and sport in Australia (Hickey), an Irish teenage boy's engagement with physical education as a student with a special educational need (Meegan), and the marginalization of Canadian young adults from physical education and sport on the basis of sexuality, gender, physical dis/ability and body shape/size (Sykes).

Taken together, the chapters highlight the different approaches, methodologies and populations that contribute to such a growing literature base of young people's experiences and engagement with sport and physical activity. Each chapter strives to provide evidence of young people's understanding of, and experiences in, sport and physical activity while some provide insights into students' experiences as researchers and co-researchers. Authors also report the challenges of giving young people a voice in favour of merely reporting research undertaken with young people and the implications of the research projects highlighted for future research, policy development and programme development.

Organization of the book

The book is divided into three sections, as described below.

Exploring student voice in different settings

The first section explores student understandings and experiences in different settings, such as school physical education and school sport, as well as the role of physical activity as part of their lives.

The first chapter, Chapter 2 by Jessica Lee, explores the voices of 20 Australian young people, recruited from three very different schools, on their experiences in physical education, sport and physical activity as they move through school and beyond school. While epidemiological data show decreasing levels of activity by adolescents Lee argues that these studies do not assist in identifying solutions to this problem as little or no attention is given to how class, gender, school and location shape their engagement with physical activity over time. The chapter shares findings from longitudinal data (three years) of the Life Activity Project (LAP) about young people's engagement with physical education, sport and physical activity as part of the total biography of their lives. The longitudinal nature of the project is positioned within a poststructural perspective and captures young people's voices during a number of important transitions in their lives (secondary school to college or work, from living at home to moving to new towns and/or to living with a partner or friends). Lee shares interesting data about the physical activity patterns of these young people, from the intersection of school, gender and social class, and the implications of these findings for health promotion policy.

In Chapter 3, Kimberly Oliver draws on 13 years of activist research in the United States to highlight how intersections of gender, race and sexuality influence how girls experience their bodies and how they experience physical activity. The chapter shows ways of collaborating over time with girls as co-researchers, in developing a language of critique and possibility that allows them to challenge cultural practices and messages that limit their health and physical activity participation. Oliver uses innovative research methods (magazine exploration, photo critique and inquiry-based projects) to learn about the girls' perspectives, such as what African-American girls view as fashionable. From another project she describes how she worked with Mexican-American adolescents to create games to enact alternative possibilities to being physically active as 'girly girls'. The last section of the chapter describes how, using photos, young students were encouraged to name and change the inequities that prevented them from being physically active at their elementary school.

In Chapter 4, the last of the first part of the book, Donetta Cothran discusses students' perspectives of the purposes of physical education programmes in the United States, and the implications for their meaningful engagement with physical education. While much of the research in this area has been qualitative in nature, Cothran includes a number of different studies that have used mostly quantitative techniques (e.g. Q-sort methodology, attitudinal survey research and critical incident recall). In the chapter, she examines students' values of physical education, how those values are met, or not met, by different curricula and how students attempt to shape the curriculum through their actions. The first section of the chapter summarizes five student value patterns (Playful Friends, Competitors, Friendly

Learners, Cooperative Learners, Social Comparison) and how students experience the same curriculum quite differently, and often related to gender, race and ability. The later section of the chapter outlines the conflicting values between the teacher's educational mission for the curriculum and the students' greater concern for fun and friends. Data from students has highlighted how they have at times resisted, accommodated or redefined their school experience. Cothran recommends an authentic role for students in the design of physical education curricula, ensuring multiple goals could be met simultaneously and creating a curricular path of mutual worth.

Multiple identities of adolescent populations

The second part of the book includes four chapters that highlight the multiple identities and perspectives of adolescent populations, and include disaffected youth, a student with a special educational need, boys and male adults reflecting on their experiences of ableism, heterosexism and body discrimination in school physical education, and students who were marginalized during physical education because of their sexual or gender identity, physical disability or the size and appearance of their body.

In Chapter 5, Rachel Sandford, Kathleen Armour and Rebecca Duncombe investigate youth voice in education research, providing examples of ways in which participants' voices, particularly those of disaffected youth in the UK, have been sought and heard in the growing number of research projects involving disaffected youth. The significance of youth voice in public discourse is explored with an admittance that, although researchers have taken young people's views into account in evaluation studies, these are often tokenistic due to young people's contributions being directed, structured and limited by external, adult-led research agendas. The authors present four selected projects, an overview of the methodologies employed and a brief illustration of how disaffected youths' voices have been used to articulate key issues or themes in the dissemination of findings. The chapter concludes by providing an example of one potential research approach that may allow for a genuine representation of young people's voice.

In Chapter 6, Sarah Meegan presents the experiences of James, a 16-year-old Irish wheelchair user, as he attempts throughout a school year to participate in mainstream physical education. The research is grounded within the theoretical framework of negotiating the curriculum, looking to explore if, and how, James' participation in physical education impacted on inclusive curricular practices through student and teacher negotiation. Meegan discusses four key themes that provide insight into the physical education experiences of James, identifying instances where her observations appeared to contradict James' recollection of events. The methodological challenges of conducting ethnographic research in presenting the voice of an adolescent with a special educational need within a physical education setting are considered before noting recommendations for future research practice.

In Chapter 7, Christopher Hickey focuses on the engagement young males have alongside hypermasculine sporting discourses in the context of schools, and the particular curriculum practices of sport and physical education. Acknowledging that the methodological foundations of his inquiries into masculinity, sport and education are best characterized within the paradigmatic lenses of phenomenology, Hickey acknowledges the place of the researcher in the research process, and the relationship between researcher and participant. Using data collection methods associated with narrative inquiry, Hickey draws on Foucault's work on how we develop a sense of self. Reporting from different data sets compiled across a number of studies, Hickey highlights some of the drivers that produce certain sensibilities and practices around masculinity for young boys involved in the Australian Football League's introductory programme, for men reflecting on incidents or events that had shaped their lives 15 years earlier and for a 12-year-old boy sharing his understandings of a footballing identity. The chapter concludes with implications for (pedagogical) practice through which young males can locate and articulate alternative ways of being and doing.

In order to identify some continuing and changing patterns of discrimination in physical education Heather Sykes introduces, in the final chapter in this section, reflective and retrospective voices of Canadian adults who self-identified as a sexual or gender minority, having a physical disability and/or having a socially undervalued body shape/size. The chapter focuses on their experiences as students who were marginalized during physical education because of their sexual or gender identity, or the size and appearance of their body. Theoretically, the chapter explores how discourses about the body in physical education contribute to particular forms of ableism, heterosexism and body discrimination within students' experiences of schooling. The chapter focuses on adults 'looking back' on their physical education experiences as an invitation to dialogue about the continuation of physical education to create situations in which students who embody some form of queerness have to engage in difficult emotional and embodied negotiations. The chapter also focuses on 'looking sideways' at physical education by highlighting people with non-mainstream and critical perspectives about physical education. Sykes concludes by reporting revisionist histories of sex, sexology and queerness that could extend the line of inquiry offered in this chapter.

Theoretical frames and methodological approaches

The third and final section of the book explores the contributions of different theoretical frames and methodological approaches to data collection with and by young people, and how these can enrich our understandings of what engagement with physical education, health and sport means to them.

In Chapter 9, the first of this section, Lisette Burrows shares data from her New Zealand study of 9- and 10-year-old children from two very different schools, to make sense of what she calls the 'health and physical activity imperatives' that infuse their lives. She discusses how and why theoretical concepts from poststructuralism are useful tools in informing our understandings of young people's engagement with, and resistance to these discourses. She discusses the key Foucauldian concepts (such as power, knowledge, subjectivities, technologies of the self, and discourse) that underpin her poststructural inquiry, and how they can influence the kinds of research methods used to interrogate and illuminate young people's understandings of health and physical activity. Her chapter reminds us how limiting children's understandings of health can be when Burrows compares them to the more holistic notions of health emphasized in the New Zealand physical education curriculum. She uses these concepts to critique how young people engage with the New Zealand health promotion strategy, 'Push Play', and the metaphoric use of the couch in these efforts.

In Eimear Enright and Mary O'Sullivan's chapter (Chapter 10), the aim is to challenge physical education teachers and researchers to work with students to 'trouble the boundaries of what's possible in physical education, imagine what is possible, and work towards what could be'. The authors acknowledge that it is not students who are always the problem but, more often, the pedagogical contexts within which they are expected to participate and the curricula with which they are instructed to engage. Enright and O'Sullivan focus on Participatory Action Research (PAR) as a theoretical construct, a research methodology and a pedagogical framework as a more educationally meaningful and socially relevant learning experience for all students in physical education. They reference four PAR-orientated projects in physical education to provide evidence of 'pedagogies of possibility' with groups of children and adolescents ranging from 9 to 16 years of age. The chapter addresses the challenges and benefits for students, teachers and researchers associated with supporting a PAR pedagogy.

In the final chapter of this section, Clive Pope sets out to explore the experiences of young people in sport via visual research data collection methods. He describes the growing interest in user-friendly visual technology (i.e. photos and photo-elicitation discussions with three young New Zealanders) to learn about their social worlds and what their engagement in competitive rowing during a national schools championship in New Zealand meant to them. He draws on Becker's (2000) argument that photographs rather than words can more aptly display social phenomena, and shows the values of such an approach to highlight young people's voices in sport. He presents a set of nine photos created and narrated by the young rowers as a way of helping us understand the emotions, tensions, intensities and friendships associated with sporting settings and their participants. Pope's chapter shows the potential for visual research methods to help us understand the interests, needs and experiences of young people, and it is a contribution to the growing body of work in visual culture.

In closing

In the epilogue to the text, Jonathan Long and David Carless reflect on how what we do and think as researchers and insiders might shape the knowledge we produce through our research, structuring their reflections around some of the key issues and themes raised across the chapters. Reflecting on which of the many voices in physical education and sport we listen to and privilege, Long and Carless outline four reasons why some young people may be disinclined to voice their stories. They ask researchers to consider whether these stories have something new to offer, something qualitatively different from stories already told. If some voices go unheard they can have no part in constructing physical education or sport. The authors challenge us to extend our thinking on devising innovative and effective practices and methodology in encouraging young people to share their stories that allow for the enhancement of understanding of young people's needs and experiences in physical education and youth sport settings, which in turn can be used to inform and formulate policy.

Reference

Becker, H. S. (2000) 'What should sociology look like in the (near) future?', *Contemporary Sociology*, 29 (2): 333–336.

Rudduck, J. and McIntyre, D. (2007) *Improving Learning through Consulting Pupils*. London: Routledge.

Part I

Exploring student voice in different settings

2 Students' evolving meanings and experiences with physical activity and sport

Jessica Lee

Introduction

There is a growing body of literature that explores the impact of social structures such as race and gender (e.g. Azzarito, 2009), social class and location (e.g. Wright, Macdonald and Groom, 2003; Evans and Davies, 2008), and healthism and obesity discourses (e.g. Burrows, Wright and Jungersen-Smith, 2002; Evans *et al.*, 2008) on young people's conceptions of health and their participation in physical activities. What is lacking in the current literature, however, is an exploration of how young people's meanings and experiences with physical activity evolve over time. The aim of this chapter is to explore young people's voices on their experiences in physical education and sport and physical activity as they move through and beyond school. The particular question addressed in this chapter is 'How do social structures such as class, gender, school and location (place) shape young people's engagements with physical activity over time?' To address this question, data will be drawn from the Life Activity Project (LAP), an Australian longitudinal qualitative project exploring young people's engagements with physical education and sport and physical activities.

Recent literature has called for a move 'beyond epidemiology' to explore the social structures that shape 'health behaviours' such as physical activity (McGannon and Mauws, 2002; Williams, 2003; Warin *et al.*, 2008). Epidemiological research suggests that young people's participation in physical activities is inadequate and decreases with progression through adolescence, particularly among groups such as girls and ethnic minorities (Health Survey for England, 2004a, 2004b; Abbott *et al.*, 2007; Australian Government, 2008). The nature of this kind of data, however, leaves unanswered questions regarding the interplay of social structures and institutions such as class, gender, ethnicity, location (place), school and family that shape young people's meanings of, and engagements with, physical activity. Furthermore, while epidemiological and large-scale statistical research has assisted in the documentation of broad patterns of participation (e.g. Sport England, 2001; Health Survey for England, 2004a, 2004b), these studies do not assist in identifying solutions.

This chapter begins with an overview of the literature on a social understanding of young people's participation in sport and physical activities. A brief description of the LAP is provided before presenting an analysis of longitudinal data from semi-structured interviews with a cohort of Australian young people.

Young people, physical activity and physical culture

While *physical activity* is inclusive of planned activities such as *sport* and *exercise* along with leisure activities and physical forms of transport, we are also concerned with *physical culture*, defined by Kirk (1999) as the social practices involved with maintaining, representing and regulating or socially constructing the body, in and through various forms of institutionalized practices such as sport, physical recreation and exercise. In providing a supplementary way in which to locate physical activity within young people's lives, the concept of physical culture is pivotal to a social understanding of young people's engagements with sport and physical activities. The key point of focus is the consideration of 'the embeddedness of the physical in social and cultural practices' (Kirk, 1999, p. 65). This is important when examining young people's participation in sport and physical activities, as consumption of sporting goods and services is acknowledged as a prominent feature in young people's lives (e.g. Kenway and Bullen, 2001).

Physical culture as a form of discourse refers to the ways in which people speak about their bodies, what they do with their bodies and, just as importantly, the silences in their communications, what they do not say or do (Kirk, 1999). Pronger (1998) maintains that sport and physical activity play a very important sociocultural role in representing, creating and challenging certain relations. In particular, he refers to the power struggles associated with the discourses of gender, difference, masculine hierarchies, sexuality, ethnic and racial difference, and health as projects of 'boundary maintenance' (Pronger, 1998). For example, in thinking of the boundaries that constitute manhood and womanhood, Pronger (1998, p. 282) notes that:

> sport helps men set the boundaries for appropriate masculine behaviour, sense of self, and body production. Sport helps set the limits beyond which men should not venture if they are to achieve the status of man as opposed to woman, and maintain that difference through life.

In this way, sport and physical activities not only maintain binary discourses (e.g. manhood/womanhood, masculinity/femininity) but also contribute to the production of boundaries in the broader society. As such, the concept of physical culture provides a broader scope in which to locate physical activity within the total biography of young people's lives (Macdonald, 2002).

Of particular interest for this chapter is how different settings, including social and geographical aspects, shape the ways in which young people experience physical culture and, subsequently, the meanings of sport and physical activities within the broader contexts of their lives. Structures and social practices can often vary greatly across and within social and geographical locations.

Social structures and young people's physical activity (social class, gender, location, school, family)

Sociologists of sport have maintained an interest in social class and physical activity (e.g. Miller, 1999; Foote, 2003; Mehus, 2005; Stempel, 2005; Bairner, 2007). This is despite some suggestion that the issue of social class may be limited in contemporary studies of popular practices. Some argue that traditional social class variables such as occupational category and education have given way to other variables such as gender, age, family status, health, and ethnic identity, contributing to a *decentring* of work relative to these other spheres of life (e.g. Offe, 1985; Rowe, 1998). Furthermore, Rowe (1998, p. 245) claims that many aspects of contemporary culture 'stubbornly refuse to follow the contours of class'.

Alternatively, others (Walkerdine, Lucey and Melody, 2001; Evans and Davies, 2008) maintain that, as a structural category, social class is still one of the most powerful factors shaping lives and life chances, although they also acknowledge the tensions experienced in working with class alongside poststructural imperatives of complexity. Indeed, poststructuralism by its very name suggests a rejection of universal grand narratives such as social class and gender, instead foregrounding pluralism, agency and personal autonomy (McLaren and Farahmandpur, 2000), creating an opposition between the concept of postmodern multiple identities and modern class identities (Walkerdine *et al.*, 2001). Poststructuralist researchers who maintain an interest in class remain concerned with power, knowledge and discourse, while acknowledging that 'old practices of subjectivity continue to exist' (Walkerdine *et al.*, 2001, p. 19) and are deeply implicated in the production of subjectivity, as written on the body and mind. Karen Evans (2002) uses the term *bounded agency* to describe the interaction between choice (individual agency) and structural influences. Bourdieu (1987, p. 5) also contends that the notion of social class runs deeper than socio-economic categories, suggesting that 'social distances are inscribed on the body'. In this way, social class not only refers to economic categories but can be 'characterized by any kind of socially constructed trait, such as gender, age, or ethnicity' (Laberge and Kay, 2002, p. 241). This embodiment of class makes visible the signs of distinction through actions and patterns of consumption.

While previously reported data suggest that social class status has an equivalent impact on both young women's and young men's physical activity patterns, epidemiological, critical, feminist and poststructuralist research highlights how gender plays a significant role in physical activity and physical culture. Historically, in western culture sport and masculinity have been concepts that go hand in hand, which indeed has implications for both young men and young women in terms of participation and perceptions. Participation in sport and physical activity can reinforce a dominant masculinity, leading to marginalization of others including women and forms of masculinity that do not conform (Dowling Naess, 2001; Humberstone, 2002). Much social research on young women's sport and physical activities suggests that their participation is shaped by traditional notions of femininity and a concern for health and fitness including body shape (Sleap and

Wormwald, 2001). See Chapter 3 in this volume for a perspective on this issue with different girls in the USA.

The kind of school attended can be a key factor in the transmission of culture and opportunity (McGregor, 1997). The existence of both public (fully government funded) and private (fee paying) schools denotes an element of class division. Through certain traditions and practices (blazers, school songs, speech nights, sports, competitions), private schools openly seek to provide a different education for their selected pupils, and emphasize the difference between them and students at other schools (McGregor, 1997). Indeed, high-fee-paying schools frequently use physical activity and sport as pivotal in the construction of the school's ethos and the reproduction of privilege (e.g. Courtice, 1999).

The literature reviewed here suggests that young people's participation in sport and physical activities is a result of decisions negotiated within the context of their social environment, and mediated by the young person's views of self and personal goals. While they make active decisions about their sport and physical activity involvement, these are also within a wider, structural and social context. As such, in order to understand young people's participation in sport and physical activities, it is important to listen to how they express their own meanings and experiences.

Young people, choices and transitions

The emergence of adolescence as a stage of life has gradually come to dominate the youth research agenda. Roberts (1985) argued that, by the late 1970s, young people's circumstances were changing rapidly and radically, as the institutions such as employment, education and family that directly involved young people were undergoing significant changes. The distinctive circumstances of the post-1970s generation have encouraged contemporary young people to develop new approaches to life (Wyn and White, 2000). Wyn and White (2000) argued that realizing the ways in which young people themselves respond to new realities is important in understanding how social structures (e.g. labour market, education) and social divisions (e.g. social class, ethnicity, gender) affect their lives. The term *choice biographies* has been used to describe the life patterns of young people who are negotiating the paradoxical relationship between perceived choice and agency, and the social and structural conditions that direct all people's lives (du Bois-Reymond, 1998).

Karen Evans' (2002) concept of bounded agency introduced in the previous section suggests that young people's life *choices* are shaped by their past experiences, their current life chances and the perceptions of possible futures. As such, 'future possibilities [are] envisaged within contingencies of the present moment . . . influenced but not determined by structures and emphasizing internalized understandings and frameworks as well as external actions' (Evans, 2002, p. 248).

Furlong (2000) claimed that the rigidity that characterized traditional transitions has subsided, making way for a new situation where young people are actively constructing and re-constructing biographies. Engagements with sport and physical activities are part of this active construction of biographies, and are shaped by young people's negotiations with other life experiences; not least those structures outlined in the previous section – gender, economics and school/work. The Life Activity Project (LAP) is unique in that, while it is concerned with listening to young people's voices in their descriptions of the place of sport and physical activities in their own lives, it is longitudinal and captures many young people's major life transitions from primary to secondary school, from secondary school to work or further study, and from living at home with family to moving towns and living with a partner or friends. The methods of the LAP as they relate to this chapter are described briefly in the next section.

The Life Activity Project

The purpose of the LAP was to examine the place and meaning of physical activity in the context of young people's lives and, in doing so, to investigate some of the taken-for-granted assumptions about young people's participation in physical activity and the relationship between physical activity and health that underpin practices in physical education and in public health promotion. For the larger project, interview data were collected over a period of seven years (1999–2006) with a cohort of young people (n=97) from various geographical and social locations in three states in eastern Australia. One-off interviews with a sample of parents and school physical education teachers were also conducted. Of the cohort referred to in this chapter, each young person participated in two to four interviews each year over three years, focusing on topics including health and fitness, bodies and sport in the media, geographical location and local communities, and past and present participation in physical activities.

It was the intention to recruit young people from various social, ethnic and geographic locations, as well as from different types of school, although as with all forms of research, sometimes those from whom we would most like to hear are the least willing to participate. Indeed, it was sometimes difficult to engage some young people throughout the duration of a longitudinal project. To maintain young people's interest, we specifically made use of multiple methods over the years, including visual (Lee and Abbott, 2009), magazines and other popular media, and diaries. Quotes and examples used in this chapter are drawn from interviews (individual and small group) with participants recruited from three schools in Queensland (n=20). The schools were an elite private boys' college, to be known as Malcos College (note that all names of people and locations have been changed to protect participant anonymity), a co-educational rural government secondary school, to be known as Greenvalley High, and a school of distance education, to be known as Homestead School. The young people were aged between 11 (year 6, primary school) to 15 years old (year 10, last year of compulsory schooling) at the time of recruitment.

Malcos College is located in an inner suburb of a major city, which has an elite culture and a strong 'old boy' tradition and network. The school boasts a superior sports complex housing courts and equipment for various sports, and a weights room – considered to be the best in (elite) schools in the state. In addition, the college has a number of tennis courts and fields, as well as a 50-metre swimming pool. Malcos offers a wide range of competitive sports and strongly recommends that 'each student be involved in at least one physical activity per year'[1] (cited on school website). Participants from Malcos College all lived in suburban areas of a major city.

Greenvalley High was located in a socially isolated, small rural town, given the lack of local services and access to public transport between nearby towns and larger centres. Some of the young people attending Greenvalley High lived in residential housing blocks in the town, while others lived in properties up to 30 kilometres away from the school. The Homestead School caters for students who cannot, for various reasons, attend regular schools and, as such, has a high proportion of students who live in remote rural locations. The Homestead School students in this study were all rural young people who lived in isolated areas with difficult access to local schools. Distance education as carried out through the Homestead School entails students receiving hard copies of learning materials and guidance on daily work plans from teachers. Personal communication between students and teachers is usually via telephone, sometimes email (depending on access), and audio-tapes can be used for assessment. The young people studying via Homestead School lived on farming properties in four different rural locations up to 600 kilometres from the state capital and between 20 and 60 kilometres from the nearest town.

The participants described in this chapter reflect a diverse range of young people from various geographical, social and economic locations. The range allows for an exploration of various structures identified as influencing young people's experiences in sport and physical activities, social class, gender, type of school and geographical location (e.g. rural vs urban). It is inevitable however that some voices were not captured. Despite this, the strength of longitudinal qualitative data is that it allows for the generation of rich contextualized stories of young people's lives that are not captured by traditional survey methods typically used to explore experiences in physical activity.

An ideographic approach to the data analysis was taken, which is based on the view that to understand the social world, we need to gain first-hand knowledge of the subject under investigation (Sparkes, 1992). This approach is not judgemental but rather allows the subject to reveal its nature and characteristics during the process of investigation. Interview responses were coded into themes as they were observed by the researcher (that is, no pre-determined categories were used) and then further analysed to refine groupings and categories, and to search for recurrences of certain words or text within sets of documents. This process involves the interpretation of young people's voices and experiences. As interviewing and analyses were ongoing we were able to revisit topics and themes with young people to check for our own understanding as well as for consistencies and contradictions. This study is positioned within the poststructural theoretical perspective because of its emphasis on discourse and power, however a focus on the wider structural and institutional processes that impact on rural young people's lives remains. Specifically, it is implied that rural young people are actively involved in negotiating a physical activity identity, while there remains significant evidence to suggest that their lives continue to be constrained by very real, material limits and lack of opportunities. In this way, Bourdieu's work building upon notions of structure and agency is useful in theorizing the findings.

Young people's experiences in sport and physical activities: a longitudinal perspective

Gender and geographical location will be explored as they intersect with the two main headings in this section: 'Through school and beyond' and 'Experiencing social class'.

Through school and beyond

Findings from the LAP highlight the importance of the school in shaping young people's conceptions of health and fitness, and their participation in sport and physical activities. Indeed, for some young people, the school's influence is still present up to two years post-school. The three different types of school as outlined earlier are examined in this chapter. The schools – through their ethos, facilities and physical education curriculum – afforded different opportunities for their students.

Malcos College, with its prestige facilities, wide range of sport and physical activities on offer, and a policy that each student must participate in one sport or physical activity per year, theoretically offered the most opportunities out of the three schools in this study. Indeed many of the boys kept heavy sporting schedules alongside their academic commitments.

> On Mondays I have Photography Club and that goes until five o'clock. Tuesday and Thursday I have public speaking and debating. On Tuesday morning, oh, after school I have soccer as well on Thursdays, soccer coaching as well. On Friday I have my normal debate at night. So basically I don't get home until six-thirty every night . . . . I used to do volleyball but that's over so I've got nothing on Wednesday. I have soccer training on Tuesday mornings. [*Int.*: And are you coaching soccer at school as well?] Yeah the thirteen Ds. (Anthony, aged 17)

Participation in organized team sports among the Malcos College students was indeed very high compared to those from the other schools. The culture of sport in the school however tended to be interpreted by some students as very elitist and privileged certain sports over others.

> *Int.*:   How important do you think sport and other physical activities are inside the school culture?
> *S*:   Oh very high. School places a big importance in sport and it defines you as a person a lot in schools . . . It's just such a fierce rivalry between, in

the school and out of the school. [Later in the same interview] If you don't do rugby or rowing then you're a wimp . . . For instance, tables, you know at lunchtime, people, people sit at different tables and you've got all the rugby players, you got all the rowers together and yeah. (Steve, aged 15)

Int.:   How does something like soccer compare with rugby?
A: There's sort of a culture to rugby which soccer doesn't really have. It's different to what it used to be but rugby is very, all the old boys are there. Soccer's not as big a deal but I mean we put in the same amount of work but it's probably not as big a deal.
Int.:   So how prestigious was your role as soccer captain?
A: Well within the soccer community it was. I mean that's a pretty good achievement, but it doesn't have the same kudos within the school as say a rugby captain just because of the way our school works (Aidan, aged 17)

Participation in sport in general was considered a good thing and certainly encouraged, with many sports on offer. Comments such as, 'I mean if you don't play anything at school you're very, you're a nobody' (Aidan, aged 17), were not uncommon. Fierce rivalry and emphasis on rowing and rugby union, however, had the effect of turning some young men away from certain sports. Therefore, although some sports were easily accessed, as evidenced by Aidan and Steve's heavy participation in soccer and basketball respectively, there was a clear culture favouring certain sports and elite participation. While Aidan found the sporting culture at school favoured rugby union, his own participation in the more marginalized sport of soccer was still easily accessed in terms of training routines and facilities.

Given the requirement of at least some participation in sport, it was interesting to note that none of the Malcos College young men in the cohort continued physical education after the compulsory years (years 11 and 12). They generally enjoyed physical education in their younger years because 'it was a bludge'[2] and let them relax away from the 'more academic' subjects. The most cited reasons for not continuing physical education in the senior years was that it would not contribute towards their career (e.g. 'I won't be needing it at uni') and that they already do enough physical activity (e.g. 'I don't have the energy to do that because I'm also doing sport after school'). Therefore, despite being physically skilled, as evidenced by their participation in various sports, the Malcos young men still did not find physical education appealing in their senior years. This trend has been explored in the academic literature (e.g. Tinning, 2000).

A number of the Malcos College young men completed school and continued on to university throughout the course of the study. As a result of this transition they found that their lives in general, and particularly their participation in sport and physical activities, became a lot less structured (Lee, Macdonald and Wright, 2009). None of them continued competing in their respective sports.

Aaron: It's a little different, you've got to sort of motivate yourself to do stuff; you don't have anyone sort of relying on you to be doing this work if you don't want to. I guess I sort of prefer the way that school was organized because then you always had things to do like to do with sport; you know it was a lot easier to get into back then. (Aaron, aged 18)

Anthony: Because school was so routine I was able to fit everything in. But now everything just, even though I have more free time it's not as routine. (Anthony, aged 18)

It was clear that the young men felt that their school experiences had set them up for very smooth transitions into the academic and social side of university but the structure of the sporting programme made it somewhat more difficult to continue in sport and physical activities post-school. Many of the Malcos young men's experiences in sport and physical activities during and after school are linked to social class which will be discussed further in the following section.

The Greenvalley High students' experiences of school sport and physical education were quite different from those of the Malcos College young men. As mentioned in an earlier section, the school and town had somewhat limited facilities and opportunities. Due to geographical isolation Greenvalley High also had a very limited inter-school sport programme. As such, the Greenvalley High students', particularly the young women's, sport and physical activity participation patterns tended to focus (with some exceptions) more on recreational physical activities with siblings, physical labour, and active transport (Lee and Macdonald, 2009).

Int.: What physical activity are you doing at the moment?
Jacinta: I don't think any, any more. I'm sort of like finished and I'm just doing things at home . . . Well usually if I'm doing anything, I go out and talk to my sister who's usually outside on the trampoline. We just start talking and then we go down the road, we go for a walk down the road because there's nothing else to do . . . [I also] Dance to music. I turn on 'Rage' and I'm just standing there dancing. (Jacinta, aged 15)

While the school's geographical location certainly restricted sporting opportunities, being a government-funded school also meant financial priority was given to 'academic' functions. Unlike Malcos College and other private schools, sporting opportunities and achievements were not a selling point for Greenvalley High.

The Homestead School students mostly lived on isolated properties and had no access to competitive school sport programmes. An advantage they did have was an abundance of space to participate in recreational sport and physical activities. In addition to using formal equipment in the home, some of the Homestead young people innovatively made their own equipment, along with their siblings and sometimes with help from their parents. This goes some way to overcome the barrier of lack of formal sport and physical activity facilities in their local areas.

> *Mouldy*:   . . . we made a mini golf course . . . Well we just decided where we were going to put the holes, teed them, then we dug a hole and put a tin in the ground and covered it with some dust so the grass would grow through it and it's pretty good. (Mouldy, male aged 12)

While both rural young men and young women (from Greenvalley High and Homestead School) participated in physical labour, the young men were keen to demonstrate how theirs contributed to their physical activity, whereas the young women considered themselves physically inactive, despite participating in physical labour (Lee and Macdonald, 2009).

> *Sally*:   At a turf farm . . . I roll turf . . . For about an hour and half, two hours every morning and then I go to school.
> *Int.*:   So that involves pushing the turf along and running along behind it?
> *S*:   And picking it up and loading it on the truck. (Sally, aged 15)

> *Wadiken*:   . . . as I say I get a fair bit of physical activity like yesterday afternoon after I did my exams I went up for a ride [motorbike] up the front just to check on things . . . and I went up to a dry dam and there was three sheep stuck in there, in the mud. The mud would have sucked against them right? So it's really tough work, you've got to be really fit to pull them out . . . basically by myself and then we lifted them into the trailer and take them back here and wash the mud off them and feed and water them. So you know, it's a fair bit of fitness is needed to do things like that. (Wadiken, male aged 14)

Indeed, physical labour also appeared in young men's descriptions of their leisure time. Tyrone rode his push bike around his property and incorporated his recreation time with his chores.

> *Int.*:   So what sort of stuff do you normally do at home, when you're not doing your school work or your chores, what sort of other stuff do you do at home?
> *Tyrone*:   Bike riding, straight away. If Mum wants me to go and check the trough over there and make sure it's not overflowing or anything and I'll be back about an hour later, just checking the trough and I'll go up the road and up the other side there, coming down the other side there's good [tracks], I think it's eight kilometres or seven. (Tyrone, aged 14)

Brandon was the only Greenvalley High student to be involved in extra-curricular sport; he was a successful competitor in volleyball and triathlon with the school teams, and swimming, golf and touch football with local clubs. From the Homestead School, Lemming and Mouldy were involved in club cricket and Lisa was a nationally ranked dressage competitor. In contrast to the Malcos College students, this involved a considerable time and financial commitment from parents as the rural young people's sports participation was mostly club based. Parents' own views illustrate the extent of their commitment in rural young people's sport and physical activities. (See Chapter 11, which looks at young people's view of parental involvement.)

> With Friday night is a thing where we go to swimming club . . . and Terrence [husband] helps with the barbecue or whatever you know. (Brandon's mother)

> Well I'm quite involved in club cricket. I usually score and help [my husband] set up things, so pretty much the whole family is involved. (Lemming and Mouldy's mother)

Both the parent and student interviews revealed the importance of the children's sport involvement in terms of family time spent together.

Physical education for the rural young people presented an interesting story for Greenvalley High and Homestead School students. Greenvalley High offered two physical education options in the post-compulsory years: Senior Physical Education and Recreational Studies. The former, aimed at students interested in pursuing sporting excellence and keen to develop their sporting prowess, had low student enrolment. In contrast, the emphasis of Recreational Studies was on participation and enjoyment for students who wished to broaden their knowledge and experiences in recreational pursuits such as orienteering, archery, tennis, golf, kayaking and lawn bowls, which attracted almost double the enrolment of Senior Physical Education (Greenvalley High Physical Education HoD, email communication, 9 September 2004). While none of the students in the Greenvalley High cohort participated in Senior Physical Education, Recreational Studies (also called 'Rec Studies' or 'Health and Rec' by the students and teachers) was a more popular choice.

> *Brett:*   Yeah, it's [Recreational Studies] going pretty good. We're doing lawn bowls at the moment, did kayaking last term. I got a B in kayaking, that was pretty fun. We're supposed to be doing a coaching session, coaching lesson for two terms. We've got to coach the primary schoolers across the road. (Brett, aged 17)

The popularity of Recreational Studies over Senior Physical Education is noteworthy given that the focus of the former is on participation and enjoyment, and broadening students' physical activity experiences, and that of the latter is on pursuing excellence in, and theoretical analysis of, traditional physical activities. It appears that Recreational Studies suits the rural young people's lived experiences of sport and physical activities more so than Senior Physical Education.

For the students of Homestead School, it was compulsory to participate in physical education until the end of grade eight. Practical work was still focused on traditional sports such as basketball, soccer, athletics and swimming. For the
participants in this study, the absence of a class context made participation in these
types of activities difficult. Challenges included having to participate with siblings
and/or parents, constructing their own facilities to use at home (e.g. basketball
hoop), and extensive travel to facilities such as pools. Restraints such as these often
resulted in the students disengaging with physical education altogether.

> *Lemming*:   I do not do physical activity for my school work at the moment
> or any more. I did HPE [Health and Physical Education] in
> year eight but I don't do it now. I didn't enjoy it much. I had
> to play basketball and dancing with my mum. I reckon it
> would have been better if I could do it with other kids instead of
> with my family . . . The things that I did in it were basketball,
> athletics and swimming . . . It's a bit hard by yourself too, I had to
> travel for an hour to get to the pool in swimming so that was hard
> and we don't have any water around here. (Lemming, male
> aged 14)

In contrast to the Malcos College students, the rural young people from
Greenvalley High and Homestead School tended to experience sport and physical
activities outside of school and, where sport was played in clubs, this required a
high parental time and financial commitment. All of the Homestead School students remained in full-time education throughout the course of the study so their
engagements with sport and physical activities over time were mostly consistent.
No major transitions were observed for these young people. Some of the
Greenvalley High young people either completed school or left school during the
study. As they had not previously been involved in school sport, however, this
major life transition did not affect their engagements with sport and physical activities. Brett went on to further study at a technical college and part-time work while
continuing to be involved competitively in pistol shooting with his father and
grandfather. Adam began full-time work at a local supermarket and eventually
joined the army. Physical fitness continued to be important for him as a means of
being successful in his employment. The rural young women who finished school
continued to have minimal involvement with sport and physical activities. Any
engagement was restricted to active transport for commuting to work or some irreg-
ular recreational activity like push-bike riding and walking for pleasure. While
these young women still felt that sport and physical activity was important for their
general health and fitness, they also felt that time and financial restrictions were
major barriers to their participation. Perhaps for all the young people, their engagements with sport and physical activities both during and post-school years is best
understood at the intersection of school and social class. The following section
addresses this issue.

Experiencing social class

While the previous section focused on the influence of school on young people's experiences of sport and physical activities, the differences observed could well be attributed to social class. As noted previously, the mere fact that both public (fully government funded) and private (fee paying) schools exist denotes an element of class division.

During their school years the Malcos College young men mainly had their sporting opportunities provided for them by the school. Through the school fees, the families invested in the physical culture of the school and in a way contracted out the commitment to sport and physical activity. The rural families, however, did not have this opportunity and participation in outside school sports teams required significant parental support. It was observed that during the school years the rural young people participated in less sport but more physical recreation and physical labour compared to the Malcos College young men. Therefore, one impact of type of school and social class was on the types of sport and physical activities that were most common among the groups.

Perhaps the most substantial difference observed at the intersection of sport and physical activity and social class came post-school. The Malcos College young men made smooth transitions to further education. The social and cultural capital (Bourdieu, 1986) acquired through attending such a school ensured their success within this field. Their main barrier to participation in sport and physical activities at that stage appeared to be adjustment to the more flexible university schedule, and they found the lack of a regimented provision of sport and physical activity as experienced at school somewhat difficult. While they were no longer competing in the sports they did at school, each of the Malcos young men continued to value sport and physical activities in their lives, some continuing to participate in less structured activities (e.g. running, weights) and felt they could easily resume their chosen activities in the future. In this way, the Malcos young men's privileged social class allowed for positive experiences in sport and physical activities. They found their participation simple, albeit in certain sports within a restrictive culture, with few barriers and took it for granted that it would remain a part of their lives.

For the Greenvalley High young people who made the transition from school to work or further study, gender differences emerged as to their participation in physical activities. The young women felt that time constraints due to work and family commitments, and lack of financial stability were barriers to their participation in sport and physical activities.

> . . . it might have something to do with me if I was better financially you know, if I had more money to spend on things like that [physical activities]. So if I lived close to like a place where you play tennis or you play squash or something I could get into a club and I could go there but then I'd have to be more financially well for it you know. (Jacinta, aged 17)

> If there were more things around it would be good and if it were cheaper as well. Like there'll always be student discounts and stuff but what about the

> people who are working and you can't make enough money sometimes and you just want a little bit of help. (Sharon, aged 18)

At this point in their lives, the rural young women did not feel that physical activity was important to them, nor among their peer groups.

In contrast, the rural young men who had left school either continued with sport with the support of the family (e.g. Brett in pistol shooting) or were employed in jobs requiring physical labour and training.

> Basically the job I've got now I'm lifting fairly heavy objects anyway, so the more I work the fitter I get. (Adam, aged 17)

The rural young men and Malcos College young men had somewhat different experiences of sport and physical activity post-school. This may be observed as an intersection between the construction of masculinities and social class (Lee *et al.*, 2009). Laberge and Albert (2001, p. 202) suggest that upper-class boys are most often socialized with the aim of occupying management or leadership positions, meaning that 'they are unlikely to aspire to occupations requiring physical strength, thereby lessening the importance of physical sturdiness in the evaluation of maleness'.

This description appears to describe the Malcos College young men very well as they pursued university degrees in international business, commerce and engineering, and while they continued to value physical activity, they no longer competed in the sports of their school years. Their upper-class culture valued intelligence and sociability as characteristics of masculinity (Laberge and Albert, 2001). On the other hand, the rural working-class young men valued physical strength in order to express power and masculinity (Laberge and Albert, 2001), and utilized this power in continued sporting participation and through employment.

These distinctions, however, are not based on economic differences alone. Bourdieu (1978, p. 838) highlights the importance of cultural obstacles or 'hidden entry requirements', such as family tradition and early training, clothing, and techniques of sociability, that keep certain sports, and their privileges, closed to people of lower classes. These hidden requirements of particular forms of cultural and social capital are less obvious markers of distinctions, however they underscore how inequalities are not simply about money, but linked to subtle forms of differentiation that are taken as natural attributes of individuals. Although some sports were more privileged at Malcos College, it was clear from the young men's comments that participation in any sport was held as prestigious (e.g. 'If you don't play sport then you're nobody'). Having been socialized in this way, the Malcos College young men had the advantage of having accrued social and cultural capital in the form of support structures and a greater number of opportunities allowing for their smooth transitions into university. In contrast, working-class networks such as those of the rural young people were relatively smaller and more homogenous, providing them with relatively fewer opportunities and a less certain pathway into mainstream options, both in sport and physical activities and further study or employment.

Discussion

This chapter has presented an exploration of structural categories (social class, geographical location, schooling, families) as ways of understanding how young people experience physical activity over time. The data from young people's and parents' interviews demonstrated how the intersections of schools, families, geographical location and social class have an impact on amount and type of participation in sport and physical activities. Social class in particular provided differential access to cultural and social capital, which had a great influence in the post-school years. On the other hand, the data also demonstrate how geographical and school location are not sufficient to predict the future capitals of these young people in any kind of totalizing way. For example, the rural young men from Greenvalley High utilized opportunities to remain physically active, which had benefits for their employment in physical jobs; thus their physical capital was converted into economic capital. In terms of a more general analysis, however, the Malcos College young men's participation in a variety of team and individual sports (e.g. rugby, rowing, basketball, karate, golf, tennis) through their school provided them with forms of physical and social capital that have higher symbolic value in contemporary western societies (Bennett *et al.*, 2001). As also observed by others (Laberge and Albert, 2000; Light and Kirk, 2001) the private school young men experienced socialization into middle-class culture through participation in sports, and were able to convert this into university studies and lucrative future career prospects.

While DiMaggio (1987) suggested we were emerging (at least in the late 1980s) into a period of cultural declassification where boundaries between social groups were more porous and choices more diverse, there was generally little evidence of the young people moving outside their delimited life courses. In this situation, the young people's options can be described as *bounded agency* (Evans, 2002). For example, while it was evident that the rural young people from Greenvalley High and Homestead School had fewer traditional sport and physical activity opportunities, most still managed to participate in some form of physical activity, including sports (e.g. swimming, volleyball, equestrian, cricket), recreational physical activity (e.g. playing with siblings, using home equipment), physical labour and active transport, albeit their participation patterns were more recreational and less formal in comparison to the Malcos College young men. These young people, while perhaps considered *marginalized* in terms of sport and physical activity options, are making their own choices about participation and building their own identities around sport and physical activity within their local social and cultural worlds. The case of Lisa (Homestead School) being the only young woman to participate in a sport demonstrates her possession of the necessary social capital (access to equestrian clubs and coaches) and cultural and economic capital (knowledge of horse training and grooming methods, possession of land and equipment for horse riding), which afforded her the agency to participate in the sporting activity of equestrianism. Lisa's access, however, was only available to an activity that is considered appropriate and legitimate for female participants (Lee and Macdonald, 2009). Rather than being structurally forced into certain actions, Lisa chose a sport that was consistent with her habitus. While Lisa differed from the other young women, her personal trajectory still conformed to the social and cultural expectations of her social and geographical location.

In Bourdieu's terminology, bounded agency is demonstrated in the following quote: 'Agents shape their aspirations according to concrete indices of the accessible and inaccessible and, of what is and is not *for us*' (Bourdieu, 1990, p. 64, emphasis added). It is important to point out that this is not a conscious effort on behalf of the individual to match their aspirations to their perceived chances of success (Bourdieu, 1990). It is the interplay between the habitus and the social setting that results in the generation of dispositions that are compatible with social conditions, 'the most improbable practices are therefore excluded as unthinkable' (Bourdieu, 1990, p. 54).

The perpetuation of capital through schools and families that was observed in the school years continued to have an impact in the post-school years as the young people's habitus (plural) had been shaped by the social conditions of their early experiences. Their historical interactions with the physical culture in their local settings served as a form of boundary maintenance as we observed the young men and young women, higher and lower social classes, and rural versus urban, shaping their choice biographies within their own particular place of the possible. The Malcos College young men took for granted their early experiences and the valuable capital accrued, which meant their participation in sport and physical activities remained just another social and cultural asset they could draw on as they made transitions into adulthood. For the rural young men, continuation in sport and physical activities post-school meant affirming their masculine identities. For the rural young women, however, sport and physical activity was not a priority, and economic, social and geographical barriers remained.

Participants from these cohorts (and others), as proposed by Bourdieu (1990), formed a habitus consistent with their social and cultural fields, and geographical location. Structural factors such as gender, place, schooling and social class clearly had a powerful influence on identity construction. This supports perspectives of Evans (2002) and others of an interplay of structural forces with an individual's (and their family's) agency in taking up physical activity and physical culture practices and dispositions in nuanced ways not acknowledged in epidemiological studies.

Conclusion

Bourdieu's theory of capital and habitus has been useful in this analysis in deconstructing structural categories and allowing for an acknowledgement of individual agency. In this way structuralist concepts such as class, sex and geography were analysed from a poststructuralist perspective to explore issues of difference, diversity and complexity. This approach is consistent with recent calls to retain our 'structuralist memory' (e.g. Crotty, 1998; McLaren and Farandmandpur, 2000) in acknowledging the ongoing influence of structures such as gender and social class in the lives of young people. Qualitative data of this kind have the benefit of being longitudinal, in-depth and drawn from multiple methods. These characteristics of qualitative research allow us to come to understand the particularities of the groups that statistics identify as the least active, such as those from lower social classes, which have been the targets of – mostly unsuccessful – physical activity and health promotion campaigns. For example, despite the reported success of the Physical Education School Sport and Club Links (PESSCL) strategy in England, the best results were found in schools that had 'smaller proportions of pupils eligible for free meals, were in more affluent areas, and had a lower proportion of children from an ethnic minority heritage', and participation rates were also lower in girls-only schools (DCSF, 2007, p. 3). In Australia, national campaigns such as Active After School Communities (Australian Government, 2009) and the Healthy Active Ambassador Program (Australian Government, 2007) overlook many barriers to participation and make assumptions about young people's engagements with physical culture (Lee, 2008). If we are going to promote sport and physical activities as part of the concept of lifelong learning, then it is vital that those involved in both promotion and the teaching of physical activity understand the social and cultural frames of reference within which many young people construct their notions of sport and leisure (Deem and Gilroy, 1998). It is here that the challenge lies in extending research with young people into informing policy and curriculum. A continuation of qualitative research of this kind is necessary to add to the somewhat hollow stories of participation statistics and to contribute to a greater understanding of inequalities and differences in participation in physical activities. The issues raised in this chapter (social class/gender/bounded agency) and the impact they have on participation clearly have implications for how we promote sport and physical activities more broadly in the public health sector. We therefore need to continue longitudinal research, and give a voice to young people to inform equitable sport and physical activity promotion policy and curriculum.

Notes

1   All of the sports/physical activities are competitive and run in seasons, not as one-off events, so to participate would mean a whole-season commitment.
2   'Bludge' is an Australian and New Zealand slang term meaning to shirk responsibility or hard work.

References

Abbott, R.A., Macdonald, D., McKinnon, L., Stubbs, C.O., Lee, A.J., Harper, C. and Davies, P.S.W. (2007) *Healthy Kids Queensland Survey 2006 – Summary Report*. Brisbane, Australia: Queensland Health. Online. Available at: http://www.health.qld.gov.au/ph/documents/hpu/32848.pdf (accessed 4 November 2009).

Australian Government (2007) *Healthy Active – The Healthy Active Ambassadors Program*. Online. Available at: http://www.healthyactive.gov.au/internet/healthyactive/publishing.nsf/Content/ambassadors (accessed 11 August 2008).

Australian Government (2008) *2007 Australian National Children's Nutrition and Physical Activity Survey – Main Findings*. Online. Available at: http://www.health.gov.au/

internet/main/publishing.nsf/Content/66596E8FC68FD1A3CA2574D50027DB86/$Fil
e/childrens-nut-phys-survey.pdf (accessed 4 November 2009).

Australian Government (2009) *Participating in Sport*. Online. Available at:
http://www.ausport.gov.au/participating/schools_and_juniors/aasc/about (accessed 4
November 2009).

Azzarito, L. (2009) 'The panopticon of physical education: pretty, active and ideally white',
Physical Education and Sport Pedagogy, 14 (1): 19–39.

Bairner, A. (2007) 'Back to basics: class, social theory, and sport', *Sociology of Sport
Journal*, 24: 20–36.

Bennett, T., Emmison, M. and Frow, J. (2001) 'Social class and cultural practice in contemporary Australia', in T. Bennett and D. Carter (eds) *Culture in Australia: Policies, Publics
and Programs* (pp. 193–216). Cambridge: Cambridge University Press.

Bourdieu, P. (1986) 'The forms of capital', in J.G. Richardson (ed.) *Handbook of Theory and
Research for the Sociology of Education*. New York: Greenwood Press.

Bourdieu, P. (1987) 'What makes a social class? On the theoretical and practical existence
of groups', *Berkeley Journal of Sociology*, 32: 1–17.

Bourdieu, P. (1990) *The Logic of Practice*, trans. R. Nice. Stanford, CA: Stanford University
Press.

Burrows, L., Wright, J. and Jungersen-Smith, J. (2002). '"Measure your belly": New
Zealand children's constructions of health and fitness', *Journal of Teaching in Physical
Education*, 22 (1): 39–48.

Courtice, R. (1999) 'All-male schooling: speech night and the construction of masculinities', in C. Symes and D. Meadmore (eds) *The Extra-ordinary School: Parergonality and
Pedagogy*. New York: Peter Lang Publishing.

Crotty, M. (1998) *The Foundations of Social Research: Meaning and Perspective in the
Research Process*. St Leonards: Allen & Unwin.

DCFS (2007) *School Sport Survey 2006/07*. Online. Available at: http://www.teachernet.
gov.uk/docbank/index.cfm?id=11991 (accessed 18 September 2008).

Deem, R. and Gilroy, S. (1998) 'Physical activity, life-long learning and empowerment –
situating sport in women's leisure', *Sport, Education and Society*, 3 (1): 89–104.

DiMaggio, P. (1987) 'Classification in art', *American Sociological Review*, 52: 440–455.

Dowling Naess, F. (2001) 'Narratives about young men and masculinities in organized sport
in Norway', *Sport, Education and Society*, 6 (2): 125–142.

du Bois-Reymond, M. (1998) '"I don't want to commit myself yet": young people's life concepts', *Journal of Youth Studies*, 1 (1): 63–79.

Evans, J. and Davies, B. (2008) 'The poverty of theory: class configurations in the discourse
of Physical Education and Health (PEH)', *Physical Education and Sport Pedagogy*, 13
(2): 199–213.

Evans, J., Rich, E., Davies, B. and Allwood, R. (2008) *Education, Disordered Eating and
Obesity Discourse: Fat Fabrications*. London: Routledge.

Evans, K. (2002) 'Taking control of their lives? Agency in young adult transitions in
England and the New Germany', *Journal of Youth Studies*, 5 (3): 245–269.

Foote, S. (2003) 'Making sport of Tonya: class performance and social punishment',
Journal of Sport and Social Issues, 27 (1): 3–17.

Furlong, A. (2000) 'Introduction: youth in a changing world', *International Social Science
Journal*, 164: 129–134.

Health Survey for England (HSE) (2004a) *The Health of Children and Young People*.
Online. Available at: http://www.archive2.official-documents.co.uk/document/deps/doh/
survey02/hcyp/hcyp01.htm (accessed 14 May 2007).

Health Survey for England (HSE) (2004b) *Health Survey for England 2004: The Health of Minority Ethnic Groups*. Online. Available at: http://www.ic.nhs.uk/webfiles/publications/healthsurvey2004ethnicfull/HealthSurveyforEngland210406_PDF.pdf (accessed 14 May 2007).

Humberstone, B. (2002) 'Femininity, masculinity and difference: what's wrong with a sarong?', in A. Laker (ed.) *The Sociology of Sport and Physical Education: An Introductory Reader*. London: Routledge Falmer.

Kenway, J. and Bullen, E. (2001) *Consuming Children: Education-Entertainment-Advertising*. Buckingham: Open University Press.

Kirk, D. (1999) 'Physical culture, physical education and relational analysis', *Sport, Education and Society*, 4 (1): 63–73.

Laberge, S. and Albert, M. (2000) 'Conceptions of masculinity and gender transgressions in sport among adolescent boys', in M.A. Messner and D. Sabo (eds) *Masculinities, Gender Relations, and Sport*. Thousand Oaks, California: Sage.

Laberge, S. and Kay, J. (2002) 'Pierre Bourdieu's sociocultural theory and sport practice', in J. Maguire and K. Young (eds) *Theory, Sport and Society*. London: JAI.

Lee, J. (2008) 'Mapping young people's own meanings of physical activity and health against physical activity promotion initiatives', paper presented at the annual conference of the Australian Association for Research in Education (AARE). Queensland University of Technology, Brisbane, November.

Lee, J. and Abbott, R. (2009) 'Physical activity and rural young people's sense of place', *Children's Geographies*, 7 (2): 191–208.

Lee, J. and Macdonald, D. (2009) 'Rural young people and physical activity: understanding participation through social theory', *Sociology of Health and Illness*, 31 (3): 360–374.

Lee, J., Macdonald, D. and Wright, J. (2009) 'Young men's physical activity choices: the impact of capital masculinities and location', *Journal of Sport and Social Issues*, 33 (1): 59–77.

Light, R. and Kirk, D. (2001) 'Australian cultural capital – rugby's social meaning: physical assets, social advantage and independent schools', *Culture, Sport, Society*, 4 (3): 81–98.

Macdonald, D. (2002) 'Extending agendas: physical culture research for the 21st century', in D. Penney (ed.) *Gender and Physical Education: Contemporary Issues and Future Education*. London: Routledge.

McGannon, K.R. and Mauws, M.K. (2002) 'Exploring the exercise adherence problem: an integration of ethnomethodological and poststructuralist perspectives', *Sociology of Sport Journal*, 19: 67–89.

McGregor, C. (1997) *Class in Australia*. Ringwood, Victoria: Penguin Books Australia.

McKay, J. (1991) *No Pain, No Gain? Sport and Australian Culture*. Sydney: Prentice Hall.

McLaren, P. and Farahmandpur, R. (2000) 'Reconsidering Marx in post-Marxist times: a requiem for postmodernism', *Educational Researcher*, 29 (3): 25–33.

Mehus, I. (2005) 'Distinction through sport consumption: spectators of soccer, basketball, and ski-jumping', *International Review for the Sociology of Sport*, 40 (3): 321–333.

Miller, T. (1999) 'Hating sport', *Journal of Sport and Social Issues*, 23 (1): 3–4.

Offe, C. (1985) *Disorganized Capitalism: Contemporary Transformations of Work and Politics*. Cambridge: Polity Press.

Pronger, B. (1998) 'Post-sport: transgressing boundaries in physical culture', in G. Rail (ed.) *Sport and Postmodern Times*. Albany: State University of New York.

Roberts, K. (1985) 'Youth in the 1980s: a new way of life', *International Social Science Journal*, 37: 427–440.

Rowe, D. (1998) 'Rethinking power and resistance in sport', *Journal of Sport and Social Issues*, 22 (3): 241–251.

Sleap, M. and Wormwald, H. (2001) 'Perceptions of physical activity among young women aged 16 and 17', *European Journal of Physical Education*, 6: 26–37.

Sparkes, A.C. (1992) 'The paradigms debate: an extended review and a celebration of difference', in A.C. Sparkes (ed.) *Research in Physical Education and Sport: Exploring Alternative Visions*. London: The Falmer Press.

Sport England (2001) *Disability Survey 2000: Young People with a Disability and Sport*. Online. Available at: http://www.sportengland.org/research/tracking_trends.aspx (accessed 14 May 2007).

Stempel, C. (2005) 'Adult participation sports as cultural capital: a test of Bourdieu's theory of the field of sports', *International Review for the Sociology of Sport*, 40 (4): 411–432.

Tinning, R. (2000) 'Unsettling matters for Physical Education in Higher Education: implications of "New Times"', *Quest*, 52: 32–48.

Walkerdine, V., Lucey, H. and Melody, J. (2001) *Growing Up Girl*. Hampshire: Palgrave.

Warin, M., Turner, K., Moore, V. and Davies, M. (2008) 'Bodies, mothers and identities: rethinking obesity and the BMI', *Sociology of Health and Illness*, 30 (1), available at: http://www.blackwell-synergy.com/toc/shil/0/0.

Williams, G.H. (2003) 'The determinants of health: structure, context and agency', *Sociology of Health and Illness*, 25: 131–154.

Wright, J., Macdonald, D. and Groom, L. (2003) 'Physical activity and young people: beyond participation', *Sport, Education and Society*, 8 (1): 17–33.

Wyn, J. and White, R. (2000) 'Negotiating social change: the paradox of youth', *Youth and Society*, 32 (2): 165–183.

3 The body, physical activity and inequity

Learning to listen *with* girls *through* action

Kimberly L. Oliver

Introduction

> The boys told me I couldn't play with them because I was a girl and I was Black
> . . . Some boys don't want the girls to play because they are girls and I think
> that's a real problem because we should all be able to do what we want to do.
> We should all be able to play – Maggie Mae, age 10. (Oliver and Hamzeh,
> 2010)

The purpose of this chapter is two-fold. In the first part, I will highlight three studies that illuminate some of what we have learned about how the intersections of gender, race and sexuality influence how girls experience their bodies, and how they experience their physical activity opportunities and participation. In the second part, I will discuss what we have learned about how to understand girls through collaborating with them to practise strategies for changing body and physical activity inequities as *they* see them.

Data for this chapter come from 13 years of doing activist research with African-American, Hispanic, Mexican-American and European-American girls. Activist methodologies are rooted in the belief that 'valid knowledge is produced only in collaboration and in action' (Fine, 2007, p. 613). From this perspective, researchers position participants as 'architects' rather than research 'subjects' and thus they can become co-researchers who contribute to both research design and knowledge production. A central theme in activist research methodologies is the 'fundamental right to ask, investigate, dissent, and demand what could be' (Fine, 2007, p. 613).

Over the years we have found that feminist, poststructural, and critical theories can help scholars move away from only documenting *what is* and begin to explore with their participants *what might be*. We can do this by engaging in research projects that collaborate with participants in developing both a language of critique and a language of possibility. That is, assisting participants in identifying forms of inequity that threaten their health and well-being, and then working together to name and enact possibilities for change so that transformation might begin (Fine, 1994; Giroux, 1997). Giroux (1997) wrote:

> a critical pedagogy has to begin with a dialectical celebration of the languages
> of critique and possibility – an approach which finds its noblest expression

in a discourse integrating critical analysis with social transformation . . .
[around] problems rooted in the concrete experiences of everyday life.
(p. 132)

By making girls' everyday experiences central to the research we are able to see the
circulating discourses that shape their subjectivities, search for places to explore
their agency and work collaboratively with them to practise change (Weiler, 1988;
Weedon, 1997; Davies, 2000; Weis and Fine, 2004).

Subjectivity is the name given to the 'conscious and unconscious thoughts and
emotions of the individual, her sense of herself and her ways of understanding her
relation to the world' (Weedon, 1997, p. 32). People's subjectivities are dynamic
and multiple, constantly positioned in relation to the circulating discourses and
practices; 'Further, the discourses and practices through which we are constituted
are also often in tension, one with another, providing the human subject with multiple layers of contradictory meanings which are inscribed in their bodies and in
their conscious and unconscious minds' (Davies, 2003, p. 11). Girls, as thinking
and feeling subjects, constantly read, negotiate, accept, reject and alter the social
discourses they experience. Thus, subjectivity is always in process, and therefore is
open to change (Davies, 2000).

From a feminist poststructural perspective, viewing subjectivity as a process
open to change does not mean denying the importance of any particular form of
being (Weedon, 1997). Rather, it provides insights into the values and practices that
hold existing norms in place. Through recognition of how norms function in girls'
lives we can begin to see these norms not as absolutes, but rather as structures that
can be acted upon by both individuals and groups. While the constitutive power of
normative structures must be recognized, 'the possibility that it can also be laughed
out of existence, played with, disrupted, or used to manufacture new possibilities,
can also be recognized' (Davies, 2003, p. 200).

This recognition of new possibilities creates opportunities for girls to explore
their agency. According to Davies (2000), agency is:

> the discursive constitution of a particular individual as having presence (rather
> than absence), as having access to a subject position in which they have the
> right to speak and be heard . . . author of their own multiple meanings and
> desires . . . one who can go beyond the given meaning in any one discourse
> and forge something new . . . through imagining not what *is* but what *might be*'.
> (p. 66, original emphasis)

Authorizing student perspectives

If researchers and teachers hope to focus on *what might be* in order to take steps
towards challenging oppressive practices that limit either girls' experiences of
their bodies or their physical activity participation/opportunities, it is important
that we value girls as viable co-researchers who can collaborate with us to find
solutions to everyday problems: 'Educators must embrace what Welch (1990) calls

a "feminist ethic of risk" – the willingness to take small steps toward changing oppressive practices even if complete change seems or is unattainable' (Cook-Sather, 2002, p. 6).

I believe that if we are to better understand girls' experiences then our research needs to include authentic spaces where girls can contribute to what is studied, how it is studied and what is done with the information learned. I agree with Cook-Sather (2002), who claims that students have unique perspectives about what goes on in their worlds and, as long as 'we exclude these perspectives from our conversations about schooling and how it needs to change, our efforts at reform will be based on an incomplete picture of life in classrooms and schools and how that life could be improved' (p. 3). If we take her idea and apply it to health-related issues, we can begin to see the importance of including students' perspectives in how to challenge cultural practices and messages that limit their health and physical activity participation (Oliver, Hamzeh and McCaughtry, 2009). By listening and learning from students' perspectives we begin to see the particular experiences of their worlds from their points of view.

However, to more fully authorize student perspectives means more than simply including them in conversations that name and critique local normative discourses that threaten their health or physical activity participation. Rather, it means that we create valued spaces where students can speak, and where we as researchers re-tune our ears so that we can hear what they are saying and redirect our actions in response to what we hear (Cook-Sather, 2002). It is in the response that we can begin to collaborate with students to practise strategies for changing inequities as *they* see them.

Jennifer Gore (1993) claims that we should use our power as researchers 'in an attempt (that might not be successful) to help others exercise power' (p. 59). In an attempt to collaborate with students as co-researchers to help them practise strategies for challenging the physical activity inequities they identify, we agree with Weiler (1988), who claims that it is important to recognize 'the limits of what is possible to accomplish . . . and recognize the value and importance of *doing* what is possible' (p. 153, emphasis added).

Understanding girls through collaboration and action

I have organized this chapter around three different research projects (Oliver, 1999; Oliver and Lalik, 2001; Oliver, Hamzeh and McCaughtry, 2009; Oliver and Hamzeh, 2010). Findings from each of these different projects all come from the ways we worked with our research participants as co-researchers (Cook-Sather, 2002). For a more detailed and theoretical discussion of activist research methodologies, sometimes called participatory action research processes, please see Enright and O'Sullivan's chapter in this book (Chapter 10).

The findings described in this chapter emerged through using data-collection techniques that involved all of our participants studying topics that they believed were pivotal to how they experienced their bodies or how their activity participation was influenced. While there were differences between the studies described in this chapter, what was similar between each of these research projects was our commitment to transformative practices and our focus on using the girls' interests as a starting point for inquiry and understanding. For some of the studies the girls engaged in magazine inquiries with the intent of naming and critiquing how they were learning to think about their bodies and the bodies of others (Oliver, 1999). In other studies the girls engaged in the inquiry processes with the intent of learning more about how their activity participation was constrained and what we could do to increase their opportunities to play (Oliver, Hamzeh, and McCaughtry, 2009; Oliver and Hamzeh, 2010). These processes included: (a) identifying and/or selecting a topic of study; (b) informally interviewing peers, family members or teachers; (c) creating a survey to learn more about their topic; (d) surveying others; (e) analysing survey and interview data; (f) creating a representation of their learning; and (g) practising change or publicly speaking out.

Girls' experiences of their bodies and physical activity: intersections of gender, race and sexuality

> The boys also say that we are dumb, stupid and wouldn't last five seconds [in sports] . . . and that you're a woman and you need to stay in your place – Maggie Mae, age 10. (Oliver and Hamzeh, 2010)

> Some girls don't pay attention to me because I wear a scarf, and I don't like that. I just feel like taking my scarf off. When I do, I think everyone will like me, even the boys. I think I have a nice figure, but I can't show it. In my religion, the women are only allowed to show their figure to their husband [only] – Khalilah, age 13. (Oliver and Lalik, 2001, p. 313)

'Fashion In' and 'Fashion Out'

This section highlights how three African-American girls and one European-American girl used the phrases 'Fashion In' and 'Fashion Out' (Oliver, 1999) to describe how they experienced their bodies. This story emerged when I asked the girls to go through magazines and cut out pictures that captured their attention. Through fashion these four were constructing multiple meanings of their bodies. Their bodies were a central part of how they were learning about normality, their relationships with others and what society values in women. These girls were learning that their bodies could be, or needed to be, manipulated and controlled to create the desired images they associated with 'Fashion In' (Oliver, 1999; Oliver and Lalik, 2000).

The two predominant criteria for being 'Fashion In' were 'looking right' and being 'normal'. According to Nicole, Khalilah, Alysa and Dauntai, to 'look right' and be 'normal' girls need 'healthy hair', the 'right clothes and shoes' and the right 'body shape', and they must 'look feminine'. These girls described others, and could be described by other girls, as being 'Fashion In' or 'Fashion Out' depending on whether they met or failed to meet the above criteria.

Those who could model the fashion became what the girls called 'role models'. These role models set the standard for what the girls perceived as right and normal. 'Fashion In' and 'Fashion Out' were the girls' terms, the interpretive codes they used to describe what looking right and being normal were all about. A more critical interpretation of their terms 'Fashion In' and 'Fashion Out' illuminates how these girls' bodies were a space for them to learn to internalize various forms of sexism, racism, classism and heterosexism.

The specific criteria the girls identified for being 'Fashion In' centred on healthy hair, clothes and shoes, body shape and being 'feminine'. However, the underlying factor in determining whether the images were acceptable was whether a girl 'looks right' and, thus, is 'normal'. Being normal was about 'looking' a certain way. While these girls individualized this normalized image, they did so within the criteria of 'Fashion In'.

'Healthy hair'

The girls identified 'healthy hair' as a necessity for the image associated with the perfect woman. Healthy hair was one of the criteria that determined whether a girl would be considered by her peers as 'Fashion In' or 'Fashion Out'. Among some of the looks they associated with healthy was hair that looked 'conditioned', 'shiny', 'sparkly', 'has no split ends', 'no new growth that can be seen' and 'is straight'. The girls perceived healthy hair as something they could create by purchasing and using certain products.

Nicole:	Well see with us three [Dauntai, Khalilah and Nicole] we get perms . . . you know how if you got a perm it makes your hair more straight . . . We get one [a perm] because this, [points to wavy part] you can see where it grew . . . So you have to get a new perm cause you got new growth . . . And you have to treat that with the perm too.
Researcher:	Oh, it makes your hair straight when you get a perm? . . . But what if you don't perm your hair?
Nicole and Dauntai:	It looks a mess!
Khalilah:	It gets all wrinkly and stuff. . . . It looks terrible!
Nicole:	See your hair is not like ours.
Researcher:	Oh OK, so does everybody perm their hair?
Khalilah:	No, if you need it.
Nicole:	No, if you cannot afford a perm. I mean some people's hair is just so, you know, it's not funny because they look like a doggy . . . and you know it makes their hair real thick . . . it just be coming down and it look like wool . . . It looks a mess.
Khalilah:	You feel like just going out and buying um a perm. Ask um when their birthday is and go buy them a perm.
Nicole:	You do!

Dauntai, Nicole and Khalilah would tell you that, if you are an African-American or Indian girl with 'wrinkly' or 'woolly' hair, you'd better change what is natural if you want to fit the image so you do not 'look a mess'. These girls were learning that healthy is a look they could create. Yet the look is not natural for everyone, thus not a realistic image of 'health' for some. For a girl to be 'Fashion In', her hair needs to 'look right', which means it needs to be 'straight'. So, within this particular criterion – that is, 'healthy hair' – a girl's race and hair type contribute to whether she would meet the criteria naturally or if she would need economic power to buy the image; an image they called 'healthy' (see Oliver, 1999, for more detail on the other criteria).

Women should be feminine

Femininity was not a criteria identified by the girls for being 'Fashion In'. However, femininity was tied in with looking right; and looking right was part of the criteria for being 'Fashion In'. Femininity was an underlying factor for their normalized image of the perfect woman.

Researcher:	What do you think of her? [I pointed to a tall African-American woman dancer; you can see the muscles in her legs]
Alysa:	That's sick . . . Too muscular. . . . I just think women should be feminine . . . you know, not where you can see the muscle cause I think that's masculine.
Researcher:	Oh, so muscular is a masculine trait?
Alysa:	No it's just seeing the muscle.
Researcher:	What does feminine look like?
Alysa:	Just like you can have muscle but not really see a lot of it. You don't look fat you just don't have muscle.

Not only are well-developed muscles a sign of strength, but muscle is important to our metabolic functioning (US Department of Health and Human Services, 1996). Alysa did not perceive women that looked muscular as feminine. In her view it was all right for girls to have muscle as long as you could not see the muscle as that would not be feminine.

Researcher:	I'm still curious Alysa, why you don't think it's OK for too much muscle to show.
Alysa:	I don't know, I just think that men . . . everybody should have the muscle, but men should show it and women shouldn't.
Dauntai:	I don't agree with her.
Researcher:	You don't what Dauntai?
Nicole:	I don't either.
Dauntai:	I don't agree with her [Alysa] cause she said that men should show, men don't necessarily have to show their muscles, I don't think so.
Researcher:	What do you think about women?

Dauntai: Women they don't have to necessarily not show their muscles. It's all, it depends, it depends upon you how you are, how you want to look like, and what looks best on you, what you think looks best on you.

Many of the cultural stories of women these girls were seeing, hearing and telling did not centre on how they function as healthy human beings, or develop into whole people, but rather how girls and women can manipulate their bodies to create visual images that conform to cultural norms. These girls were learning that the 'look' is what is important (Featherstone, 1991). The concerns these girls had about how they looked are real; not looking right eliminates them from gaining access to social power. On the surface, their conversations about their bodies may seem like simple adolescent chitchat about fashion. Yet the stories girls tell to others become their ways of acting together (Gilbert, 1994). When girls' conversations are laced with internalized sexism, racism, classism and heterosexism, the possibilities they are creating for themselves and others become limited and, therefore, freedom is lost. Not only can listening to the stories adolescent girls tell about their bodies help us to better understand how their health may be affected, their stories will help those who are different from them to understand them better. Or as Dauntai wrote, 'This group . . . gave me a chance . . . to tell an older person how younger people are because some older people don't understand and they act like they don't want to take the time to listen to what other younger people are like or what they think' (Oliver, 1999, p. 242).

'Girly girls can play games too'

This study highlights how the intersections of gender, race and sexuality create barriers to 11 girls' (eight Mexican-American, two Hispanic, one European-American) physical activity participation (Oliver, Hamzeh and McCaughtry, 2009). Early in the research the girls introduced the construct of 'girly girl' as pivotal to understanding what prevented them from being physically active at school. It surfaced during a photo analysis where we asked them to 'take pictures of things that prevent girls from being physically active'. They explained that being a 'girly girl' often hindered some girls' activity participation because a 'girly girl' does not want to 'sweat', 'mess up her hair and nails', 'mess up her nice clothes' and sometimes wears 'flip flops'.

Sunshine explained that 'girly girls' do not like to play sports like football and soccer because 'you get all sweaty and yucky'. In addition to not wanting to sweat, Matilda explained that 'girly girls' are worried about their 'hair standing up', as well as being 'scared they'd break a nail'. Suzette claimed that girly girls 'like looking perfect'. Thus, according to Niecy, girly girls 'don't want to participate in physical activity because they care more about their hair and nails than running or anything'.

It would be easy to interpret this passage as girls buying in to and thus regulating their bodies around notions of heteronormative femininity (Butler, 1993). Without trying to listen and learn more about how the enactment of girly girl manifested in these girls' lives, and specifically their physical activity participation patterns, we might have continued to perpetuate the notion that the girls are the problem and, more specifically, that Mexican-American girls are the problem. We worked hard to listen to these girls without making the judgement that a girly girl or heteronormative Mexican values are a problem. Thus, we left ourselves open to learn more about how these girls' fluid embodiment of girly girl positioned them as active agents in their worlds (Davies, 2000; Azzarito, Solomon and Harrison, 2006).

The girls' description of being 'girly girl' was a fluid, temporal and partial embodiment (Davies, 2000). As Kat stated, 'I'm like 80 per cent girly girl and 20 per cent not girly girl.' Likewise, Niecy reported, 'I'm sometimes a girly girl.' 'It depends on how my day is already going . . . if you smell good . . . or are clean and fresh . . . then you want to be a girly girl,' claimed Amy. She further elaborates, 'It also depends on the days we have PE. If it's a PE day I will be really really active . . . We are more girly girl on a non PE day.'

These girls were often strategic in performing girly girl when it served their mood or physical activity opportunities. Sunshine explained, 'Sometimes if I don't like the sport they are playing in PE, then I'm a girly girl.' Kim asked, 'So on PE days, most of the time you are not girly girl right? Unless you don't like an activity . . . so girly girl becomes your excuse for not doing the sport. Is that how it works?' Sunshine continued, 'Yeah.' Kim responded, 'That is a really interesting strategy for getting out of being active.'

These 11 girls helped us to understand the complexity of being girly girl. On the one hand, given the way the girls described girly girl we could have read it as a fixed and unitary subjectivity (Davies, 2000) – that is, girly girls 'don't want to sweat', 'don't want to mess up their hair and nails' and 'like wearing nice clothes', and that is why they 'don't like physical activity'. However, as we continued listening we began to recognize how the girls described the fluidity of being a girly girl (Weedon, 1997; Davies, 2000).

For these girls, being a girly girl was more than 'not wanting to sweat' or not wanting to 'mess up their hair and nails' – it was a discourse that they could use to articulate one of their subjectivities and an embodiment that they could easily perform to get what they desired. However, their ability to use their girly girl discourse was a double-edged sword. On the one hand, when the girls chose to not participate in activities they didn't like, and used being 'girly girl' as their excuse, no one would acknowledge, question or challenge this embodiment because it fits so well within the dominant discourse of heteronormative femininity within the larger Mexican culture (Bordo, 1993; Butler, 1993; Anzaldúa, 2007). On the other hand, because girly girl *is* such a normalized discourse, no one questioned whether there might be some other explanation to why the girls were not participating in physical activity.

Exploring physical activity possibilities

As feminist activist scholars we believed that part of what we needed to do was to look at what we were learning from the girls as if things could be different. We wanted to use our positions of authority in ways that allowed us and the girls to see and then enact alternative possibilities that might better suit the girls' needs. After spending two sessions where the girls thoroughly explained how embodying 'girly girl' functioned in their lives or the lives of their friends, we were still trying to understand how being a girly girl worked with respect to physical activity. Sunshine's comment about using girly girl as an excuse to get out of physical activity during PE when she did not like a particular sport created an opportunity to discuss the types of activities the girls at school did not like and why they did not like them. The girls discussed not liking 'football', 'soccer', 'basketball' and 'frisbee' in PE. They explained that they did not like these sports 'because the boys kick your feet', 'trip you on purpose', 'push you down' and 'grab your hair'.

Kim asked, 'So it isn't the sport that you don't like necessarily, it's the way the sport is being played? So if the boys are kicking you or tripping you or pulling your hair or not giving you the ball, those kinds of things . . .' – Sunshine cut her off, 'You feel left out and hurt.' Kim continued, 'We're trying to figure out if there are a lot of girls that are girly girls or identify as girly girls, they should be able to be active in ways that are . . .' – Sunshine cut her off again, 'Suitable for them.' 'Yes, that are suitable, wouldn't you think?' asked Kim.

Kim continued, 'How could we be more active on our girly girl days? Because you have to have your girly girl days, I understand this.' Sunshine explained that if girls 'felt comfortable with themselves [they] would be able to do physical activity'. This was a turning point in the study. It was at this moment that we began to better understand the complexity of physical activity in the girls' lives. What seemed to be happening initially was that the girls talked about their physical activity barriers only in relation to being 'girly girl'. But as we listened longer what we began to hear was how the girls used their girly girl language of embodiment as a way to express additional barriers that hindered their physical activity participation – that is, the girls did not like the choices of activities available at school, did not like how the activities were played (when playing with boys), did not like getting hurt or being left out, and wanted to be able to play and 'feel comfortable with themselves'. Thus, rather than play in situations they identified as unsuitable, they chose not to participate.

Practising change through game play

For the next seven sessions, we worked with each group of girls from the McAuliffe and Frida Kahlo schools to co-create games that girls could play while simultaneously being 'girly girl'. For each theme that the girls identified as part of being 'girly girl' and therefore a barrier to their physical activity (i.e. don't want to sweat, mess up hair or nails, mess up nice clothes, and wear flip flops), as well as days when they 'didn't have equipment' (McAuliffe) or 'the boys wouldn't let them play' (Frida Kahlo), we: (a) made up games; (b) played the games; (c) decided what modifications or changes were needed to the games; (d) wrote up the games using a form we designed to help structure game creation; (e) tested the games with the other group of girls; and (f) discussed whether they liked the game, and why or why not. In the next section, a description of this process is provided.

For these girls, initially, their available physical activity spaces and opportunities were constricted because in their view they did not allow for them to be girly girl *and* physically active simultaneously. This partly resonates with a variety of physical education scholars who have noted girls' participation in physical activity is often limited by perceived gender barriers (Wright, 1999; Flintoff and Scraton, 2001; Azzarito, Solmon and Harrison, 2006). However, girly girl is not just about gender. Girly girl is also a language and embodiment that illuminates the intersection of gender discourse with Mexican culture and values (Cruz, 2006; Anzaldúa, 2007).

Anzaldúa (2007) writes that for a *mexicana* the 'ultimate rebellion she can make against their native culture is through her sexual behavior' (p. 41). As a lesbian she claims that for a *mexicana* to be anything but heterosexual places herself at risk of 'being abandoned by the mother, the culture, *la Raza*, for being unacceptable, faulty, damaged . . . totally rejected. . . . To avoid this rejection, some of us conform to the values of the culture' (Anzaldúa, 2007, pp. 40–42). While the girls used the language of girly girl as a way of identifying barriers to their physical activity, their embodiment of girly girl resonates with heteronormative Mexican culture.

Rather than focus our attention on asking the girls to critique parts of Mexican culture that Anzaldúa (2007) claims injure women in the name of protecting them, our hope was to work with the girls in ways that focused on creating possibilities. When we began focusing on *what could be*, by acknowledging the girls' desires to be girly girl, and invited them to create games that girly girls would enjoy playing, the barriers they identified were no longer the problem. Once the games became about enacting their subjectivities without outsiders' (Hill-Collins, 1990; Anzaldúa, 2007) judgement, then not wanting to sweat or mess up their hair or nails really did not matter any more.

It was as if the moment we acknowledged their desire to be girly girl and worked *with* them to co-create games *for* them, the content of the games they created actually contradicted many of their self-identified girly girl barriers – that is, while they may have been making up games for days where they did not want to sweat or mess up their nice clothes, many of the actual games involved running, jumping, chasing and fleeing – in other words, the possibility of sweating or getting their clothes dirty. Through the process of making up and playing games we noticed that the girls began to resist the idea that being girly girl meant one cannot, or does not, desire being physically active. It was through the game creation process that the girls began to name and enact alternative possibilities for their physical activity participation.

Through practising change, these girls re-inscribed discourses of race/gender/sexuality by creating a curriculum of possibilities that allowed them to be, feel and become physically active. The games that the girls created with Kim allowed them to take ownership over their physical activity practices. It centred them as physically active through the games they created and played, and re-positioned them as girls who were willing to possibly sweat, get dirty, and mess up their hair or break their nails. According to Davies (2000), this is agency:

Agency is never freedom from discursive constitution of self but the capacity to recognize that constitution and to resist, subvert, and change the discourses themselves through which one is being constituted. It is the freedom to recognize multiple readings such that no discursive practice, or positioning within it by powerful others, can capture being an individual standing outside social structure and process. (p. 67)

'The boys won't let us play'

In this section I highlight what we learned about how the intersections of race, gender and sexuality were revealed as one African-American girl and four Mexican-American girls explored and challenged what they identified as preventing them from being physically active at school: 'the boys won't let us play' (see Oliver and Hamzeh, 2010, for the full story).

While scholars of colour remind us that the intersections of race, gender, sexuality and social class are central to girls' experiences (Delgado Bernal, 2002; Cruz, 2006; Delgado Bernal *et al.*, 2006; Anzaldúa, 2007), we are cautioned by Mohanty (2003) and Ahmed (2000) of the importance of moving away from essentializing minorities and treating them as if they were 'a singular group' (Ahmed, 2000, p. 165). Rather, they suggest a need to study the intersections of race and gender in ways that do not view minorities as the 'strange other' (Ahmed, 2000), but rather as people with whom we can engage in meaningful conversations about their day-to-day lives.

It is within these conversations we might begin to better understand how girls negotiate normative discourses that circulate in their lives and influence their physical activity participation and opportunities (Hall, 1996). By focusing on the girls' experiences within physical activity in ways that highlight the intersections of race/ethnicity, gender, sexuality, age and so forth, we might better position ourselves to attend to how girls are engaged in a process of 'resisting subjectivities that seek to classify them in particularly limited racialized, classed, gendered, and sexualized ways' (Jamieson, 2003, p. 2).

One of the first tasks we asked the girls to do was to 'photograph things that helped them to be physically active and things that prevented them from being physically active'. We agree with Sanders-Bustle (2003) that providing students with cameras and asking them to photograph their worlds creates opportunities for them to begin documenting their life experiences that may otherwise go unnoticed. Further, using images as an opener to conversation also helps young people begin to explain verbally what they know intuitively (Sanders-Bustle, 2003; Oliver and Lalik, 2004a, 2004b). Several of the girls' photos were of different spaces around the school playground, such as the basketball courts, the swings, the jungle gym and the tree borders that served as benches for the children to sit. Other images documented the girls' home lives and included pictures of computers, girls doing housework and playing in their backyards.

Using the girls' photos as a starting point for discussion, Kim asked them to explain their pictures and why they took them. 'This one . . . I took [of] a girl

[Maggie Mae] that some boys don't want to play with them.' She explained that the boys told Maggie Mae she could not play with them because 'she was too big and too tall . . . that she made most of the goals and that made the girls beat the boys . . . and because her skin was the wrong colour'.

Mary's photo stimulated a critique about what was happening at their school with respect to physical activity. During this critique the girls used several of their photographs to verbally explain how the boys and girls interacted during recess; their primary opportunity for physical activity. Mary picked up a picture of one of her friends:

Mary:	That is my friend but the boys won't let her swing because they say it's the boys' swings.
	[Marie jumps in with one of her pictures of the boys swinging and a girl standing on the side.]
Marie:	Here are the boys and they told that girl she couldn't get on [the swing] because girls don't know how to go fast.
Kim:	What do you think about that?
Marie:	It's crazy.
	[Mary continues Marie's critique of the boys.]
Mary:	This one is of me that someone took.
Kim:	Why did you have someone take that picture?
Mary:	Cause they [the boys] won't let me play soccer with them . . . cause they say I wasn't good enough and plus I have glasses.
Kim:	Did you know that a lot of people play soccer and wear glasses?
Mary:	Yah, because once I got hit they [the boys] say I can break them [my glasses] but I said that I'll be careful but they said no you can't play.
Kim:	Does this happen a lot at your school that the boys tell the girls what they can and can't do?
Girls together:	Yes!
Kim:	Do you think it's fair that the boys are allowed to do that?
Girls together:	No!
Mary:	I say that any girl can do whatever they want because sports can be for both boys and girls . . . I tell them like we should be friends and don't make fun of people, what kind of color of skin they have.

Maggie Mae suggested to the group that they create a PowerPoint presentation and give it to all the 5th-grade classes, outlining exactly how and why the boys were not letting the girls play during recess. Kim and Manal assisted the girls in studying the problem they identified and creating a presentation they could give to publicize their concerns. Figure 3.1 shows the presentation the girls created and gave to the 5th-grade classes, their PE teacher and the classroom teachers. Within their presentation we can see how the intersections of race and gender limited the girls' physical activity opportunities at school.

How Boys Treat Girls
By
Kathy, Marie, Mary, Maria, Maggie Mae, Kim and Manal

Today's Message . . .
   We want boys to treat girls fairly, equally, and respectfully during physical activities.

What is our concern?

- How some boys treat girls during physical activities.

What have we done to study our concern?

- We took pictures of things that help girls to be active and things that prevent girls from being active.
- We analysed our photos to determine what was preventing some girls from being physically active.
- We interviewed the girls on how boys treat the girls during physical activity.
- We designed a survey to learn more about how boys treat the girls during physical activity.
- We surveyed a number of girls at our school and analysed the survey data we collected.
- We made a presentation to report our learning.

What we learned . . .

- *How it makes girls feel when the boys won't let them play:*
   - It hurts our feelings.
   - We are disappointed.
   - We feel degraded.
   - It makes us angry.
   - It makes us mad and sad – especially when the boys call us names.

- *Why girls think the boys treat the girls unfairly:*
   - Some boys think girls are "girly girls."
   - Some boys think that "girls are too weak."
   - Some boys think that "the girls might get hurt."
   - Some boys think "it's a man's game."
   - Some boys think "that they are better than the girls."
   - Some boys think that the "girls are stupid or dumb to think that they can't play with the boys."
   - Some boys say the girls are "weak, too short, too fragile, or that they might break a nail."
   - Some boys don't like some of the girls so they won't let them play.

- *When the boys treat the girls unfairly in physical activity:*
   - At recess.

- Before and after school.
- During PE.
- During music.

- ***What excuses the boys make to prevent the girls from playing:***
  - Girls are too "girly girl and wear make-up."
  - "You can't play because you don't know how to make a basket."
  - The boys pretend they are not playing when the girls ask if they can play.
  - Girls are "not into sports."
  - "We already have enough players."

- ***What the boys actually do to prevent the girls from playing:***
  - "They kick the girls off the playing area."
  - Some boys "yell at the girls until they leave the playing area."
  - Some boys "throw the ball at their face or stomach to make them leave."

How we want the boys to treat girls

- *Please stop calling us names.*
- *Please start treating us fairly, equally, and respectfully during physical activities.*
- *Please stop underestimating our physical abilities.*
- *Please stop hurting our feelings by degrading us.*
- *Please realize that sports are for girls too.*

Figure 3.1 How boys treat girls

By the girls publicly challenging the racialized and gendered discourses that denied them opportunities to be active, they were successful at bringing about change in subtle ways. First, over the course of the research project, the girls' PE teacher took an active interest in what we were learning. As he became aware of the problems the girls were having during recess he began to talk with the people on recess duty about what was happening, and asked them to pay attention to the dynamics between the boys and girls and to make sure that the girls also had an opportunity to play. The girls' PE teacher also began to pay more attention to the ways the girls and boys interacted during physical education. While the girls did not talk about the boys' behaviours in PE class, their teacher actively worked to make sure that no one was denied an opportunity to participate.

When girls are given an opportunity to critically study barriers to their physical activity researchers and teachers can begin to see where girls resist racialized and gendered discourses around physical activity. Through this knowledge, we begin to see that it isn't that these 'minority girls don't like activity', it is that these girls have to negotiate and challenge forms of sexism and racism to simply have the *chance* to be active.

Implications for research and teaching

As researchers and teachers begin to better understand how the intersections of gender, race and sexuality influence girls' experiences, we can begin to find ways to work with them to name, negotiate and challenge the inequities they identify that threaten to rob them of their health and physical activity opportunities. Throughout our work with girls we have learned several things about how to understand their lives, what they value, and what they hope for with respect to things that influence how they experience their bodies and how they experience physical activity. Much of our learning has occurred as we have collaborated with girls to practise strategies for identifying and challenging such inequities.

First, and probably most importantly for researchers, we have learned that it is imperative for us to listen to girls over time. For us to more fully understand inequities that threaten girls' health and physical activity, simply interviewing them once or twice is insufficient. Delgado (2006) writes, 'the process of getting youth to voice their opinions may take a lot longer and require greater effort than most adults are willing to acknowledge' (pp. 80–81). For young girls and adolescents, finding a language to communicate what inequity looks and feels like takes time. We have learned that direct questioning, as frequently done in traditional interviews, is not the most effective way to understand young people's perceptions of inequity. As Delgado (2006) claims, 'any discussion of youth-led research is not complete without attention to the use of innovative research methods' (p. 90). We agree completely with Delgado. We have found that engaging girls in a variety of tasks aimed to help them articulate what they know (e.g. magazine explorations and critiques, photo analyses and critiques, inquiry-based projects, drawings and journals) is a more effective way to learn about their perspectives. These types of research method take time. Thus, scholars who hope to focus on student voice need to be prepared to spend a great deal of time working with young people if they hope to see below the obvious surface. We need to be prepared to get lost (Lather, 2007), and we need to be prepared to hear something we could never imagine in the first place.

Second, to more fully understand girls we need to work collaboratively with them to explore their everyday experiences. In doing this, we need to be prepared to shift our research agenda when necessary in order to respond to what we are hearing (Cook-Sather, 2002). By collaborating with girls as co-researchers in an attempt to explore *what might be* we will better understand *what is*. What we have seen consistently through the years (Oliver, 1999; Oliver and Lalik, 2000, 2001, 2004a, 2004b; Oliver, Hamzeh and McCaughtry, 2009; Oliver and Hamzeh, 2010) is that when we have asked girls to imagine something different they have become much more articulate at naming *what is*. Through this process we have been able to break through the surface and see things we never expected or could have anticipated. We have also learned that girls have very powerful ideas about what they want to see change and how to go about seeking change. What they do not have, however, is a space in school to practise change, or the know-how to actually make change happen. This is where activist research becomes most powerful – that is, activist research allows those of us committed to transformative practice to respond to girls' needs.

For teachers, we have learned that girls find value in having opportunities to explore how they experience their bodies and physical activity. It actually helps them to connect physical education to their lives outside school. There are so few spaces in schools for girls to look critically at how they are learning to think about their bodies, or to look at what prevents them from being physically active that if teachers were to include these types of learning opportunities within their physical education programmes students might find PE more meaningful and relevant.

Another important lesson we have learned, for both researchers and teachers alike, is that an element of playfulness is crucial to assisting girls as they engage in tasks designed to stimulate critique, or inspire change, because often these types of task are difficult. Consistently throughout our work we have seen the girls engage in both social and academic talk as they engaged in the various tasks designed to help them explore, critique and transform inequities that threatened their health and well-being. While a naive observer might see the girls giggling, laughing, talking about after-school functions, boys, girls, parents or teachers as 'off task', on the contrary, we have found that girls often are best able to critique when they move in and out of social and academic talk. Delgado (2006) claims, and we have found this to be true in our own work, that when working with youth the general rule of 50/50 needs to be applied – that is, 50 per cent of the time should be devoted to formal types of task specific to the research and 50 per cent of the time should be allocated to informal interactions and activities that stress fun and entertainment. While we would not say that our work followed a strict 50/50 split, we have found value in both types of interaction, and we have also learned a great deal about girls' worlds in both formal and informal settings.

Finally, as teachers and researchers, we need to remember that our knowledge about how inequity influences girls' health and physical activity may be very different than girls' own knowledge. As soon as we think we 'have the answers' we need to step back and continue to listen, and remember that young people value having their thoughts, ideas and feelings heard. I leave you with the words of Nicole, a 13-year-old African-American teen:

> I think this has been an excellent experience . . . because we got to see how much adults can, I mean, you know, really get involved with teens if they really, if they really care about what they have to say, or if they really want to learn about things, we, you know, see every day, things we talk about. (Oliver and Lalik, 2000, p. 109)

References

Ahmed, S. (2000) *Strange Encounters: Embodied Others on Post-coloniality*. New York: Routledge.

Anzaldúa, G. (2007) *Borderlands/La Frontera: The New Mestiza* (3rd edn). San Francisco: Aunt Lute Books.

Azzarito, L., Solmon, M.A. and Harrison, L. (2006) '"... If I had a choice, I would ...": a feminist post-structuralist perspective on girls in physical education', *Research Quarterly for Exercise and Sport*, 77: 222–239.

Bordo, S. (1993) *Unbearable Weight: Feminism, Western Culture, and the Body*. Berkeley: University of California Press.

Butler, J. (1993) *Bodies that Matter: On the Discursive Limits of Sex*. New York: Routledge.

Cook-Sather, A. (2002) 'Authorizing students' perspectives: toward trust, dialogue, and change in education', *Educational Researcher*, 3 (4): 3–14.

Cruz, C. (2006) 'Toward an epistemology of a brown body', in D. Delgado Bernal, C.A. Elenes, F.E. Godinez and S. Villenas (eds) *Chicana/Latina Education in Everyday Life: Feminista Perspective on Pedagogy and Epistemology* (pp. 59–75). New York: State University of New York Press.

Davies, B. (2000) *A Body of Writing, 1990–1999*. New York: AltaMira Press.

Davies, B. (2003) *Shards of Glass: Children Reading and Writing Beyond Gendered Identities*. Cresskill, NJ: Hampton Press, Inc.

Delgado, M. (2006) *Designs and Methods for Youth-Led Research*. London: Sage.

Delgado Bernal, D. (2002) 'Critical race theory, Latino critical theory, and critical raced-gendered epistemologies: recognizing students of color as holders and creators of knowledge', *Qualitative Inquiry*, 8: 105–126.

Delgado Bernal, D., Elenes, C.A., Godinez, F.E. and Villenas, S. (2006) *Chicana/Latina Education in Everyday Life: Feminista Perspective on Pedagogy and Epistemology*. New York: State University of New York Press.

Featherstone, M. (1991) 'The body in consumer culture', in M. Featherstone, M. Hepworth and B.S. Turner (eds) *The Body: Social Process and Cultural Theory*. Newbury Park: Sage.

Fine, M. (1994) 'Dis-stance and other stances: negotiations of power inside feminist research', in A. Gitlin (ed.) *Power and Method: Political Activism and Educational Research* (pp. 13–35). New York: Routledge.

Fine, M. (2007) 'Feminist designs for difference', in S. Hesse-Biber (ed.) *Handbook of Feminist Research: Theory and Praxis*. Thousand Oaks, CA: Sage.

Flintoff, A. and Scraton, S. (2001) 'Stepping into active leisure? Young women's perceptions of active lifestyles and their experiences of school physical education', *Sport, Education and Society*, 6 (1): 5–21.

Gilbert, P. (1994) '"And they lived happily ever after": cultural storylines and the construction of gender', in *The Need for Story: Cultural Diversity in Classroom and Community*. United States: National Council of Teachers of English.

Giroux, H.A. (1997) *Pedagogy and the Politics of Hope: Theory, Culture, and Schooling*. Boulder, CO: Westview Press.

Gore, J. (1993) *The Struggle for Pedagogies: Critical and Feminist Discourses as Regimes of Truth*. New York: Routledge.

Hall, M.A. (1996) *Feminism and the Sporting Bodies. Essays on Theory and Practice*. Champaign, IL: Human Kinetics.

Hill-Collins, P. (1990) *Black Feminist Thought: Knowledge, Consciousness, and the Politics of Empowerment*. New York: Routledge.

Jamieson, K.M. (2003) 'Occupying a middle space: toward a *mestiza* sport studies', *Sociology of Sport Journal*, 20 (1): 1–16.

Lather, P. (2007) *Getting Lost: Feminist Efforts Toward a Double (d) Science*. New York: Suny Press.

Mohanty, C.T. (2003) *Feminism Without Borders: Decolonizing Theory, Practicing Solidarity*. Durham: Duke University.

Oliver, K.L. (1999) 'Adolescent girls' body-narratives: learning to desire and create a "fashionable" image', *Teachers College Record*, 101 (2): 220–246.

Oliver, K.L. and Hamzeh, M. (2010) '"The boys won't let us play": 5th grade *mestizas* challenge physical activity discourse at school', *Research Quarterly for Exercise and Sport*, 81 (1): 39–55.

Oliver, K.L. and Lalik, R. (2000) *Bodily Knowledge: Learning about Equity and Justice with Adolescent Girls*. New York: Peter Lang.

Oliver, K.L. and Lalik, R. (2001) 'The body as curriculum: learning with adolescent girls', *Journal of Curriculum Studies*, 33: 303–333.

Oliver, K.L. and Lalik, R. (2004a) 'Critical inquiry on the body of girls' physical education classes: a critical poststructural perspective', *Journal of Teaching in Physical Education*, 23 (2): 162–195.

Oliver, K.L. and Lalik, R. (2004b) '"The Beauty Walk, This ain't my topic": learning about critical inquiry with adolescent girls', *Journal of Curriculum Studies*, 36 (5): 555–586.

Oliver, K.L., Hamzeh, M. and McCaughtry, N. (2009) '"Girly girls *can* play games/*Las niñas pueden jugar tambien*": co-creating a curriculum of possibilities with 5th grade girls', *Journal of Teaching in Physical Education*, 28 (1): 90–110.

Sanders-Bustle, L. (ed.) (2003) *Image, Inquiry, and Transformative Practice: Engaging Learners in Creative and Critical Inquiry through Visual Representation*. New York: Peter Lang.

US Department of Health and Human Services (1996) *Physical Activity and Health: A Report of the Surgeon General*. Atlanta, GA: US Department of Health and Human Services, Centers for Disease Control and Prevention, National Center for Chronic Disease Prevention and Health Promotion.

Weedon, C. (1997) *Feminist Practice and Poststructuralist Theory* (2nd edn). Malden: Blackwell Publishing.

Weis, L. and Fine, M. (2004) *Working Methods: Research and Social Justice*. New York: Routledge.

Weiler, K. (1988) *Women Teaching for Change: Gender, Class and Power*. Westport, CT: Bergin & Garney.

Wright, J. (1999) 'Changing gendered practices in physical education: working with teachers', *European Physical Education Review*, 5 (3): 181–197.

4 Students' curricular values and experiences

Donetta Cothran

'Why did they do that?' 'What in the world were they thinking?' Anyone who has spent time in schools teaching or observing physical education has heard or asked themselves those very questions when thinking about students, as student behaviours frequently do not meet the expectations of their teachers. The problem is that rarely have educators bothered to ask the only people who can answer that question, the students, to respond.

Fortunately, that trend is changing and educators are increasingly interested in the student perspective. For example, students provide valuable information about their learning behaviours, including help seeking (Nye, 2008) and effort (Veal and Compagnone, 1995). They share insights into classroom management (e.g. Supaporn, 2000; Cothran, Kulinna and Garrahy, 2003) and effective use of teaching styles (Cothran, Kulinna and Ward, 2000; Cothran and Kulinna, 2006). Students also provide important feedback about fitness assessment (e.g. Hopple and Graham, 1995; Garn and Cothran, 2009), conceptions of health (Yelling and Penney, 2003; Burrows and Wright, 2004) and teacher education programmes (McCullick *et al.*, 2008). We also know that students value fun in their classes and can identify practices that contribute to it (Garn and Cothran, 2006; Smith and Parr, 2007).

In addition, students can be valuable sources of information about curricula and this chapter examines students' curricular experiences with curriculum being broadly defined to include the wide range of experiences the student has in the context of the class. This chapter examines student values, how those values are met, or not met, by different curricula, and how students attempt to shape the curriculum through their actions.

One of the core facets of curricular research is to explore the underlying values and assigned meanings of the participants. Exploring the field of educational values, however, can soon become a confusing investigation due to the number of different terms and oft missing definitions used to describe similar, but different, constructs. The broader theoretical framework from which the interest in a student perspective often springs is that of beliefs. Beliefs are a 'messy construct' (Pajares, 1992) and most often are described in relation to knowledge. Pajares describes the commonly held relationship between the two as follows: 'the chosen and perhaps artificial distinction between belief and knowledge is common to most definitions:

Belief is based on evaluation and judgment; knowledge is based on objective fact'
(p. 313). Another important term is 'attitudes'; these are a collection of beliefs centred about an object or topic. Values are beliefs that are used in an evaluative manner. Because values are related to preferred end states and goals, they are often
indicators of action for individuals to achieve their goals. We know a great deal
about teachers' curricular values (e.g. Ennis and Zhu, 1991; Ennis, Ross and Chen,
1992) but little about students' curricular values and what they hope to achieve
from the class. Relatedly, we need additional information about how students
respond to teachers' values as expressed through the curriculum and how we might
better align and meet the value systems in a class to maximize the effectiveness of
the curriculum.

Students' physical education values

What do students value about physical education? To answer that question, some
researchers have asked students to rate a standard list of educational goals like
skill development and fitness. For example, Walling and Duda (1995) asked high
school students to rate ten educational goals on a five-point Likert scale. Similar
formats were used to investigate high school students' (e.g. Tannehill and
Zakrajsek, 1993) and college students' (e.g. Avery and Lumpkin, 1987) rankings of
purposes for physical education. In general students rate all items at least moder-
ately important.

Although student ratings of educational goals provide some insights to student
values, the investigative format is somewhat limited in helping us understand the
student perspective. First, the lists typically assume that students are interested only
in educational goals, and findings from general education research (e.g. Wentzel,
1992; Allen, 1995) suggest students hold non-educational goals too (see Chapter 3
in this volume). The Likert scale format also usually results in all items being
ranked fairly high, with little differentiation. It is unlikely that any student can
successfully pursue ten or more goals at one time so there must be another value
hierarchy underlying student values that is not captured by typical ranking investigations.

Cothran and Ennis (1998) attempted to solve that measurement dilemma by
using a Q-sort methodology in large urban high schools in the United States. For the
Q-sort, they recruited 42 students, a vast majority of whom were African-
American, who represented a full spectrum of class engagement, skills and gender.
Q-sort methods involve the development of a set of statements that participants
evaluate. In this case the researchers developed a set of 20 educational items based
on teacher educational values (Ennis and Chen, 1993) and 20 non-educational
items developed from student interviews and a review of literature. Since values are
a judgement system in which some items are valued more than others, the Q-sort
methodology asks participants to rank order the physical education outcomes from
most to least valued. As participants rank order the items, they discuss their
thoughts about the statement, and the investigator probes to better understand what
is important/not important and why. One of the unique aspects of Q methodology is

that it allows for multiple analyses of the data. One analysis is to simply total the rank orderings and develop a ranking table for all participants. In this case, the ranking table revealed that the students most valued fun, passing grades and spending time with friends. Non-educational items dominated the top of the students' rankings, in contrast to their teachers who also completed the Q-sort and primarily indicated value for educational items.

A second type of analysis available via Q methodology is to use a principal components analysis to identify which participants share similar rankings – in effect, clustering similar groups of people together. The third type of analysis is to analyse the interview comments as the same rating may actually mean two different things to different participants. For example, in the Cothran and Ennis (1998) study teachers and students ranked 'fun' as their top item but interview data revealed different meanings assigned to those rankings. These two additional levels of analysis by Cothran and Ennis (1997a) revealed some interesting student value patterns that offered additional insight into the many different student perspectives in class. To aid in the clarity of the discussion the authors provide a descriptive name for each group, as discussed in the text that follows.

Playful Friends

Pattern 1, the Playful Friends, was the largest group, accounting for nearly 25 per cent (10 out of the 42 students) of the sample. The students, six males and four females, assigned the highest value to non-educational items. In order of importance, those valued items were: (1) I get to play my favourite sport or do my favourite activity; (2) I have fun; (3) I have a chance to talk with my friends; (4) I get a good grade; (5) I can compete against others; (6) I can be with my friends; and (7) I get to make new friends. For this group, physical education was valued because it provided opportunities to be with friends, have fun and play, all while getting a good grade.

The value of these items was also reflected in interviews with these students. LaDonna described the characteristics of a good physical education class: 'This might be the only class you have with some friends. It's the only time you can see them if you don't have the same lunch. You can talk, associate, and play games.' For Nick, who described himself as 'not really a sports person', having friends in class made the difference between passing and failing the course. Last year he failed physical education because he never dressed out, 'I just didn't like it. There was nobody to talk to.' He was re-taking the course this year and passing because several of his friends were in the class, 'It [this year's class] is just really different. This year is much better because I have more friends this year.' The value of the course for LaDonna, Nick and the other members of this group was not inherent in the curriculum content but was a function of the people in the class. As such, learning about physical education was of little value for the Playful Friends. The 11 least valued items for the group all began with the item stem, 'I learn . . .'.

Competitors

In contrast to the Playful Friends, the Competitors did not rate the friends items highly. Instead this second pattern of values for physical education emphasized skill and its display in game play. The eight members of this group (six boys and two girls) rated the following items as their most valued outcomes: (1) I can compete against others; (2) I can see how good I am compared to others; (3) I learn new things about myself; (4) I learn how to analyse my own mistakes when I perform skills; (5) I become skilled and fit; (6) I have fun; and (7) I get to play my favourite sport or do my favourite physical activity.

This group valued the educational items most related to skill development. Cole described what he liked to learn in physical education: 'You learn about rules and how to play. In PE you learn the right way to play.' These group members also valued demonstrating their knowledge and skills in game play. Christine discussed what she liked about PE: 'I like it when the teacher is looking at you. It shows you're good and better than the others and that you're good at it. Maybe then the teacher will recommend you to a coach of a sport.'

The Competitors also found value in the competitive phase of the multi-activity approach. Caden, who was in a fitness course due to a scheduling conflict, claimed to hate fitness and wished he could be in team sports. He complained that fitness was the same activity all the time: 'Fitness is no challenge. You just do it. It's not like you can compete against nobody or something like in team sports.' The investigator responded that it looked like team sports did the same thing every day, too. Caden replied, 'No. Team sports are so much better. You've got to manoeuvre yourself and your team against obstacles. You're playing somebody different every day and it's a new challenge.' The Competitors' least valued items were those related to friends and social environment items.

Friendly Learners

The Friendly Learners, the third pattern of values, primarily valued items related to friends, but were also interested in grades and learning. For these seven students, three boys and four girls, their top-ranked items were: (1) I get a passing grade; (2) I can be with my friends; (3) I have fun; (4) I have a chance to talk with my friends; (5) I can be around members of the opposite sex; (6) I get a good grade; and (7) I learn how the skills I know are similar to ones I'm learning. Although not in the top seven items, three of the next four items were educational items related to skill development.

Leslie, a member of the Friendly Learners group, described the dual focus of what she valued about physical education, 'You get opportunities to learn but you're with your friends and moving around and stuff so it's like a break too.' As long as the learning was combined with social aspects this group was content with the course. When asked what makes a good class, Emily responded, 'PE is fun compared to my other classes 'cause in other classes you just sit there and write and do book work. In PE it's like a time when I can come and work out and have fun with my friends and I can learn at the same time.' The least valued items for the Friendly Learners were competition and social environment items.

Cooperative Learners

Four students (three girls and one boy) comprised the members of the fourth pattern, the Cooperative Learners. This group's most valued items were: (1) I have fun; (2) I learn how to work together with other students; (3) I get to just play instead of having to practise something; (4) I get a good grade; (5) I get a passing grade; (6) I learn to work well alone and in groups; and (7) I gain knowledge that is personally meaningful. This group's focus on getting good grades, getting along and learning emphasized traditionally appropriate student behaviour. Barb said she was glad that her class learned about, 'How to talk through it and don't fight. She [her teacher] don't want no fights or no riots so she tells us to talk through it and stuff.' This focus on learning appropriate behaviour made the class valuable for these participants. Julia described the need for and therefore value of working with others in PE:

> You work with a team which is kind of good 'cause in school you don't really learn to work with other people. It's just you and your peers and you have to do it. You've got to get along with them and try. You teach each other and help and so you're involved with each other. The school needs that.

Although this group valued getting along and learning how to work together, they assigned low value to being with friends in class. Competition was also rated low by the Cooperative Learners.

Social Comparison

The fifth and final pattern of values was the Social Comparison group. This group of three girls and one boy valued grades and a variety of other items related to their position in class with respect to other class members. The most valued items for this group were: (1) I learn how other people in class are different than and similar to me; (2) I have fun; (3) I get a good grade; (4) I can see how good I am compared to others; (5) I don't embarrass myself in front of anyone; (6) I get a passing grade; and (7) I learn rules and strategies for sports and games.

Those in the Social Comparison group were unique for their inclusion of the item 'I learn how other people in class are different than and similar to me', as no other group rated this item highly. The ranking may be contextual as three of the four group members were students from the most culturally diverse school in the study. This was the only pattern to value a social environment item: not being embarrassed. The least valued items for this group were those related to play, such as free choice days and playing favourite activities.

These value patterns reveal that students are not a monolithic entity with all students valuing the same things in physical education, although there are clearly trends of fun and social as primary values for many students. What else might students value about physical education? Another significant theme in the literature is that students like and value physical education for providing a break from the rest of the school day (e.g. Morey and Goc Karp, 1998; Cothran and Ennis, 2001). Physical education frequently provides opportunity to move, talk and engage with others – class characteristics that are generally in short supply throughout the rest of the day. Ironically, although students value the different learning environment of physical education they also report not always valuing the content (e.g. Carlson, 1995; Cothran and Ennis, 1999, 2001).

Student experiences in the curriculum

The previous section notes some general trends and specifics related to student values, which then prompts the question, are students' values being met by their physical education curriculum? Obviously the answer to this question is dependent on the individual student as each experiences the curriculum differently and in just about any programme there may be students whose value systems are a good match with the class curriculum. For example, the sub-group of the Competitors, described above, found a very good match between their value for competition with the multi-activity model in their schools, which was based heavily on game play and public display of skill in competitive settings. Other sub-groups of students had a less successful match between their values and the physical education curriculum. Researchers suggest that there are other significant mismatches between at least some students' values and the curriculum (e.g. Tjeerdsma, 1997; MacPhail, Kirk and Kinchin, 2004; Mowling, Brock and Hastie, 2006). A majority of the work done in this area of the student experience of the curriculum has been qualitative in nature, with field observations and interviews with students being primary data collection methods. This capturing of 'student voice' has enlightened our understanding of the student curricular perspective considerably.

One of the key understandings our field has gained is that students experience the curriculum very differently, and those differences are often related to gender and ability. The multi-activity model offered in many schools is often based on traditional team sports that reward size and power. As implemented the model often also includes a great deal of competition and public display of skill; as such, low-skilled or less confident students often report negative experiences and feeling marginalized. Portman (1995) talked with 13 low-skilled 6th graders about their physical education experience, and reported student frustration, but also acceptance, of their lack of success and meaningful involvement in class. Suomi, Collier and Brown (2003) found similar negative experiences for students who were struggling or who were identified with disabilities in their elementary physical education class. Gender also plays a role in the student experience as girls generally report liking physical education less than their male peers and they also report less activity (Azzarito and Solmon, 2009). We know much less about the influence of race on physical education experiences, although a few studies do show at least some differences in how students from different races may experience physical education (e.g. Tannehill and Zakrajsek, 1993; Azzarito and Solmon, 2009; Oliver, Chapter 3 in this volume).

Another common negative experience in physical education is that of alienation (Carlson, 1995; Ennis *et al.*, 1997). Carlson suggests that alienation arises from a lack of personal meaning and power, and from isolation. Students do not always understand their teachers' goals for their classes (Cothran and Ennis, 1998) and even then may not see the value of the topic to their lives. Students reported having little control over the class and perceived that class rules were unfair and unchangeable (Cothran and Ennis, 1997b, 1999; Martel, Gagnon and Tousignant, 2002). Courturier, Chepko and Couglin (2005) report that over 70 per cent of the 5000 urban students surveyed wished they had input into activities. In contrast, students enrolled in an elective dance class reported that the class had less alienation and more personal meaning than the rest of the school day (Stinson, 1993), perhaps due to the elective nature of the course.

One key to reducing alienation appears to be meaningful and personal links between the students and teachers. Figley (1985) used a critical incident recall technique to examine factors that influenced student memories and attitudes towards physical education. The teacher was the number one factor – a finding largely replicated by Luke and Sinclair (1991). Azzarito and Ennis (2003) also report how teachers' intentional efforts to create a social constructivist learning environment enhance student connections to each other and with their community. Attitudinal survey research (Subramaniam and Silverman, 2000) also supports the importance of the teacher and the curriculum in addition to usefulness and enjoyment, as key determinants of student attitude. Cothran and Ennis (1999, 2000) suggest the importance of teacher caring and respect to engage students.

Students enrolled in an innovative curriculum often report more positive experiences in physical education. For example, the structure of Sport Education seems to provide a strong match with students' social needs, and the structured interactions of the class help minimize student isolation. Carlson and Hastie (1997) reported on students in two different units taught with the Sport Education curricular model, and noted that students responded positively to the teamwork, leadership and responsibility portions of the curriculum. The students also reported that those same traits led to increased fun, another student value. Similar positive reports about students and Sport Education are offered by multiple investigators (e.g. Hastie, 1998, 2000; MacPhail *et al.*, 2004; Pope and Grant, 1996). Other projects note positive student curricular experiences with Adventure Education (Dyson, 1995; Hastie, 1995).

Innovative curricula, however, are not always met with acceptance by students and that rejection can be very painful for the teachers involved. New curricula can violate student expectations for physical education, leading to student disengagement and resistance. Cothran and Ennis (2001) found that a new fitness course in a large urban high school resulted in very different reactions from various students. The class was designed to offer personalized, meaningful fitness knowledge to students. The authors described three reaction patterns to the curriculum from students. The first group, the 'resisters', was the largest group and their expectations for physical education were violated by the addition of an academic component to a physical education class. Carrie explained her dissatisfaction: 'It's almost like a real class. I don't think you should learn for PE class though. It's not right.' Carrie's, and the other resisters', values for physical education clearly included having a break from the rest of the school day and the fitness class violated that value. A second group of students were classified as 'screeners'; they behaviourally complied with teachers' expectations but cognitively and affectively accepted only the topics that were directly related to weight loss and body image. The final and smallest group, the 'connecters', did seem to hold a value system very congruent with the new curriculum and therefore they expressed strong satisfaction with the new class. Lelia explained, 'It's about taking care of your body and yourself. You got to know about exercise and things. It's a lot more than a regular PE class. You can use this stuff forever.'

Student (dis)engagement shapes the curriculum

The three groupings described by Cothran and Ennis (2001) suggest students are actively and intentionally engaging/disengaging from the curriculum as it meets or fails to meet their needs and values. That active presence would be expected as values are core beliefs and as such they are related to action. Although students rarely have an official role in course curricular development, their values nonetheless shape the curriculum through informal, but powerful routes. They 'work' towards their goals of fun, friends and good grades in a number of ways, but primarily attempt to influence the course by negotiating the work demands and curricular content by giving or withholding compliance with teachers' requests.

Hastie and Pickwell (1996) reported on high school students participating in a dance unit that was not well liked. The students found numerous ways to minimize work and maximize fun without stepping outside the boundaries of class conduct in a way that would have negatively affected their grade. The teacher 'accepted' these student actions as a perceived trade-off for at least the minimal levels of student cooperation needed to maintain the class. Given its importance, positive student engagement becomes a daily negotiation point for students and teachers.

Students use their compliance and engagement not only to shape the expected work, but, at least in some schools, to shape the actual content of the curriculum. In addition to the Hastie and Pickwell (1996) report, other researchers have noted the active role students take in (dis)engaging with and/or shaping their curricular environments (Carlson, 1995; Kinchin and O'Sullivan, 2003; Azzarito, Solmon and Harrison, 2006). Cothran and Ennis (1997b) offered a detailed report of students 'rewarding' their teachers with compliance and positive interactions if the teacher offered preferred content. Students also described disengaging from activity that was not valued. The authors share a story from Nathan, who described a successful student withdrawal to influence teacher selection of curricular content, 'Last year she [teacher] tried to get us to play volleyball to start off with and we didn't want to do it so we didn't. She finally let us play football and basketball all year. That was good. She tried the volleyball, but no way. We just told her we wouldn't play. We did football and basketball and everybody had fun and we participated, so that was better so she let us keep doing it.' When asked if he thought the teacher did the right thing he replied, 'Yeah, we were happy. We never got tired of it so it was good. As long as we do what we want, we'll dress and it'll be good.'

When students weren't 'happy' the class period became a struggle for teachers to get students to participate and cooperate. Students in the Cothran and Ennis (1997b) study reported intentionally moving slowly, failing to volunteer, and 'bugging' the teacher when not happy with the content or lesson format. One student reported that whining bothered teachers and was a good way to change a teacher's mind: 'We just all groan and usually the teacher doesn't want to hear it so they keep changing it until people shut up.' A small number of students reported intentionally disruptive behaviour like being loud or misusing equipment to encourage the teacher to change activities. Another small group of students also described 'powerful personality' students who could either rally student support for a specific class topic or talk personally and positively with the teacher to express the student views.

Student disruptions and non-compliance, however, had to be carefully balanced against the teachers' assessment system as misbehaviour or lack of participation often affected the students' grades. For students who cared about their grades, the non-compliance was necessarily more subtle and occasional. A few students, however, did not care about their grades or were willing to take the academic risk, and they were therefore more willing to engage in direct confrontations and disruptions to the class.

Resolving the values conflict

To return to the questions that began this chapter . . . why do students do what they do and what are they thinking? At least with regard to curricula, student values and the ability of the curriculum to meet those values provide insights into what students do and why. Students have clear priorities in class and they act to meet those priorities within the environment established by the curriculum. Although individual student values vary significantly, in general students hold the most value for aspects of physical education (e.g. fun, friends) that do not fit the educational mission of the teachers and schools. Gasson (1973), an engineer who specialized in design issues, suggested that when faced with conflicting interests between the product designer and the customer, or in educational terms, between the teacher and the student, the designer has three options: withdraw, persuade or accommodate. I suggest that the customer/student also has those same three options.

The first option is to withdraw from the design process. Due to mandatory attendance and credit hour rules in most states and countries, a complete withdrawal from physical education is not possible. A partial withdrawal via minimal effort and engagement, however, is a common report from the research literature. The second option, persuasion, was clearly detailed by the students as they attempted to persuade the teachers to modify the course content to better match the students' values. That persuasion most commonly took the form of awarding or withholding student compliance. Similar to the New Zealand secondary students described by

Jones (1989), these students 'systematically encouraged the teacher to participate with them in certain activities and discouraged her from doing others' (p. 24). Although the students did not have enough outright power to determine the specific nature of the course content or rules, they did hold the power to determine at what pace the class would proceed and consequently greatly influenced the teacher's planning to avoid the possibility of student withdrawal and outright misbehaviour and class disruption.

The third option, accommodation to the other's wishes, was also part of the design conflict resolution for these classes. Although never formally negotiated, the daily interactions with each other nonetheless served as a negotiation process in which a 'deal' was struck by the teachers and students that accommodated each other's most valued goals and defined the nature of their work. For students, their work was to be on time, participate and cooperate. If they fulfilled those responsibilities they were rewarded with good grades, access to favoured activities and time to spend with friends – all three of which were substantially controlled by the teachers. The teachers' primary work was to maintain student order and the easiest way to gain the student cooperation that teachers needed was to offer a programme with few educational demands. Erickson and Shultz (1992) suggest that both teachers and students benefit in some ways from this type of negotiation: 'Collusion develops in which teachers do not press students to learn what may be meaningless or face-threatening for them and students do not press the teacher by disrupting class' (p. 471). Hastie and Pickwell (1996) report a similar physical education situation in which teachers traded low participation for non-disruption. In these schools, the negotiated relationship gave the illusion of at least minimal class success because students were somewhat active and cooperative, and teachers were able to maintain the class order that they and their administrators valued.

It seems that another form of accommodation might better resolve the design conflict and leave all participants with a more valued, meaningful and enjoyable physical education class. Whereas teachers and students sometimes seem to see curricular value differences as an either/or scenario in which one set of values must 'trump' the other, what if the curricular design process resulted in a curriculum that allowed for multiple goals being met simultaneously? Carlson and Hastie (1997) suggest that when students' and teachers' agendas overlap in support of each other, more positive learning environments can be created. In this scenario, both groups' valued goals are accommodated, not by ignoring the other's values, but by finding mutually meaningful learning experiences and curricular structures. As an example, students clearly held highest value for 'fun' as a class outcome and it seems likely that students might be willing to go along with teachers' other educational requests as long as students' most valued goals of having fun could also be met.

There are alternatives to the multi-activity curriculum and direct instruction models present in most schools. For example, Sport Education (Siedentop, 1994) appears to address the students' desire for a social focus and a variety of potentially fun activities (e.g. creating team posters and names, variety of competitions) while addressing the teachers' concern for responsibility and skills. Teaching Games for Understanding (Griffin and Butler, 2005) might provide the currently missing link between students' perceived lack of relevance in the curriculum and teachers' instructional methods and content. Alternately, cooperative learning (Dyson, 2001, 2002) offers a variety of course organizational formats while reinforcing the social and learning aspects of class valued by students and teachers.

A key to the success of any new curriculum will be the ability of the teacher to understand and connect the curriculum and instruction with students' values. To do so may mean that a variety of course offerings in both content (e.g. sport, dance, fitness) as well as curricular models (e.g. Sport Education, Teaching Games for Understanding) are needed to address the multiple values of both teachers and students. It is also likely to mean that students should play a formal and authentic role in curricular construction to ensure that open communication representing the student value perspective is part of the formal curricular process (see Chapter 10 in this volume for an example of this co-construction). With that inclusion, it may be possible to create a curricular path of mutual worth from which all students can benefit, and that allows them to enjoy and find meaning in the class.

References

Allen, J. (1995) 'Friends, fairness, fun, and the freedom to choose: hearing student voices', *Journal of Curriculum and Supervision*, 10: 286–301.

Avery, M. and Lumpkin, A. (1987) 'Students' perceptions of physical education objectives', *Journal of Teaching in Physical Education*, 7: 5–11.

Azzarito, L. and Ennis, C.D. (2003) 'A sense of connection: toward social constructivist physical education', *Sport, Education and Society*, 8: 179–198.

Azzarito, L. and Solmon, M.A. (2009) 'An investigation of students' embodied discourses in physical education: a gender project', *Journal of Teaching in Physical Education*, 28: 173–191.

Azzarito, L., Solmon, M.A. and Harrison, L. (2006) '"... If I had a choice I would ...": a feminist poststructural perspective on girls in physical education classes', *Research Quarterly for Exercise and Sport*, 77: 222–239.

Burrows, L. and Wright, J. (2004) 'The good life: New Zealand children's perspectives on health and self', *Sport, Education, and Society*, 9: 193–205.

Carlson, T.B. (1995) 'We hate gym: student alienation from physical education', *Journal of Teaching in Physical Education*, 14: 467–477.

Carlson, T.B. and Hastie, P.A. (1997) 'The student social system within Sport Education', *Journal of Teaching in Physical Education*, 16: 176–195.

Cothran, D.J. and Ennis, C.D. (1997a) *Curricular Accommodation as a Consequence of Students' and Teachers' Values*. Paper presented at the annual meeting of the American Educational Research Association, Chicago, IL.

Cothran, D.J. and Ennis, C.D. (1997b) 'Students' and teachers' perceptions of conflict and power', *Teaching and Teacher Education*, 13: 541–553.

Cothran, D.J. and Ennis, C.D. (1998) 'Curricula of mutual worth: comparisons of students' and teachers' curricular goals', *Journal of Teaching in Physical Education*, 17: 307–327.

Cothran, D.J. and Ennis, C.D. (1999) 'Alone in a crowd: meeting students' needs for relevance and connection in physical education', *Journal of Teaching in Physical Education*, 18: 234–247.

Cothran, D.J. and Ennis, C.D. (2000) 'Building bridges to engagement: communicating respect and care for students in urban high schools', *Journal of Research and Development in Education*, 33: 106–118.

Cothran, D.J. and Ennis, C.D. (2001) '"Nobody said nothing about learning stuff": students, teachers, and curricular change', *Journal of Classroom Interaction*, 36: 1–5.

Cothran, D.J. and Kulinna, P.H. (2006) 'Students' perspectives on direct, peer, and inquiry teaching strategies', *Journal of Teaching in Physical Education*, 25: 166–181.

Cothran, D.J., Kulinna, P.H. and Garrahy, D.A. (2003) '"This is kind of giving a secret away . . .": student's perspectives on effective classroom management', *Teaching and Teacher Education*, 19: 435–444.

Cothran, D.J., Kulinna, P.H. and Ward, E. (2000) 'Students' experiences with and perceptions of Mosston's Teaching Styles', *Journal of Research and Development in Education*, 34: 93–103.

Courturier, L.E., Chepko, S. and Coughlin, M.A. (2005) 'Student voices – what middle and high school students have to say about physical education', *The Physical Educator*, 62: 170–177.

Dyson, B.P. (1995) 'Student voices in two alternative elementary physical education programs', *Journal of Teaching in Physical Education*, 14: 394–407.

Dyson, B.P. (2001) 'Cooperative learning in an elementary school physical education program', *Journal of Teaching in Physical Education*, 20: 264–281.

Dyson, B.P. (2002) 'The implementation of cooperative learning in an elementary school physical education program', *Journal of Teaching in Physical Education*, 22: 69–85.

Ennis, C.D. and Chen, A. (1993) 'Domain specifications and content representativeness of the revised value orientation inventory', *Research Quarterly for Exercise and Sport*, 64: 436–446.

Ennis, C.D. and Zhu, W. (1991) 'Value orientations: a description of teachers' goals for student learning', *Research Quarterly for Exercise and Sport*, 62: 33–40.

Ennis, C.D., Ross, J. and Chen, A. (1992) 'The role of value orientations in curricular decision making: a rationale for teachers' goals and expectations', *Research Quarterly for Exercise and Sport*, 63: 38–47.

Ennis, C.D., Cothran, D.J., Davidson, K.S., Loftus, S.J., Owens, L., Swanson, L. and Hopsicker, P. (1997) 'Implementing curriculum within a context of fear and disengagement', *Journal of Teaching in Physical Education*, 17: 52–71.

Erickson, F. and Shultz, J. (1992) 'Students' experiences of the curriculum', in P.W. Jackson (ed.) *Handbook of Research on Curriculum* (pp. 465–485). New York: Macmillan.

Figley, G. (1985) 'Determinants of attitudes toward physical education', *Journal of Teaching in Physical Education*, 4: 229–240.

Garn, A.C. and Cothran, D.J. (2006) 'The fun factor in physical education', *Journal of Teaching in Physical Education*, 25: 281–297.

Garn, A.C. and Cothran, D.J. (2009) 'Correlates of a high 2 x 2 achievement goal profile in a fitness testing context: a qualitative analysis', *Sport and Exercise Psychology Review*, 5: 30–46.

Gasson, P. (1973) *Theory of Design*. New York: Barnes and Noble.

Griffin, L. and Butler, J. (2005) *Teaching Games for Understanding: Theory, Research and Practice*. Champaign, IL: Human Kinetics.

Hastie, P.A. (1995) 'An ecology of a secondary school outdoor adventure camp', *Journal of Teaching in Physical Education*, 16: 88–103.

Hastie, P.A. (1998) 'The participation and perceptions of girls within a unit of Sport Education', *Journal of Teaching in Physical Education*, 17: 157–171.

Hastie, P.A. (2000) 'An ecological analysis of a Sport Education season', *Journal of Teaching in Physical Education*, 19: 355–373.

Hastie, P.A. and Pickwell, A. (1996) 'Take your partners: a description of a student social system in a secondary school dance class', *Journal of Teaching in Physical Education*, 15: 171–187.

Hopple, C. and Graham, G. (1995) 'What students think, feel, and know about physical fitness testing', *Journal of Teaching in Physical Education*, 14: 408–417.

Jones, A. (1989) 'The cultural production of classroom practice', *British Journal of Sociology of Education*, 101: 19–31.

Kinchin, G.D. and O'Sullivan, M. (2003) 'Incidences of student support for and resistance to a curricular innovation in high school physical education', *Journal of Teaching in Physical Education*, 22: 245–260.

Luke, M.D. and Sinclair, G.D. (1991) 'Gender differences in adolescents' attitudes towards school physical education', *Journal of Teaching in Physical Education*, 11: 31–46.

MacPhail, A., Kirk, D. and Kinchin, G. (2004) 'Sport Education: promoting team affiliation through physical education', *Journal of Teaching in Physical Education*, 23: 106–122.

Martel, D., Gagnon, J. and Tousignant, M. (2002) 'Physical education teachers' and students' views of injustices in the gymnasium', *AVANTE*, 8: 55–68.

McCullick, B., Metzler, M., Cicek, S., Jackson, J. and Vickers, B. (2008) 'Kids say the darndest things: PETE program assessment through the eyes of students', *Journal of Teaching in Physical Education*, 27: 4–20.

Morey, R.S. and Goc Karp, G. (1998) 'Why do some students who are good at physical education dislike it so much?' *The Physical Educator*, 55: 89–100.

Mowling, C.M., Brock, S.J. and Hastie, P.A. (2006) 'Fourth grade students' drawing interpretations of a Sport Education soccer unit', *Journal of Teaching in Physical Education*, 25: 9–35.

Nye, S.B. (2008) 'Students' help seeking during physical education', *Journal of Teaching in Physical Education*, 27: 368–384.

Pajares, M.F. (1992) 'Teachers' beliefs and educational research: cleaning up a messy construct', *Review of Educational Research*, 62: 307–322.

Pope, C.V. and Grant, B.C. (1996) 'Student experiences in Sport Education', *Waikato Journal of Education*, 2: 103–118.

Portman, P.A. (1995) 'Who is having fun in physical education classes? Experiences of sixth grade students in elementary and middle schools', *Journal of Teaching in Physical Education*, 14: 445–453.

Siedentop, D. (1994) *Sport Education*. Champaign, IL: Human Kinetics.

Smith, A. and Parr, M. (2007) 'Young people's views on the nature and purposes of physical education: a sociological analysis', *Sport, Education & Society*, 12: 37–58.

Stinson, S.S. (1993) 'Meaning and value: reflections on what students say about school', *Journal of Curriculum and Supervision*, 8: 216–238.

Subramaniam, P.R. and Silverman, S. (2000) 'Validation of scores from an instrument assessing student attitude toward physical education', *Measurement in Physical Education and Exercise Science*, 4: 29–43.

Suomi, J., Collier, D. and Brown, L. (2003) 'Factors affecting the social experiences of students in elementary physical education classes', *Journal of Teaching in Physical Education*, 22: 186–202.

Supaporn, S. (2000) 'High school students' perspectives on misbehaviour', *Physical Educator*, 57: 124–135.

Tannehill, D. and Zakrajsek, D. (1993) 'Student attitudes towards physical education: a multicultural study', *Journal of Teaching in Physical Education*, 13: 78–84.

Tjeerdsma, B. (1997) 'A comparison of teacher and student perspectives of tasks and feedback', *Journal of Teaching in Physical Education*, 16: 388–400.

Veal, M.L. and Compagnone, N. (1995) 'How sixth graders perceive effort and skill', *Journal of Teaching in Physical Education*, 14: 431–444.

Walling, M.D. and Duda, J.L. (1995) 'Goals and their associations with beliefs about success in and perceptions of the purposes of physical education', *Journal of Teaching in Physical Education*, 14: 140–156.

Wentzel, K.R. (1992) 'Motivation and achievement in adolescence: a multiple goals perspective', in D.H. Schunk and J.L. Meece (eds) *Student Perceptions in the Classroom* (pp. 287–306). Hillsdale, NJ: Erlbaum.

Yelling, M. and Penney, D. (2003) 'Physical activity in physical education: pupil activity rating, reason, and reality', *European Journal of Physical Education*, 8: 119–140.

Part II

Multiple identities of adolescent populations

5 Finding their voice

Disaffected youth insights on sport/physical activity interventions

Rachel Sandford, Kathleen Armour and Rebecca Duncombe

Introduction

Contemporary concerns about youth disaffection/disengagement have resulted in a call for action to be taken to 'fix' the problem. Such action includes a plethora of programmes and projects designed to re-engage and rehabilitate young people within an educational context. Reflecting a historical belief (in theory and in public policy) in the potential of sport to build 'good character', many of these initiatives make use of physical activities, both within and outside of school, in order to foster positive youth development and facilitate young people's socio-moral education (Holt, 2008). A growing body of evaluation research is providing increasing evidence that sport/physical activity initiatives can indeed have a positive impact on the young people who participate in them; both immediate impact and, in some cases, sustained impact (e.g. Crabbe *et al.*, 2006b; Sandford, Armour and Duncombe, 2008a). Moreover, knowledge is slowly building about how future initiatives can be designed in order to maximize the potential benefits for young people and facilitate the sustainability of positive impact (e.g. Sandford, Duncombe and Armour, 2008b). Nonetheless, significant questions remain about whether and how young people can transfer positive impact beyond the boundaries of a specific programme to broader school and community contexts (Armour and Sandford, 2006; Theokas *et al.*, 2008). It could also be argued that much of the data available on school-based positive youth development programmes are what might be termed 'adult-centric', reflecting the priorities of programme funders, teachers, activity leaders and youth mentors. Thus, although most researchers have taken young people's views into account in evaluation studies (e.g. Duncombe and Armour, 2005; Armour and Sandford, 2008), the data have tended to address the adults' research agendas. What is missing, we argue, is a genuine youth insight into the process of being 'engaged' through sport/physical activity initiatives.

This chapter investigates the issue of youth voice in education research. The significance of youth voice in public policy/discourse is explored and the implications for contemporary sport/physical activity research considered. Examples are provided of ways in which participants' voices have been heard in recent youth sport research, with a particular focus on disaffected youth voices. While acknowledging the valuable data yielded by existing research, it is also argued in this chapter that the approach taken is often tokenistic in nature because young people's contributions tend to be directed, structured and limited by an external, adult-led, research agenda. The chapter concludes by making the case for research that allows for a genuine representation of youth voice, and an example of one potential research approach is provided. Essentially, it is argued that young people should be involved in the design and undertaking of research where the issue under investigation requires their input. Without such genuine youth insights, it could be concluded that youth sport/physical activity research on disaffected young people is unlikely to offer any new knowledge to aid the development of future initiatives.

Contemporary significance of youth voice

It is generally accepted that young people's voices have been largely muted, silenced or ignored in much of the youth research and policy development to date (Prout and Hallett, 2003; Alderson and Morrow, 2004; Brownlie, Anderson and Ormston, 2005). This silence is often attributed to the fact that traditional views of childhood have been grounded, theoretically, in developmental or psychological conventions, thus regarding young people as 'incomplete adults' (James *et al.*, 1998). It is argued that such views have, ultimately, served to deny young people agency, as well as positioning them primarily as the 'objects' of research and viewing them as a largely homogenous social group (e.g. James, Jenks and Prout, 1998; Punch, 2002). However, there is a growing shift towards acceptance of, and support for, viewing young people as competent and skilled social agents who are capable of reflecting upon, understanding and articulating their experiences (Christensen and James, 2008; Heath *et al.*, 2009). As such, there is evidence within public policy and discourse of young people's views being recognized and respected, with ever-increasing opportunities for youth voices to be heard (Roberts, 2003). Indeed, it is now widely accepted that young people are the primary source of knowledge about their own views and experiences, and that they should be understood as active rather than passive recipients of information or services (Alderson, 2008). This view has led to calls for an authentic inclusion of youth voices in research, evaluation and consultation practices (Halsey *et al.*, 2006).

At a policy level, the significance of young people's thoughts and perspectives is recognized in Article 12 of the United Nations Convention on the Rights of the Child (UNICEF, 1989). Enshrined within this is the notion that respect for the views of children is a central tenet of young people's human rights, and Prout (2003) has argued that this view has become part of the 'rhetorical orthodoxy' (p. 11) of much social policy discourse. In addition, a number of countries have appointed national children's commissioners as a means of foregrounding the views and interests of children in public policy. Within the UK, there are children's commissioners for each of the home countries. These posts are independent of government and have the overarching aim of hearing and respecting young people's voices. In addition, the UK government's Children and Young People Unit has expressed a desire for 'joined up' policy with regard to children's participation and voice, suggesting that young people should be heard, valued and treated as responsible citizens (CYPU, 2000). Within education in the UK there is also increasing evidence that youth voice has become established in policy and discourse. For example, young people's active participation in decision making and consultation practices is central to the Government's Children's Plan (DfCSF, 2007). Moreover, the Every Child Matters strategy highlights the need to engage pupils in decision making and has, as a core aim, the requirement to support young people to make a positive contribution to policies and services that affect them (HM Treasury, 2003). Likewise, the Children's Act 2004 requires Local Authorities to take the views of young people into account when making decisions about youth services. Consultation with pupils is also enshrined in the 2002 Education Act, is a feature of many Ofsted inspections (since the Education Act 2005) and is a criterion for meeting the Healthy School Standard (DfEE, 1999).

Underpinning the promotion of youth voice in education is the belief that the process of hearing students' voices is a valuable learning strategy for pupils themselves. In particular, making spaces for youth voice can encourage citizenship and, indeed, it could be argued that the introduction of citizenship education into the school curriculum is a mechanism for facilitating young people's active engagement through debate and discussion. It has also been suggested that meaningful engagement of youth voice can have a role to play in tackling disaffection and disengagement within schools. For example, Sandford, Armour and Warmington (2006) have argued that citizenship education can also be seen as evidence of the expectation placed on schools to capture the interest of pupils, particularly those who are disaffected or disengaged from traditional education approaches. Similarly, a current DfCSF guidance document appears to endorse this view, when it proposes that allowing young people a say in decisions that affect them can challenge elements of disaffected behaviour by helping, in particular, to 'improve engagement in learning, help develop a more inclusive school environment and improve behaviour and attendance' (DfCSF, 2008, p. 1).

It is apparent, therefore, that there is a strong belief in contemporary UK education policy, underpinned by international conventions, of the need to promote youth voice and the potential benefits that can result for individuals and organizations. The questions to be addressed in this chapter are therefore: how should a focus on youth voice in education impact upon education research and, specifically, sport/physical activity research?

Educational research and youth voice

As has been noted, there is growing support for providing authentic opportunities to hear young people's voices within society, and to allow them to share their thoughts and views on matters that directly concern them. It follows, therefore, that young people have a key role to play in research on policies that affect them and programmes in which they are or will be involved (Clark and Moss, 2001; Flutter and Rudduck, 2004; Alderson, 2008). It has also been argued that there is a case for moving from simply *consulting* pupils to actively engaging them in the research process (e.g. Thomson and Gunter, 2006). Thus, young people are increasingly taking on the role of researchers who explore and examine youth experiences. Indeed, a recent government guidance document acknowledges that allowing pupils to undertake researcher roles can be a valuable means of encouraging their active participation in decision making processes (DfCSF, 2008). The potential benefits of youth involvement as researchers are oft cited in the literature and include, for example, helping young people to gain confidence and learn new skills (Bryant, Lee and Levin, 1997), providing possibilities for empowerment (Bland and Atweh, 2003) and presenting a fresh perspective on familiar things (Rudduck, 2005).

Essentially, ascertaining young people's views can not only help researchers and policy makers to understand more about issues within schools, it can also help them to identify potential solutions and pathways to change (Prout and Hallett, 2003; Flutter and Rudduck, 2004). In this way, it has been suggested that schools have much to gain by listening to pupils, and, in particular, to disaffected pupils, although it is acknowledged that their voices are often more difficult to hear. As Rudduck (2005) has noted, 'one of the strengths of consultation is the opportunity it provides to hear from the silent (or silenced) pupils and to understand why some disengage and what would help them to get back on track' (p. 2). Riley and Docking (2004) also add, '*all* voices need to be heard, not just those of the more able or artic- ulate' (p. 178, original emphasis) and, along with Mitra (2001, cited in Bland and Atweh, 2003), they acknowledge that disaffected pupils can talk clearly and hon- estly about issues that affect them if given the chance.

Despite strong and numerous assertions that pupil voice should be heard and val- ued within schools, a number of researchers have commented that there are still few opportunities for young people to contribute meaningfully to shaping their school experiences (Alderson and Arnold, 1999; Wyse, 2001). Cook-Sather (2002), for example, has noted that students represent the 'missing voices' of educational research (p. 5). Moreover, while many researchers acknowledge the importance of pupil voice, it is clear that the process of actually hearing pupils' voices, and acting upon them, is far from straightforward. Gibbons (2006) has noted that the involve- ment of young people in research should lead to empowerment and enhance learn- ing capacity, but that this is not always the case. Indeed, it is clear that much previous research conducted with young people has been designed and framed entirely by adults (Roberts, 2000; Woodhead and Faulkner, 2000). Moreover, even where young people have been involved in the generation and collation of data, they have rarely been given the opportunity to analyse or interpret that data, or pres- ent and disseminate research findings to policy groups. Thus, there is a danger that adult researchers' or sponsors' agendas can dominate this type of research, muting pupil voices and leading to a misinterpretation of information, the perpetuation of stereotypes, and lack of serious engagement by the youth participants.

There are a number of key points that can be taken from the youth voice literature and applied to contemporary youth sport/physical activity research. In particular, it is evident that the inclusion of youth voice should be considered in many research designs. However, it is also apparent that the precise nature of young people's inclusion in the educational research process is important, and there is a need for researchers to work hard to ensure that pupils are given legitimate opportunities to speak and be heard. As the DfCSF (2008) report 'Working Together' notes, 'participation which is tokenistic or unreflective will lead to cynicism and feelings of powerlessness among children and young people' (p. 14). Thus, there are two key challenges for youth sport researchers: structuring research to allow youth voices to be heard in genuine ways; and seeking to overcome tokenism by, where feasible, involving young people in research design, data collection/analysis and the presentation of findings.

So, what of existing youth sport research? There are certainly many examples of research projects within the field of youth sport/physical activity, and indeed physical education, that have, in one form or another, sought to gain a youth perspective (e.g. Girls in Sport, School Sport Partnerships, New Opportunities in Physical Education and Sport, Sport Unlimited, Chance to Shine). In addition, there is evidence that some projects have employed innovative techniques in an attempt to gain access to youth voice (e.g. Oliver and Lalik, 2000; Holroyd, 2003; Fitzgerald and Jobling, 2004; MacPhail and Kinchin, 2004). Of interest to this chapter, however, are the growing number of research projects involving disaffected youth that have sought young participants' perspectives on programme involvement.

Disaffected youth in the UK

Before presenting research examples, it may be helpful to outline the notion of disaffection as it is understood within this discussion, as well as provide a brief overview of the key concepts underpinning remedial sport/physical activity programmes for disaffected youth within the UK. Although not a core focus of this chapter, these issues do provide some broader context with which to frame the discussion. As noted earlier, concerns about youth disaffection abound within contemporary society, both within the UK and beyond (Smink, 2000; Hayward and Sharp, 2005). In particular, concerns have been expressed about some young people's participation in unhealthy or risky behaviours, as well as their involvement in crime (NYA, 2006; Wilson, Sharp and Patterson, 2006). Certainly, negative perceptions concerning young people have helped to fuel a sense of moral panic in the UK about the threat they pose to social and moral order (Davies, 2005). The concept of disaffection is, however, a complex one. There is a distinct lack of consensus between academics and policy makers as to the precise causes and expressions of youth 'disaffection', and there are considerable difficulties in defining the notion because the word itself has become something of a 'catch-all' term, applied to a cluster of behaviours, attitudes and experiences (Steer, 2000). Social policy makers, in particular, have appropriated the concept and use it in conjunction with other terms (e.g. social exclusion, social marginalization and disenfranchisement) when defining groups of individuals who lack access to various social resources or benefits (see Sandford *et al.*, 2006). Despite the lack of consensus in definition, however, Heathcote-Elliott and Walters (2000) note that 'one feature common to all reports on the subject is that being labelled "disaffected" has negative connotations for the individual' (p. 1). To summarize, 'disaffection' can be understood as a complex and multi-dimensional phenomenon that is influenced by numerous interrelating factors (e.g. poverty, low self-esteem, broken families, drug use), and manifested in various, often highly individualized, ways including disengagement from mainstream activities, disruptive or anti-social behaviour, or engagement in risky or criminal behaviour (Steer, 2000). In short, young people, or rather some young people, are perceived to be a 'problem' and one manifestation of that problem that is seen to be particularly concerning is their disengagement from school, and from education and training more broadly (Kendall and Kinder, 2005; Newburn and Shiner, 2005). The young people who fall into this latter category are the main focus of this discussion.

Concerns about the behaviour of a minority of children and young people in schools are not new (Klein, 2000) and there is a large body of evidence to suggest that youth disaffection, broadly defined, is a key mediating factor in truancy, exclusions, poor discipline and apathy in schools. Indeed, the DfES (2005) stated that disruptive behaviour within classrooms interrupts pupils' learning, resulting in alienation from education for many young people. However, youth disaffection is not always expressed as disruptive or deviant behaviour; indeed Brown and Fletcher (2002) coined the term 'disruptive engagement' to describe the behaviour of the young people in their research. Moreover, Heathcote-Elliott and Walters (2000) conceptualize a 'continuum of disaffection' reflecting levels varying between active and passive and mild and severe, which recognizes that the term 'disaffected youth' can apply to both the overtly disruptive and the quietly disengaged.

In response to concerns about youth disaffection within schools, a series of educational policies, programmes and initiatives has been implemented in the UK in order to 'fix' the problem, e.g. the Every Child Matters/Youth Matters agenda, National Behaviour and Attendance Strategy, Respect Action Plan, Behavioural Improvement Programmes and the availability of alternative curricula. All are evidence of the government's desire to challenge anti-social behaviour, promote social inclusion and re-engage young people in education and wider society (Sandford *et al.*, 2008b). A central feature in many of these policies and programmes is the use of sport and physical activity as a means of both engaging disaffected youth and facilitating their personal and social development. The prevalence of such activities suggests an enduring belief that sport is, in some way, 'good' for young people; a belief probably originating in the nineteenth-century (gendered) notion, in England at least, that engagement in sport is 'character building' (Nichols, 2007). Certainly, there is a growing body of international research to suggest that involvement in constructive leisure facilities can lead to positive youth development (e.g. Hellison, 2003; Larson and Silverman, 2005; Holt, 2008), as well as helping young people to build resilience and address problems of disadvantage and social exclusion through the generation of social capital (e.g. Bailey, 2005; Delaney and Keaney, 2005). In summary, then, youth disaffection/disengagement is perceived to be a pressing contemporary problem and sport/physical activity a potential solution. It is out of this context that the 'social problems industry' (Pitter and Andrews, 1997) of physical activity programmes for personal development, of which the four following projects are examples, has sprung.

Physical activity and disaffection: research examples

What follows is a brief description of the four selected projects, an overview of the methodologies employed within them, and a brief illustration of how young people's voices have been used to articulate key issues or themes in the dissemination of findings. It should be noted at this point that all four projects represent examples of independent evaluation research and were funded externally by various project sponsors in order to determine, principally, the *impact* that programme activities had on young participants. In other words, the research was intended to highlight, for example, individuals' thoughts/feelings concerning programme involvement, their perceptions of skills acquired or benefits gained, and their understanding of their own personal development. Thus, opportunities for the young participants to influence the nature of the research were restricted, although there is some evidence that their views influenced the nature of the programmes themselves. Lessons learned from these projects offer insights into the ways in which youth voice could be strengthened in evaluation research in the future.

Sky Living For Sport

Sky Living For Sport (SLFS) is a school-based behaviour improvement programme intended for young people who are having difficulties with one or more aspects of school life, resulting in active, passive or, even, potential disaffection. It is a national initiative that encourages schools to run their own projects within a broad framework developed by the programme sponsors (Sky) and organizers (Youth Sport Trust), and it takes the form of a specific intervention that uses physical activity to re-engage a target group of selected young people. Launched as a 'pilot' scheme in January 2003, SLFS is now in its sixth year and involves schools in England, Scotland and Northern Ireland. In the words of the YST, SLFS 'recognises that sport can create a spirit of adventure and creativity, inspiring 11 to 16 year olds and helping to improve attitude and behaviour' while also helping schools meet their behaviour improvement targets (Youth Sport Trust, 2007, p. 5). Teachers organizing Sky Living For Sport projects within their schools can select any activity, or combination of activities, for pupils (e.g. climbing, abseiling, horse-riding, skiing, tennis, football, martial arts, aerobics) and, indeed, pupils often work with their teachers and support staff (e.g. teaching assistants) to identify particular activities in which to engage, and also to set personal targets and goals. The projects can last from one term to one academic year, and project sizes have varied from 4–75 pupils, although groups of 8–16 pupils are most common. Each SLFS project culminates in a sport event, which is often a tournament or competition organized by the project pupils, and completion of the 'course' is marked by a celebration event. A number of schools that undertake SLFS serve areas of high social and economic deprivation, and many of the young people face challenging personal and social circumstances.

Throughout the life of the programme, an evaluation of impact has been under-taken by the Institute of Youth Sport at Loughborough University, using a range of qualitative methods to collate data from schools and pupils. Primarily, teachers are asked to use school statistics and/or their own judgement to provide profile data relating, in particular, to pupil behaviour, attendance, physical education atten-dance, self-esteem/confidence and social skills, for all participating pupils at the start and end of project activities. There is also some follow-up with schools, where possible, to determine the sustainability of impact. In addition to this, evaluators undertake interviews with lead teachers and focus groups with pupils in order to ascertain their views about project activities and outcomes. The comments and opinions of pupils and teachers are used, along with the profile data, to illustrate key findings to the programme sponsors/organizers and a wider academic audience (e.g. Duncombe and Armour, 2005; Armour, Duncombe and Stewart, 2007; Sandford *et al.*, 2008a). More specifically, young people's words are used, in direct quotes, to highlight their views of project involvement (e.g. their likes/dislikes regarding project activities or perceptions of benefits gained/skills learned) in reg-ular presentations to the programme sponsors, annual project reports and academic publications. These extracts of young people's conversation are presented both as stand-alone citations and, as shown below, in the formation of broader school case studies.

Illustrative example: Rockford School (from Sandford *et al.*, 2008a, pp. 101–102)

[This is an extract from a case study.]

Rockford School elected to participate in the first year of SLFS, with project involvement being led by Peter, a learning mentor. The project involved 10 pupils (aged 14 years), who were selected because they were all participating in an alternative curriculum. A number of the pupils had been diagnosed with autistic spectrum disorder but all found communicating with others problem-atic and most had some form of learning difficulty. As such, it was felt that they could benefit from the social and collaborative nature of the SLFS project. As a qualified climbing instructor, Peter chose to use his own skills and the school's climbing wall as the focus for the project. At the end of the project, Peter remarked that he was 'amazed by all the pupils . . . I am very impressed with them and pleased for them . . . it was quite emotional watching them do so well'. The impact on one individual was particularly memorable. At the start of the project, Holly was described by her learning mentor as 'shy and sulky'. It emerged that she struggled to communicate with her peers and rarely spoke to adults. In addition, she had 'forgotten' her PE kit every week since she started secondary school and, as a result, had never participated in PE. During the case study visit, Holly was asked if she would mind talking to the researcher about the project and she obliged happily. Holly talked for about 10 minutes, explaining with confidence that 'I think I have changed as a result of the project . . . I talk to adults more, take charge of things and behave better'. She was observed instructing primary pupils (during the final sports event) and co-operating with the other young people in the group.

HSBC/Outward Bound project

The HSBC[1]/Outward Bound (HSBC/OB) project was a corporate-sponsored initiative intended to help re-engage disaffected young people in education by involving them in outdoor/adventurous activities. The project ran for five years between September 2003 and August 2008, and an evaluation study was funded by the sponsor to run throughout the lifetime of the initiative. Based within the deprived Docklands area of London, the project involved a partnership between HSBC in the Community, the Outward Bound Trust and five schools local to HSBC's head office in the heart of the financial district. Over the course of five years, approximately 750 young people (aged 13–14 years) participated in the initiative, taking part in an organized programme of outdoor activities designed to challenge and develop skills such as team building, communication and responsibility. The young people were supported by a number of HSBC staff, who acted as volunteer mentors, and who were trained to work with schools and pupils both within the project activity sessions and in follow-up activities within the schools.

The evaluation of the HSBC/OB project was undertaken by the Institute of Youth Sport at Loughborough University. The evaluation employed a range of methods in order to gain an in-depth understanding of participants' thoughts and experiences of project involvement, and to determine the extent to which programme aims and objectives were achieved (Armour and Sandford, 2008). The evaluators generated data from the analysis of baseline and six-monthly updated pupil profiles, participant observation of activities and ethnographic field notes, as well as through methods such as individual and group interviews, open-ended surveys and journal writing. In addition, a number of activity-based tasks, such as ranking, drawing and mapping exercises (Holroyd, 2003), were used within focus-group discussions to facilitate recall and stimulate discussions about the young people's outdoor activity experiences. The long-term nature of this evaluation project meant that the evaluators were able to use the young people's feedback, together with that from the teachers and mentors, to guide and shape the development of the project over its lifetime. Data were also used in the development of conference presentations and publications, with young people's voices being used to illustrate key findings (e.g. Sandford *et al.*, 2008a, 2008b). As in the previous project, this is primarily in the form of direct quotes being used, in reports, presentations and publications, to highlight pupils' views on core themes within the data (e.g. their thoughts on the transfer of skills from the physical activities to the school context, as shown in the example below) or, in conjunction with teachers'/mentors' comments, to provide a rationale for any recommendations for programme development being made by the evaluators. For example, the evaluators noted that a common theme in the feedback from pupils, teachers and mentors from cohorts 1 to 3 of the project was a desire to have more opportunities for all project schools to meet together. This led to a core change in project structure for cohorts 4 and 5 of the HSBC/OB project, which saw pupil numbers reduced slightly so that all five schools could attend the week-long residential activity sessions at the same time.

Illustrative example (from Armour and Sandford, 2006, pp. 28–29)

[Relating to a discussion with pupils on the transfer of skills.]

Once pupils had given their opinions about the skills and attributes learnt through participation in the HSBC/Outward Bound project, they were asked to consider why they were important. Skills were viewed as important because they were positive attributes that would help pupils to socialize, communicate and work with other people:

> All of these qualities help you progress hugely as a person, both mentally and physically.

> Because in Outward Bound we were around other people, people we didn't know, and around different genders and so on, so it means that in future we will be able to mix easily and socialize with other people.

> When you are older you might have different things (to do) and move away, so you have got to learn how to make new friends and adapt to the environment.

For some pupils, the skills they had learnt were also deemed to be important for 'the future', helping them to gain employment or cope with a move away from home. As one pupil commented, 'all of these things are going to affect us in our future jobs, you know'. The experience of the HSBC/Outward Bound project was deemed to have given pupils a greater sense of independence, personal responsibility, and awareness of others, and this was felt to equip them for their lives outside of school. In particular, the confidence gained through participation in the HSBC/OB project was deemed to have a positive impact on pupils' responses to different situations:

> The activities I did gave me more courage and helped me when I needed to make speeches, like at HSBC I had to make a speech and I did one at Buckingham Palace . . . It was really scary, but the courage I gained from doing the activities at Outward Bound helped me to get over that.

NOPES disaffection case study

Undertaken by the Centre for Developing and Evaluating Lifelong Learning (CDELL) at the University of Nottingham, the aim of this one-year case study evaluation was to identify and evaluate the impact of NOPES (New Opportunities in PE

and Sport) funding on disaffected youth, defined as 'young people who may be considered disaffected, at risk of exclusion from school or [who] belong to a marginalized group' (Gibbons, 2006, p. 4). The research represented part of a wider, six-year
evaluation of the NOPES initiative, a lottery-funded programme. Launched in 2002,
the NOPES programme comprised £750 million, which was made available to local
authorities to improve sports and physical education facilities. The new or upgraded
facilities were mainly located on school sites in areas of social deprivation, and the
programme aimed to improve social, physical and educational outcomes both for
young people at school and the local adult community. A particular focus of the case
study research presented here was to examine the impact of the funding on disaffected and marginalized young people in the NOPES facility areas, and to report on
and evaluate 'any impact with particular reference to participation, sustainability,
social impact, attitudinal and cultural change' (Gibbons, 2006, p. 4).

In order to explore these issues, research was undertaken with six separate geographical cases in five locations across the UK (one location being the site for two
separate case studies). Characteristic of the NOPES programme, many of these locations were areas of high social deprivation. The case studies involved a total of 49
young people (31 boys/18 girls) and included both school- and community-based
projects targeting young people at risk of offending, exclusion or disadvantage due
to marginalization. The methodology was underpinned by 'bottom up' approaches
– essentially a belief that research should be done *with* and not *on* young people, thus
ensuring the targeted young people were directly involved in the generation of data.
Data-collection strategies included photo-narratives, semi-structured group interviews and individual reviews of videoed group discussions, and were undertaken
either independently or with the assistance of a researcher. This inclusive methodological approach meant that the research was able to highlight something of the
'complicated physical geographies and social boundaries' of young people's worlds
(Gibbons, 2006, p. 24), facilitating an understanding of whether and how the
NOPES facilities funding had made an impact on individuals' lives. Young people
were invited to keep a scrapbook of photographs they had taken during the research,
and records of their discussions. They were also presented with certificates to record
their involvement in the research process – a means of thanking young people and
showing them that their opinions were valued. Indeed, when discussing the impact
of research involvement on the young people, Gibbons (2006) noted that many individuals were pleased to have had their contribution recognized in this way. Extracts
from the young people's discussions were used in the construction of the case study
narratives in the final case study report, as illustrated below. These, together with
adult leaders' comments, led to recommendations for future programme development – for example, to develop activities specifically targeted at particular groups
and to ensure that any staff involved are responsive to young people.

Illustrative example: Hallam High (from Gibbons, 2006, pp. 20–21)

[Relating to a discussion about new facilities and aspirations for future activity involvement.]

When pressed on the facilities for sport they conceded that the facilities like the gym and the hall are much nicer but they've lost their football pitch as the school building has been re-sited there and the new MUGAs (Multi Use Games Areas) are on the site of the old school. The new pitches are not ready and they feel that their use will be restricted even when they are. However the hall facility does mean that PE is once again taught in gendered groups, which according to Captain was:

> loads better; the girls can't do nowt.

The girls in this group eventually became more adventurous in their aspirations and wanted to try new things. They both had a plan for what they would do when they left school although not in relation to sport. Tammy would one day own her own garage and be too busy for sport because it would be 'work, eat, sleep, party, sleep' and Misa wants to go to college, get her exams and go to university and get a good job, have a nice house, a car and a family – but not too soon . . .

. . . The boys' plans were along the lines of stay in bed, smoke dope and play football. Captain in particular couldn't wait to leave school to lie-in in the mornings and go round to his friend's house to smoke dope. However as we got to know Captain better it could be that this at least represents a plan where as the alternatives were nothing at all or things too awful to contemplate. With regards to lunchtime activities they felt they were too busy doing other things like spending time with their mates. Red, who was generally quiet, scoffed at the idea of after-school clubs:

> It's bad enough when you've got to come in to school. Why would you want to come in when you don't have to?

Distance and travelling time made it impossible for most of them to attend anything after school, they felt. Lunch-time was a possibility but they would only go if their mates were going. Taking the first steps seemed something they were unwilling to do alone. Yet when asked about their mates it seemed they did go to lunch-time activities – just not ones they were that interested in being involved with.

Positive Futures: case study research

Positive Futures (PF) was launched in 2000 and is a national social inclusion programme that aims to engage disadvantaged, disaffected and socially marginalized young people through sport and leisure activities (Home Office, 2006). Initially set up within the Home Office's Drug Strategy Directorate, and still funded through it, the project is now managed by a national charity (Rainer Crime Concern), and is delivered by a range of organizations such as local authorities, sports clubs and crime-reduction agencies. With overarching aims to facilitate young people's engagement with education, training and employment, as well as encouraging sustained project participation, the programme is located as a developmental rather than a purely diversionary approach, and seeks to provide new opportunities for young people aged 10–19 years who are disadvantaged or facing challenging situations. For example, PF programmes offer young people opportunities to enhance their education, learn skills such as leadership or coaching, play sport competitively, or volunteer within the local community. There is a focus on positive social interaction throughout all projects and the activities are seen as 'a basis for establishing relationships with young people who have otherwise become alienated and distanced from mainstream social policy agencies and "authority" figures' (Crabbe *et al.*, 2006b, p. 6).

Crabbe *et al.* (2006b) carried out a case-study evaluation of six Positive Futures projects as part of a wider evaluation of the initiative. The focus of this research was to 'gain a more complete picture of the ways in which projects (rather than just sports or other activities) influence participants' attitudes, engagement, interests, education, employment, peer groups and relationships' (p. 7). Given the focus on relationships, the evaluators sought to develop a research methodology that was flexible, inclusive and appropriate to the particular demands of the individuals and contexts in which and with whom they were working. As such, the degree of involvement of the researchers varied from non-participant observer to full participation in project activities, depending upon what was deemed necessary for each particular context. Moreover, the research was guided by a desire to ensure that the young people's voices were central to the study. In order to achieve this, participants were involved in the generation of data through the use of cameras, videos and what they termed 'mapping tools'. Young people's voices were articulated within the presentation of data in the form of individual or project case studies and to illustrate key themes within the data (as shown below). In keeping with their desire to employ a Participatory Action Research approach (see Chapter 10 in this volume), the evaluators noted that they, in addition to the national project management and some individual projects, were keen to 'use learning from the study to inform practice and future direction' (Crabbe *et al.*, 2006b, p. 8). Indeed, they note how lessons learned from early case study work led to the piloting of a new monitoring and evaluation framework, which moved away from the search for causal links between sport and crime reduction towards a focus on impact as an individual 'journey'.

Illustrative example (from Crabbe *et al.*, 2006a, p. 25)

[Relating to the theme of how PF influences the use/perception of neighbourhood space.]

Working through the images produced by the young people, along with conversations with staff and the young people, enabled us to build up a richer sense of the backgrounds and every day lives of the young people we have been working with, as well as making links between PF activities and how they might impact on experiences outside of the project and vice versa. What was particularly revealing about these exercises was the extent to which they further contributed to a vision of disadvantaged young people as disempowered victims rather than contributors to social disadvantage, crime and anti-social behaviour. When asked what would make their area 'better', Billie said:

> More things to do because there's nowt to do . . . There's a park but it got all sharp edges, we had things like tops on [the sharp edges] but people keep pulling them off, there's only about two left or summat and they're really high . . . and cars just drive over't green . . . I think they could like build a park on our field cos they've got a big field and there's nowt doing on it.

Notwithstanding the possible exaggeration with these kinds of comments, reflecting on this lack of things to do Terri added:

> I don't like, do you know round [that area] . . . well I live [there] right but there's park at the bottom right and one up top but if I go down to bottom you get beat up and you go to the top it's boring . . . there's a wood near the reservoir and everyone says people have died there in the reservoir and the woods . . . in the woods there's burnt cars and that and it's dangerous.

For others, the disposable camera work revealed their affinity with their environment and great love for friends and family. A number of Sonny's shots have beautiful local scenery as a backdrop; shots of the old factory, pen and scrub land where he plays, his family clearing the garden where he tells of how he 'fixes things' such as his sister's bike.

Disaffected youth voices in youth sport research: the state of play?

It is well documented that conducting research with young people in ways that generate authentic youth voices is fraught with challenges. In particular, the notion that power within a research situation resides with the adult researcher (Kvale, 1996) has implications for hearing pupils' voices, and can result in a research process that is far from authentic for young people. For example, Coleman, Catan and Dennison (1997) suggest that unless power is equal in a conversational situation, individuals can doubt their capacity to be heard. It is important, then, for researchers not only to find ways of *listening* to young people but, more importantly, to actively *hear* what is being said (Oliver and Lalik, 2000; Oliver, Chapter 3 in this volume). In other words, researchers need to pay attention to young people's views and seek to get to the heart of the issues that they highlight, in order to represent them accurately.

Conducting evaluation research with disaffected young people can be particularly challenging, because of the need to find appropriate, acceptable and ethical ways in which they can be engaged to provide views on programme involvement. In addition, traditional means of generating data (e.g. surveys, interviews or focus group discussions) can be problematic for these young people who, often, have poor reading, writing or communication skills, and who are apathetic about or antagonistic towards school work. Indeed, Gibbons (2006) noted that some young people agreed to participate in her evaluation research only when they were assured that there was no written work required. It should also be remembered that disaffected youth can be vulnerable and insecure young people, despite appearances to the contrary, and so there is a need to take time to establish trusting relationships.

Nonetheless, although entering the territory of student voice in research is fraught with some difficulty and uncertainty, the end goal of hearing the missing voice of young people is, surely, worth pursuing. Certainly, the examples given above give an indication of some of the ways in which attempts are being made to hear disaffected youth voices in recent youth sport research. They show that spaces have, indeed, been created for young people to share opinions and give their views on their experiences of physical activity programmes. Moreover, they also provide some evidence of how researchers are seeking to overcome the challenges – for example, in using a range of verbal, written and visual research methods (e.g. HSBC/OB), allowing young people to take an active role in generating data (e.g. NOPES), building relationships with participants through a focused case study approach (e.g. PF), and using young people's own words to illustrate project findings (e.g. SLFS).

Having said this, there are still some important limitations in the existing research. For example, while the case study approaches of the NOPES and Positive Futures research allowed researchers time to get to know the young participants, contact between researchers and young people in the large-scale evaluation studies of Sky Living For Sport and the HSBC/Outward Bound project was often limited to single, focus-group conversations, which are barely conducive to making young people feel at ease or hearing their voices. Moreover, it is worth noting that the participation of the young people in these discussions was, to a large extent, determined by adults (first, via parental permission and, second, via teacher selection of focus-group participants) rather than by personal choice. Gibbons (2006) also highlighted the role played by adult gatekeepers in her study, noting that their decisions can lead to the exclusion of some young people from the research process and, hence, the silencing of their voices. In addition, while it is true that most recent evaluations of youth sport/physical activity initiatives have taken young people's views into account, the data – as was the case in both the SLFS and HSBC/OB projects outlined above – have generally been collected by adults from young people (through interviews, focus groups or structured feedback surveys) and, thus, the young people are invited to comment on the adults' research agendas.

The NOPES (CDELL) and Positive Futures case studies were a little different in that the data collected through these community-based projects were generated, in part at least, by young people themselves. Nonetheless, even in these cases the key aims of both projects provided a strong framework within which research tasks were undertaken and researcher discussions with the participants were developed.

As Gibbons (2006) noted, questions relating to the project outcomes still formed 'a constant reference point for the researcher and the case study participants during the process' (p. 6). In the same way, the presentation of findings in reports and publications is often structured by project aims, outcomes or the interests of project organizers/sponsors. So, rather than seeing young people's views in full there is a tendency to present decontextualized snippets of thoughts or opinions, shaped by the researchers to illustrate appropriate themes or ideas (as with the HSBC/OB, NOPES and PF examples above). In these cases we hear young people's voices as one viewpoint among many in the generation of broad case studies (as illustrated in the example from the SLFS project). This is not to say that this form of presenting findings is worthless, but its limitations must be recognized.

There is no intention here to undermine the value of the four research projects cited above, some of which have involved the authors of this chapter. On the contrary, the existing data provided by these evaluation studies make a valuable contribution to understanding what is likely to 'work' for disaffected young people in physical activity/sport programmes and how future initiatives may be structured to facilitate maximum impact. Moreover, they do allow for participants to articulate some of their views concerning their project experiences, and offer important opportunities for their voices to be heard, albeit indirectly for the most part, by project organizers/sponsors and, even, policy makers. Furthermore, the decisions about whether to take note of young people's views, and which views, lies with the sponsors. Questions remain, therefore, about whether such tightly framed studies offer opportunities to gain a genuine insight into disaffected young people's experiences of youth sport initiatives.

It could be argued that what has been missing in disaffected youth research is what might be termed a 'kids'-eye' perspective on the experience of being selected for and then 'engaged' through such programmes in school settings. Essentially, we know very little about youth engagement in sport/physical activity initiatives from 'the inside' because much of the existing data takes the form of tightly specified evaluation data collected externally, by adults, on behalf of programme funders. As a result, it could be argued that assumptions have been made by researchers about young people's experiences of physical activity initiatives based on the achievement of specific programme objectives.

What, then, can we learn from projects such as those outlined above, and how can we move forward towards more inclusive youth sport research? We would argue that the key task here is to tread carefully and take advice from the pupil voice research literature with regard to the development of future projects – for example, providing training for young people as fledgling researchers, involving young people in decision making and identifying research questions, and providing opportunities to share findings with adults/decision makers etc. (e.g. France, 2000; Fielding, 2001). Such advice has been heeded by the authors in the conceptual development of a new research design, intended to provide fresh youth insight into disaffection, disengagement from education and sport/physical activity interventions. This proposed research approach is outlined in the final section of this chapter, below.

Looking to the future: contributing to an Olympic legacy

Taking into account the literature on youth voice in education research, and the examples from existing research in youth sport/physical activity, the final task of this chapter is to draw the evidence together and to offer an example of a research design that is seeking to both listen to and hear youth voice in authentic ways. It is suggested that hearing disaffected youth voices concerning the experience of being selected for and engaged in physical activity initiatives for personal development can offer unique insights for such programmes. Moreover, with the enthusiasm generated by London hosting the 2012 Olympics, it is argued that expectations of a broad youth legacy are high within the UK, and that such programmes are likely to proliferate. Indeed, faith in the ability of sport/physical activity to bring about positive benefits for young people formed a central part of the London 2012 Olympics bid, with numerous predictions of a physical, social and economic legacy from the Games (DfES, 2005). Moreover, a Cultural Olympiad and a domestic educational programme have been developed to complement the Games (London 2012 website) testament to the desire for the Olympics to have 'a lasting impact on the lives of learners' (DCMS website). The DfCSF has also suggested that the 2012 Games can add value to existing educational initiatives by driving strategies that will 'help address young people's under-achievement and disaffection' (DCMS website) and a government report on learning and behaviour also alluded to the significance of the Olympic legacy, suggesting that 'it is important that this exceptional opportunity is exploited across the country' (DfES, 2005, p. 50). It would seem logical to assume, therefore, that sport/physical activity programmes aimed at engaging and re-engaging young people are likely to be a strong feature of any Olympic legacy, and, if this is the case, there is a clear need for programme developers and policy makers to have best knowledge of effective programme design. We would argue that young people who have experienced similar programmes are a fundamental source of such knowledge, and that research in which youth voices are privileged has a key role to play in informing programme and policy design. Interestingly, a recent report has noted that in measuring the Olympic legacy there is a need for research to be contextualized and to explore impact and behavioural change (EdComs, 2007). How better to provide contextual information than to hear about impact directly from those young people involved?

As noted above, the authors have drawn upon the evidence from recent projects and the advice offered in the research literature on youth voice in order to develop a research design aimed at facilitating the generation of youth-centred knowledge. The proposed research intends to add fresh insights to the existing literature and largely adult-centric data on the value of sport/physical activity programmes in re-engaging disaffected youth, and to provide opportunities for the young participants to take an increasingly active and leading role in the research. Within the proposed approach, a number of young people would be trained as youth researchers (all would have been previous participants in a sport intervention programme aimed at addressing various aspects of their disaffected behaviour) before being invited to conduct their own research with another group of young people who are currently involved in a similar programme. The youth researchers would not only collect data from the youth participants but would also, where feasible, contribute to an evolving research agenda, e.g. through the design of research questions, choice of research methods and identification of focus areas. They would also collaborate with the adult researchers in the data analysis process in order to help preserve the integrity of the youth voice (Bland and Atweh, 2003). Finally, the youth researchers would also be involved in the presentation of findings to their school and, if possible, practitioners and policy makers.

This kind of inclusive approach to research is deemed to be important because, as Ellis and Caldwell (2001) note, 'the purpose of encouraging the development of youth voice is to clarify youth perceptions, opinions, ideas, needs and wants. If that voice is tainted or biased by adult influence (politics, in a sense), the original goal is lost' (p. 5). By fully involving young people, deemed to be disaffected, in the research process, and by privileging their so-called 'silenced' (Rudduck, 2005) or 'less articulate' (Riley and Docking, 2004) voices in the analysis and presentation of findings, it is hoped that an authentic youth insight into the value/impact of physical activity programmes for personal development can be achieved. Moreover, it is intended that the experience of being included in key decision making processes, and having opportunities to direct the research agenda to cover issues of perceived interest or importance, will help the young people challenge conceptions of themselves (both their own and others) as deviant, worthless or lacking control within their educational experiences. By doing so, it is also hoped that the research process can help these individuals re-engage, in some way, with the educational process, and provide skills to facilitate their ongoing learning and development. However, it is acknowledged that gaining support for such a youth-directed approach will itself be difficult as it entails placing significant responsibility for generating/collating data with young people, who are often not perceived as being capable, dependable or accountable. Indeed, one of the reviewer comments from a recent (rejected) grant submission stated: 'I don't think the time and resources spent motivating and training the youth researchers will be as valuable as paying skilled researchers to do the research work.' Such views, we argue, fail to recognize the need for authentic pupil voice, and serve to reinforce the adult-centric nature of much contemporary youth research. The quest will continue to obtain funding for this type of research.

Conclusion

In summary, this chapter provides an overview of some of the key issues and challenges relating to hearing the voices of disaffected young people in youth sport/physical activity research. The perceived significance of youth voice in public policy/discourse, and a corresponding interest in educational research, have resulted in a growing number of research projects in which the thoughts and opinions of young people are actively sought. However, the overtly adult-directed/structured nature of young people's involvement in this research is felt to stifle their voices and limit the capacity for generating genuine youth insights. In presenting and discussing four examples of recent youth sport/physical activity research involving disaffected youth, we have attempted to highlight how, although yielding valuable data and contributing to a growing knowledge base, they have not always allowed for an authentic story of disaffected young people's experiences to be told. It is proposed, therefore, that in order to take the field forward, not only should we build on the valuable data and insights already gained from existing research, but also go one step further and seek to undertake research projects in which disaffected youth are able to play a more central role. In this way, it is believed that we can hear more authentic youth voices and gain genuine youth insights of being engaged, and re-engaged, through sport/physical activity projects. Of course, we understand the process of fully involving young people, particularly those who are disaffected or disengaged, in all aspects of the research process is neither simple nor straightforward. However, we believe the potential benefits to be accrued far outweigh the challenges. Indeed, it is hoped that more youth-centred research will allow for new lessons to be learned concerning the experiences and needs of disaffected youth, and that findings from studies, such as the one proposed in this discussion, will contribute to the growing interest in youth voice in sport/physical activity research and educational research more broadly, as well as contributing to a lasting youth legacy through the development of future programmes and policies.

Note

1 The HSBC Group plc is a global financial organization. The project outlined here was funded by HSBC in the Community, a sub-group of the corporation that has the responsibility for promoting positive relationships between the organization and the local community.

References

Alderson, P. (2008) 'Children as researchers: participation rights and research methods', in P. Christensen and A. James (eds) *Research with Children: Perspectives and Practices* (2nd edn) (pp. 276–290). London: Routledge.

Alderson, P. and Arnold, S. (1999) *Civil Rights in Schools. ESRC Children 5–16 Programme Briefing No. 1.* Swindon.

Alderson, P. and Morrow, G. (2004) *Ethics, Social Research and Consulting with Children and Young People.* Ilford: Barnardo's.

Armour, K.M. and Sandford, R.A. (2006) *Evaluation of the HSBC/Outward Bound Partnership Project and the HSBC Education Trust Kielder Challenge and Tall Ships Projects: 30 Month Report.* Loughborough: Institute of Youth Sport.

Armour, K.M. and Sandford, R.A. (2008) *Evaluation of the HSBC/Outward Bound Partnership Project and the HSBC Education Trust Kielder Challenge and Tall Ships Projects: Final Report.* Loughborough: Institute of Youth Sport.

Armour, K.M., Duncombe, R. and Stewart, K.E. (2007) *Combined Report for Years 1–3 of YST/BSkyB 'Living for Sport'.* Loughborough: Institute of Youth Sport.

Bailey, R. (2005) 'Evaluating the relationship between physical education, sport and social inclusion', *Educational Review*, 57 (1): 71–90.

Bland, D.C. and Atweh, B. (2003) 'A critical approach to collaborating with students as researchers'. Paper presented at the Faculty of Education Postgraduate Student Conference, 'Performing Research', Kelvin Grove Campus, QUT, 24–25 October.

Brown, K. and Fletcher, A. (2002) 'Disaffection or disruptive engagement? A collaborative inquiry into pupils' behaviour and their perceptions of their learning in modern language lessons', *Pedagogy, Culture and Society*, 10 (2): 169–192.

Brownlie, J., Anderson, S. and Ormston, R. (2005) Children as researchers. Scottish Executive Education Department. Online. Available at: http://www.scotland.gov.uk/Resource/Doc/930/0030738.pdf (accessed 20 July 2008).

Bryant, C., Lee, L.E. and Levin, B. (1997) 'Developing student voice: a follow-up study with students as researchers'. Paper prepared for the American Educational Research Association's Annual conference, Chicago, March.

Children and Young People's Unit (CYPU) (2000) *Tomorrow's Future: Building a Strategy for Children and Young People*. London: CYPU.

Christensen, P. and James, A. (2008) *Research with Children: Perspectives and Practices* (2nd edn). London: Routledge.

Clark, A. and Moss, P. (2001) *Listening to Young Children: The Mosaic Approach*. London: National Children's Bureau/Joseph Rowntree Foundation.

Coleman, J., Catan, L. and Dennison, C. (1997) '"You're the last person I'd talk to"', in J.T. Roche and S. Tucker (eds) *Youth in Society* (pp. 227–234). London: Sage.

Cook-Sather, A. (2002) 'Authorizing students' perspectives: toward trust, dialogue, and change in education', *Educational Researcher*, 31 (4): 3–14.

Crabbe, T. *et al.* (2006a) 'Going the distance: impact, journeys and distance travelled' (third interim national Positive Futures case study research report). Positive Futures. Online. Available at: http://www.positivefuturesresearch.org.uk (accessed 30 October 2009).

Crabbe, T. *et al.* (2006b) 'Knowing the score'. Positive Futures Case Study Research: Final Report. London: Home Office.

Davies, B. (2005) 'Threatening youth revisited: youth policies under New Labour', *Encyclopaedia of Informal Education*. Online. Available at: http://www.infed.org/archives/bernard_davies/revisiting_threatening_youth.html (accessed 18 July 2006).

Delaney, L. and Keaney, E. (2005) *Sport and Social Capital in the United Kingdom: Statistical Evidence from National and International Survey Data*. London: DCMS.

Department for Children, Schools & Families (DfCSF) (2007) *The Children's Plan: Building Brighter Futures*. London: The Stationery Office.

Department for Children, Schools & Families (DfCSF) (2008) *Working Together: Listening to the Voices of Children and Young People*. London: The Stationery Office.

Department for Education & Employment (DfEE) (1999) *National Healthy School Standard Guidance*. London: The Stationery Office.

Department for Education & Skills (DfES) (2005) 'Learning behaviour: the report of the practitioner's group on school, behaviour and discipline'. Online. Available at: http://www.dfes.gov.uk/behaviourandattendance/about/learning_behaviour.cfm (accessed 20 October 2007).

Duncombe, R. and Armour, K.M. (2005) *YST/BSkyB 'Living for Sport' Programme: Year 2 End of Year Report*. Loughborough: Institute of Youth Sport.

EdComs (2007) *London 2012 Legacy Research: Final Report*.

Ellis, J. and Caldwell, L.L. (2001) *Increasing Youth Voice through Participation in a Recreation-Based Teen Center*. College Park, PA: Author.

Fielding, M. (2001) 'Students as radical agents of change', *Journal of Educational Change*, 2: 123–141.

Fitzgerald, H. and Jobling, A. (2004) 'Student centred research: working with disabled students', in J. Wright, D. Macdonald and L. Burrows (eds) *Critical Inquiry and Problem Solving in Physical Education: Working with Students in Schools.* London: Routledge.

Flutter, J. and Rudduck, J. (2004) *Consulting Pupils: What's in it for Schools?* London: Routledge Falmer.

France, A. (2000) *Youth Researching Youth: The Triumph and Success Peer Research Project.* Leicester: National Youth Agency.

Gibbons, C. (2006) *A Case-Study Evaluation of the Impact of NOPES Funding on Disaffected Youth: Final Report.* Nottingham: CDELL.

Halsey, K., Murfield, J., Harland, J.L. and Lord, P. (2006) *The Voice of Young People: An Engine for Improvement? Scoping the Evidence.* London: CfBT Education Trust.

Hayward, R. and Sharp, C. (2005) 'Young people, crime and anti-social behaviour: findings from the 2003 crime and justice survey (Home Office Findings no. 245). London: Home Office.

Heath, S., Brooks, R., Cleaver, E. and Ireland, E. (2009) *Researching Young People's Lives.* London, Sage.

Heathcote-Elliott, C. and Walters, N. (2000) Combating Social Exclusion Occasional Paper 9: ESF Objective 3 Disaffected Youth. Online. Available at: http://www.surrey.ac.uk/ Education/cse/paper9.doc (accessed 9 April 2003).

Hellison, D. (2003) *Teaching Responsibility through Physical Activity* (2nd edn). Champaign, IL: Human Kinetics.

HM Treasury (2003) *Every Child Matters* (Green Paper). London: The Stationery Office.

Holroyd, R.A. (2003) 'Fields of experience: young people's constructions of embodied identities' (unpublished PhD). Loughborough: Loughborough University.

Holt, N. (ed.) (2008) *Positive Youth Development through Sport.* London: Routledge.

Home Office (2006) Positive Futures: be part of something. Online. Available at: http://http://drugs.homeoffice.gov.uk/publicationsearch/183400/be_part_of_something. pdf?view=Binary (accessed 29 April 2009).

James, A., Jenks, C. and Prout, A. (1998) *Theorizing Childhood.* Cambridge: Polity Press.

Kendall, S. and Kinder, K. (2005) *Reclaiming those Disengaged from Education and Learning: A European Perspective.* Slough: NFER.

Klein, R. (2000) 'Fighting disaffection', *Improving Schools*, 3 (1): 18–22.

Kvale, S. (1996) *Interviews: An Introduction to Qualitative Research Interviewing.* London: Sage.

Larson, A. and Silverman, S.J. (2005) 'Rationales and practices used by caring physical education teachers', *Sport, Education and Society*, 10 (2): 175–194.

MacPhail, A. and Kinchin, G. (2004) 'The use of drawings as an evaluative tool: students' experiences of Sport Education', *Physical Education and Sport Pedagogy*, 9: 87–108.

Mitra, D. (2001) 'Opening the floodgates: giving students a voice in school reform', *Forum*, 43 (2): 91–94.

Newburn, T. and Shiner, M. (2005) *Dealing with Disaffection: Young People Mentoring and Social Inclusion.* London: Willan Publishing.

National Youth Agency (NYA) (2006) 'Knives, guns and gangs', Spotlight: Briefing Papers from the National Youth Agency, 37, September.

Nichols, G. (2007) *Sport and Crime Reduction: The Role of Sports in Tackling Youth Crime.* London: Routledge.

Oliver, K.L. and Lalik, R. (2000) *Bodily Knowledge: Learning About Equity and Justice with Adolescent Girls.* New York: Peter Lang.

Pitter, R. and Andrews, D.L. (1997) 'Serving America's underserved youth: reflections on sport and recreation in an emerging social problems industry', *Quest*, 49 (1): 85–99.

Prout, A. (2003) 'Participation, policy and the changing conditions of childhood', in C. Hallett and A. Prout (eds) *Hearing the Voices of Children: Social Policy for a New Century* (pp. 11–25). London: Routledge Falmer.

Prout, A. and Hallett, C. (2003) 'Introduction', in C. Hallett and A. Prout (eds) *Hearing the Voices of Children: Social Policy for a New Century* (pp. 1–8). London: Routledge Falmer.

Punch, S. (2002) 'Interviewing strategies with young people: the "secret box", stimulus material and task-based activities', *Children and Society*, 16: 45–56.

Riley, K. and Docking, J. (2004) 'Voices of disaffected pupils: implications for policy and practice', *British Journal of Educational Studies*, 52 (2): 166–179.

Roberts, H. (2000) 'Listening to children: and hearing them', in P. Christensen and A. James (eds) *Research with Children: Perspectives and Practices* (pp. 225–240). London: Falmer Press.

Roberts, H. (2003) 'Children's participation in policy matters', in C. Hallett and A. Prout (eds) *Hearing the Voices of Children: Social Policy for a New Century* (pp. 26–37). London: Routledge Falmer.

Rudduck, J. (2005) 'Pupil voice is here to stay!' Online. Available at: http://www.qca.org. uk/libraryAssets/media/11478_rudduck_pupil_voice_is_here_to_stay.pdf (accessed 9 June 2008).

Sandford, R.A., Armour, K. and Duncombe, R. (2008a) 'Physical activity and personal/social development for disaffected youth in the UK: in search of evidence', in N. Holt (ed.) *Positive Youth Development through Sport* (pp. 97–109). London: Routledge.

Sandford, R.A., Duncombe, R. and Armour, K.M. (2008b) 'The role of physical activity/sport in tackling youth disaffection and anti-social behaviour', *Educational Review*, 60 (4): 419–435.

Sandford, R.A., Armour, K.M. and Warmington, P.C. (2006) 'Re-engaging disaffected youth through physical activity programmes', *British Educational Research Journal*, 32 (2): 251–271.

Smink, J. (2000) 'Foreword', in R. Klein (ed.) *Defying Disaffection: How Schools are Winning the Hearts and Minds of Reluctant Students*. Stoke on Trent: Trentham Books.

Steer, R. (2000) *A Background to Youth Disaffection: A Review of Literature and Evaluation Findings from Work with Young People*. London: Community Development Foundation.

Theokas, C., Danish, S., Hodge, K., Heke, I. and Forneris, T. (2008) 'Enhancing life skills through sport for children and youth', in N. Holt (ed.) *Positive Youth Development through Sport* (pp. 71–81). London: Routledge.

Thomson, P. and Gunter, H. (2006) 'From "consulting pupils" to "pupils as researchers": a situated case narrative', *British Educational Research Journal*, 32 (6): 839–856.

UNICEF (1989) *Convention on the Rights of the Child*. New York: UNICEF.

Wilson, D., Sharp, C. and Patterson, A. (2006) 'Young people and crime: findings from the 2005 offending, crime and justice survey', *Home Office Statistical Bulletin*, 17/06. London: Home Office.

Woodhead, M. and Faulkner, D. (2000) 'Subjects, objects or participants? Dilemmas of psychological research with children', in P. Christensen and A. James (eds) *Research with Children: Perspectives and Practices* (pp. 9–35). London: Falmer Press.

Wyse, D. (2001) 'Felt tip pens and school councils: children's participation rights in four English schools', *Children and Society*, 15: 209–218.

Youth Sport Trust (YST) (2007) Youth Sport Trust Update. Online. Available at: www.
e-gfl.org/e-gfl/custom/files_uploaded/uploaded_resources/4474/yst_july07.doc (accessed
29 April 2009).

Websites

DCMS: http://www.culture.gov.uk/what_we_do/2012_olympic_games_and_par-
alympic_games/3426.aspx/ (accessed 1 October 2009).
London 2012: http://www.london2012.com/.

6 Using ethnography to explore the experiences of a student with special educational needs in mainstream physical education

Sarah Meegan

> I don't hang around in a group and everyone is aware of how bad I am at team sports so no one ever wants me on their team. The familiar hustle and bustle, murmuring and giggling that follow the instruction 'Get into teams' are always followed by 'Aw Sir, do we have to?' or 'No way are we having him' as games teacher allocates me to a random team, rather like a spare piece of luggage that no one can be bothered to carry.
>
> (Jackson, 2002, p. 129)

Introduction

This chapter will examine the physical education experiences of an adolescent with a special educational need (SEN).[1] There are three foci to the chapter: (1) to present the physical education experiences of an adolescent with SEN participating in mainstream physical education; (2) to consider the methodological challenges of conducting ethnographic research in presenting the voices of young people with SEN within a physical education setting; and (3) to provide recommendations for future research practice in examining the experiences and voices of young people with SEN.

Including students with SEN in mainstream physical education has gained increased attention in physical education discourse, largely due to broader changes within society that have aimed to promote inclusive education practices (Fitzgerald, 2006; Meegan and MacPhail, 2006b). Inclusive education has been defined as 'a process by which a school attempts to respond to all pupils as individuals by reconsidering and restructuring its curricular organisation and provision and allocating resources to enhance equality of opportunity' (Sebba and Sachdev, 1997, p. 9). Within an Irish context, inclusive education has partly resulted from the introduction of legislation and policy documents including the *Special Education Review Committee Report* (Government of Ireland, 1993), *A Strategy for Equality: Report of the Commission on the Status of People with Disabilities* (Government of Ireland, 1996), the *Education Act* (Government of Ireland, 1998), the *Education for Persons with Special Educational Needs Act* (Government of Ireland, 2004) and the *Disability Act* (Government of Ireland, 2005). Recommendations contained within policies, and enacted within the legislation, mandated for a rights-based movement towards inclusive education for children with SEN. Consequently, legislation and policy introduction, as well as parental pressure for increased inclusion in mainstream schools, grounded special education provision in Ireland. Mainstream schools are required to include and accommodate students with SEN and, in doing so, we have seen a significant increase in the number of children with SEN being placed in inclusive learning environments (Meegan and MacPhail, 2006a).

This chapter is based on an ethnographic study that was carried out to examine the experiences of an adolescent with a disability, James, attending a mainstream secondary school. The aim was to examine his experiences by hearing what he had to say about, and by observing how he participated in, physical education. The research was grounded within the theoretical framework of curriculum negotiation (Brooker and Macdonald, 1999) that explored if, and how, James' participation in physical education impacted on (inclusive) curricular practices through teacher and student negotiation. Negotiating the curriculum was explored as disengagement from physical education among children with disabilities and other groups, such as girls, is not uncommon (Fitzgerald, 2005; Penny, 2006; Enright and O'Sullivan, 2007).

Lack of student negotiation is not uncommon within the realms of physical education curriculum development (Brooker and Macdonald, 1999; Penny, 2006). Brooker and Macdonald (1999, p. 84) reported that, 'While the curriculum supposedly exists to serve the interest of learners, their preferences, if sought at all, are marginalised and their voices are mostly salient in curriculum making.' In relation to people with disabilities, Rose and Shelvin (2004) argue that the discourse of professionals and policy makers has assumed a dominant position that resulted in young people with disabilities having remained on the periphery of decision making processes in education, despite the outcome of these decisions having a profound impact on their lives. Specific to physical education, researchers such as Barton (1993, 2009) and Fitzgerald, Jobling and Kirk (2003) have argued that both researchers and policy makers seem uninterested in engaging with young people with disabilities in relation to physical education. Indeed, Barton (1993) contended that adopting a curriculum for able-bodied students without critical dialogue is unacceptable. He stressed that essential to physical education teaching is listening to the voices of young people with disabilities. It is clear that the issue of disability within physical education curriculum development has received little focus from researchers or policy makers. One may argue that, in order for this to be addressed, it is necessary to *listen* to what young people with disabilities have to say about physical education before any curriculum developments or policies are introduced.

Previous research has examined the physical education experiences of young people with disabilities. Goodwin (2009), in a review of studies examining student voice, reported nine studies that explored these experiences. Goodwin summarized the studies by stating that young people with disabilities enjoy, and want to be involved in, physical activity with their able-bodied classmates. Peers can provide support that facilitates involvement in class and that inclusion in physical education can provide positive social opportunities. Other studies specifically adopted student-centred research incorporating student voice, and employed methods including questionnaires, diaries, peer interviews, surveys, photographs, thinking boxes, posters and discussion (Fitzgerald *et al.*, 2003; Fitzgerald and Jobling, 2004; Fitzgerald, 2005). These studies found that student-centred research was a valuable tool in exploring the experiences of young people with disabilities and, in relation to physical education, illustrated that there exists a concept of normality in physical education that is grounded upon an ideal body, masculinity and high motoric ability. Additionally, the studies found young people with disabilities' reliance on significant others to engage in physical activity, frustration with lifestyle restrictions resulting from having a disability and declaring that physical education teachers offered activities that the students did not like, despite the teacher believing otherwise. The aforementioned research employed a variety of predominantly qualitative research methods. Ethnography as a distinct research tool was not pursued.

Ethnography: participant and process

At the centre of the ethnographic research reported in this chapter was James, an adolescent with a disability. To remain true to the literal concept of ethnography, i.e. to write about people (Marvasti, 2004), I will aim to portray James as best I can. James was 16 years old and an intelligent student who succeeded academically at school. James was a wheelchair user when I met him but this was not always the case. James was ambulant when he first began secondary school, but his mobility regressed and he was a wheelchair user before he reached third year. James' eyesight was also deteriorating over time. There was no formal diagnosis of James' disability as doctors were unable to identify his degenerative condition.

James was a popular student who was liked by both peers and teachers. James' sense of humour, albeit sometimes wicked, was his most redeeming character, often making others, and me, laugh. Such an occasion where James' witty character and ability to 'ruse' his teachers occurred on a day when an important hurling game (Irish national sport) was happening in the school. I noted:

> The class were very giddy and did not settle for the teacher despite his best efforts. James wheeled up to the front of the class and told him [the teacher] he was playing in the hurling match today. He said he needed to leave class as he had to warm up; the class and I could not stop laughing (although I was discreet!). The teacher was literally lost for words, he didn't know whether he was serious or joking. He told James to return to his desk. James slowly wheeled back, still saying he had to leave class as he was playing full-forward for the game and he needed to warm up. The class were backing James up by saying 'Ya sir he's playing today.' The poor teacher, I felt sorry for the predicament that James had placed him in even though I found the occasion hilarious.

When I first met James, he was friendly but quiet and not very forthcoming with information. I explained I was attending his classes to try to understand his experience of participating in a mainstream school, with a particular focus on his physical education experiences. I also focused on any issues he might have with the study. I subsequently spent three days a week throughout a school year with James, and will present his voice and experiences of physical education class as well as the use of ethnography to explore these experiences.

Embedded within ethnographic research is the establishment and maintenance of relationships between researcher and participants. Researcher bias (discussed below) is a salient feature of ethnographic research (Merriam, 1998). To this end, it is necessary to contextualize my reason for conducting the research. Prior to beginning the research, I spent five years working with people with disabilities in physical activity and physical education settings. This included working with one of the largest disability providers in Ireland where I was employed as a physical education instructor. I also spent six months conducting research on motor development among young people with Down syndrome at the University of Alberta, Canada. During this time I gained experience coaching children with disabilities in a variety of sports and physical activities. As I gained more experience in working with young people with disabilities, and speaking to them and their parents about experiences in physical education, it became apparent that the majority of young people I spoke to did not have positive physical education experiences. I became increasingly interested in exploring how young people with disabilities experienced mainstream physical education. This was the catalyst for embarking on the current ethnographic study.

Ethnography takes the position that human behaviour and the ways in which people construct and make meaning of their worlds and their lives are highly variable and locally specific. Ethnography assumes that we must first discover what people actually do and the reasons they give for doing it, before we can assign to their actions interpretations drawn from our own personal experience or from our professional or academic disciplines (Le Compte and Schensul, 1999). The American National Research Council (2002) highlighted that ethnographic research detailing localized educational settings is 'particularly important when good information about the group or setting is nonexistent or scant' (Shavelson and Towne, 2002, p. 105). Although studies have examined the physical education experiences of young people with SEN, ethnographic research in this area is limited.

The ethnographic study entailed spending three days a week throughout a full school year in a mainstream secondary school located in an urban area of Ireland. Data were generated through two processes that are common to ethnographic research (Merriam, 1998): (1) field observations, and compiling field notes based on these observations; and (2) conducting interviews with James about his physical education experiences, as well as interviews with his physical education teachers. Observation of James occurred across all subjects to gain a deeper understanding of how he experienced mainstream education, although the primary focus was on his physical education experiences. Observation of James in his physical education class allowed me to observe in the natural field setting and have a first-hand encounter with the phenomenon of interest, i.e. how he participated in physical education. Similar to Place and Hodge (2001), who observed children with disabilities in a mainstream physical education class, I stood or walked unobtrusively around the hall during physical education. From these positions, I gained optimal vantage points whereby unobtrusive observation of James' participation in physical education was permitted. Immediately after the physical education class, I wrote field notes based on my observations. The value of field notes lies in the premise that what is written down or mechanically recorded from a period of observation becomes the raw data from which a study's findings eventually emerge (Merriam, 1998).

During the ethnographic study I interviewed James and his two physical education teachers on two individual occasions. Although this may appear limited, it must be noted that, due to the nature of ethnography, I had daily conversations with both James and his physical education teachers where many of my questions were addressed. Additionally, observing James provided rich visual data that contributed to a deeper understanding of his participation in, and experiences of, physical education. Finally, another factor contributing to the limited number of interviews conducted was due to James not always being forthcoming with information. Consequently, interviews were carried out only when research questions could not be addressed from informal conversation or observation.

The rationale for conducting semi-structured interviews with James was not only to hear what he had to say about his physical education experiences but, while other research instruments focus on the surface elements of what is occurring, 'interviews give the researcher more of an insight into the meaning and significance of what is happening' (Lindlof, 2002, p. 44). I interviewed James' physical education teachers to determine what they thought about teaching physical education to James, as well as to understand their perception of his participation. Questions for the semi-structured interviews were predominantly informed from the field notes. Within ethnographic interviews 'the field is the social context that guides the interview in terms of what questions are asked, which people are interviewed, and how their answers are interpreted' (Marvasti, 2004, p. 22). Examples of questions I asked James included: 'Tell me what you think of PE class?', 'Have you ever experienced difficulty participating in PE?', 'Do you think it's possible for you to be included in all PE activities?' and 'Have you any suggestions on how you could enjoy PE more and become more involved?'

The observation field notes and interviews were analysed using the constant comparative method, which is when a researcher 'begins with a particular incident from an interview, field notes, or document and compares it with another incident in the same set of data or in another set' (Merriam, 1998, p. 159), thereby allowing for the information to evolve into themes or topics pertinent to the area of research. Resulting from this process, themes expressed through James' voice and his experiences in physical education were identified. As the focus of this chapter is on James' voice, I will discuss what James expressed from the interviews and incorporate my field notes, as well as findings from physical education teacher interviews, to provide a more comprehensive portrait of his physical education experiences. It is important to note that contained within the field notes were accounts of informal conversations I had with James and his teachers. As an ethnographic study, it is necessary to include this information as true representation of his physical education experiences.

Experiences of a student with special educational needs in physical education

Findings from the ethnography study highlighted four key themes that provide insight into the physical education experiences of an adolescent with a SEN: (1) enjoyment, (2) challenges experienced, (3) the importance of autonomy, and (4) the importance of peer support and camaraderie.

Enjoyment of physical education

James identified physical education as his favourite subject in school, as well as expressing the enjoyment he experienced from participating in certain physical education activities. From interviewing James, I explored how he felt about physical education. James' comments indicated that he enjoyed the subject: 'Ya, PE is probably my favourite [subject] ... Well PE is fun like, you get to mess around, you know in class it's all serious.' One occasion when I observed James' enjoyment of physical education and the notion of 'messing around' was when he was involved in playing frisbee:

> During PE class today James had a lot of fun. The class were playing frisbee. James was paired with a peer and they took turns passing the frisbee to each other. It seemed liked they were trying to hit each other with the frisbee rather than practise the skill!

Interviews with James' teacher also highlighted his enjoyment of physical education, particularly the social aspect:

> I think the side of coming out of school [the main school building], coming over to the PE building, the little bit of messing that goes on the way over, in the changing rooms, the messing that goes on there, carrying him down the steps [to access the physical education hall], I think all that side of it James enjoys.

Interestingly, in an interview James stated he did not enjoy physical education prior to becoming a wheelchair user (he started using the chair in third year): 'Well before I used not like it [physical education], when I was not in the chair, before I had the chair, but now that I have the chair, I like it [physical education].' When I further explored this, James stated that he had enjoyed physical education since he became a wheelchair user as he was no longer required to take part in the same activities as his able-bodied peers:

> Cos the teachers, they just tried to get me to do what everyone else was doing and it was harder . . . Well it's easier now cos they [physical education teachers] know what I can do and what I like, what I don't and it's easier now.

This comment indicated that James was expected to participate in physical education the same as his peers before he became a wheelchair user. What is noteworthy is that, according to James, since he became a wheelchair user (thereby having an obvious and visual disability), the teachers changed their approach towards his participation where they knew what activities he could participate in. From my observations, the teachers had limited understanding of James' abilities. They made little attempt to include him in many physical education activities and, on occasion, involved him in activities that were arguably exclusive and discomforting. On one such occasion, I noted:

> For PE today, James' class played tennis. For most of the time James was watching his peers who were trying to hit each other with the ball as opposed to play tennis. The teacher eventually came towards him and told him to play some tennis on the first court. He didn't hit the ball once. The teacher then asked him to get out of his wheelchair and try to play sitting down on the court. James was lifted out of his chair by two peers and placed on the ground, his peers walked away after doing this. James managed to hit the ball once or twice but he kept falling over as he has poor balance. Many people could see him falling over and it was clear he was struggling to hit the ball. The teacher called a halt to play and began demonstrating how to disassemble the nets. During this time James was left sitting on the court ground and all his peers were walking past him returning equipment. James called two of his peers to lift him back into his chair and he wheeled into the change rooms while the class returned equipment. I have been told by James' teachers that he dislikes attention been drawn to his disability and yet, it could not have been made any more obvious by taking him out of his chair and placing him on the court ground.

In relation to the activities James participated in, he repeatedly stated he enjoyed soccer (playing the role of goalkeeper) and frisbee:

> Indoor soccer, I can do that by just going into goals . . . . Ya I enjoyed soccer and frisbee because I was able to do the stuff . . . . Ya I like frisbee, I enjoyed that and soccer.

Previous studies (e.g. Fitzgerald *et al.*, 2003) also identified soccer as a favourite physical education activity among students with disabilities. Although James expressed through interviews that he enjoyed physical education, his enjoyment and preference of activities appeared to be limited to participation in soccer and frisbee as he never mentioned other activities. Participation in limited physical education activities is not uncommon for young people with disabilities (Sport England, 2001; Fitzgerald, 2006), and is an area that needs to be addressed by physical education teachers and policy makers if we want young people with disabilities to experience a broad range of activities that will contribute to lifelong physical activity participation.

Research into the experiences of young people with disabilities appears inconclusive as to whether or not these students enjoy physical education and physical activity. Some studies reported positive experiences (e.g. Kristen, Patriksson and Fridlund, 2003), others reported negative experiences (e.g. Blinde and McCallister, 1998; Place and Hodge, 2001), while yet others reported both positive and negative experiences (e.g. Goodwin and Watkinson, 2000; Hutzler *et al.*, 2002; Suomi, Collier and Brown, 2003). It is clear that additional research is required to further examine the determining factors influencing enjoyment of physical education among young people with disabilities.

Challenges experienced in physical education

Despite James enjoying physical education, he experienced challenges and difficulties in participating. These challenges included accessibility to the physical education hall, as well as difficulty partaking in certain physical education activities. An inaccessible physical education environment was a source of frustration for James. There were steps leading down to the hall as well as steps up to the weights room. To gain access to the hall, James was either lifted up or down the steps by his class peers or he had to leave the building and enter through the emergency exit doors from outside. In an interview he stated: 'The door into the hall is tiny, there's steps and there's no wheelchair toilet . . . people normally carry me down [steps to hall].' I asked James how he felt about this. He commented that he used to be embarrassed, but not any more:

> Well accessibility everywhere is a problem really, in town and you know, well in class . . . there's only one wheelchair toilet [in the school] and it's way away but I have a key for it so I can go whenever . . . but I always have someone with me to open doors . . . they don't really have to push me but for opening doors and getting up steps and stuff.

During an interview, I asked the physical education teacher her opinion about the lack of accessibility to the physical education hall:

> The door into the gym is tiny, there's no wheelchair toilet and there's steps down to the hall. There are three steps down into the hall from the changing rooms. There is an emergency exit at the far end of the sports hall . . . he can leave the building and wheel around and come in the emergency exit, but I think it is dreadful. He has to come in, get changed, leave again and have to go all the way around the outside of it [the building] to have to come in an emergency fire exit. There is something that doesn't really sit right with me about it.

To further illustrate the inaccessible physical education environment and the impact this had on James I noted:

> We went toward the weights room and I was surprised to see where the teachers expected James to go. It was a small door (like the bottom half of a door)

where one had to crouch down to enter. In addition, there were three high concrete steps to enter the room, which were completely blocked by equipment. I could not see the teacher. Three students came along and lifted James up the steps. The combined weight of the chair and James was very heavy and awkward to lift. It was very dangerous. The students did not have a secure hold on James' chair and they had to lift him up quite high to mount the ledge. As they were lifting him, his wheel got caught against the ledge and the chair began to tilt sideways. Luckily they managed to lift the chair onto the ledge without James falling out. The teacher arrived after he was lifted up the steps.

Accessibility has been identified as one of the greatest barriers to physical activity participation for people with disabilities (National Disability Authority (NDA), 2005). Inaccessibility to a physical education facility compounds existing challenges and difficulties many students with disabilities already face when participating in the subject. Despite built environment legislation such as the Building Control Act (Government of Ireland, 1990) many schools in Ireland are still inaccessible for students with disabilities (NDA, 2005). Schools should endeavour to make their physical education facilities fully accessible for all students as an accessible environment is a core feature of an inclusive and equal society. Accessibility to physical education should be a universal right, not a privilege.

Another challenge experienced by James in physical education was his difficulty with participation in certain activities. Many of these activities were team-based and competitive in nature. These activities included hockey, tennis, trampoline, basketball and volleyball. In an interview James stated:

> You know like hockey or when we have to bend down, I can't really do that . . . We do trampoline and I can't do that either cos I can't stand up on the trampoline . . . Basketball, the net is so high . . . Volleyball is difficult cos moving around and the ball is so fast. Tennis, again because of the ball, it's going so fast and it's hard to move to it.

I similarly observed James experiencing difficulties, and the impact this had on his participation:

> During physical education class James participated on his own for most of the time. The class were playing basketball and were practising shots at the hoop. James was told by the teacher to practise against the wall on his own as he could not throw the ball into the hoop.

On another occasion I noted James experiencing frustration with being unable to participate successfully in an activity:

> The physical education teacher sat beside me and we both noted how James was having difficulty passing a badminton shuttle to his partner. I suggested to

the teacher that maybe he would have better luck with a tennis racket as it had a bigger head. He went into the storeroom and got a tennis racket for James. James' success slightly improved but it was clear that he was getting frustrated playing with his partner as he could not return the shuttle to him.

Teachers made little attempt to adapt any of the activities to accommodate James' needs and abilities. I noted:

> Lack of adaptation made it difficult for James to successfully execute motor skills and participate in activities within the class as he utilized and adhered to the same equipment and rules as everyone else.

To further illustrate this, during an interview with the physical education teacher he stated:

> Tennis wise, I'd just wonder is there much we can do there, suppose it's a bit like badminton except with a tennis racket, the racket would be so heavy for him. How you adapt it then is that you can't play with a badminton racket, it's tricky. I've never really thought about it you know.

In asking James if he thought anything further could be done in physical education to help him increase his participation in activities he experienced difficulty with, he responded: 'No, Amy and Paul [two physical education teachers] do everything they can. They would try get me involved in everything.' In asking James to provide examples of how the teachers would try to include him into different activities, he was unable to respond. I probed examples of how activities he had difficulty with could be adapted:

Sarah: OK, well let's think about basketball as you said you find it difficult because of the height of the net
James: Ya
Sarah: If you had a basketball net that was lower down, do you think it would be easier for you to shoot the ball into?
James: Ya, it probably would
Sarah: Or how about tennis, as you said you have difficulty with the ball moving so fast, do you think having a bigger ball for you to hit would make it a bit easier?
James: I suppose it would ya

It was clear from our interview and my observations that James had not experienced or considered such adaptations in physical education. Additionally, his teachers had not attempted or considered adapting the class for him. Adapting variables such as equipment and rules of activities is often the key to including children with disabilities into physical education (Sherrill, 2004; Morley *et al.*, 2005). It is interesting that James perceived his teachers as doing all they could to help him participate in activities when this appeared not to be the case. Having never experienced a physical education class that was adapted or individualized for him, James did not realize the extent to which he could participate in many activities were he provided with appropriate opportunities.

Curriculum negotiation between James and his physical education teachers did not occur. There was an overt absence of dialogue between both parties regarding how the physical education curriculum offered within the school could be adapted to accommodate his abilities. To this end, the curriculum was delivered for an able-bodied cohort of students. It is important to note that lack of curriculum negotiation with James may, or may not, have been isolated as I did not glean whether whole class–teacher negotiation occurred. There was no overt observation of class–teacher curriculum negotiation during my time at the school. It is arguable that if curriculum negotiation were to occur, it should be done at whole class–teacher level rather than student with SEN–teacher level. This leads to an understanding by *all* students of curriculum content and delivery, including how content may be modified to include students with different abilities. It simultaneously embraces the inclusion concept where all students, regardless of ability, are accommodated within the negotiation process. To this end, many students with disabilities are being required to 'fit' in to the curriculum within mainstream physical education (Smith, 2004). Merely adopting a curriculum for able-bodied people without some critical dialogue with students with disabilities is unacceptable (Barton, 1993). The absence of curriculum negotiation between student and teachers resulted in James not having the opportunity to participate to the best of his abilities in many, if not all, of the physical education activities. This is despite the junior cycle physical education curriculum (Department of Education and Science/National Council for Curriculum and Assessment, 2003, p. 4) (Irish secondary level physical education curriculum) stating, 'Schools should facilitate, as far as possible, the inclusion of students with disabilities in all physical education activities . . . it is essential to present each student not only for participation but also for progression.' This commendable aim of physical education for students with disabilities was arguably not achieved for James. Essentially, he lost out on the opportunity to maximize his participation in physical education. Had curriculum negotiation occurred, such as that in Enright and O'Sullivan's (2007) study on curriculum negotiation with teenage girls, James may have been empowered within a learning environment that was cognisant of his abilities thereby experiencing a sense of ownership of *his* physical education curriculum.

It must be noted that, despite the lack of curriculum negotiation and adaptation, James asserted that he enjoyed physical education, particularly the activities of soccer and frisbee. The importance of autonomy in physical education appeared to be the reason for this.

Autonomy in physical education

Exercising autonomy and control in physical education class was important to James' pattern of participation, with James deciding what activities he did and did not participate in. When asked in an interview if he felt it important that he had a choice over what activities he participated in, James stated:

> Ya, it makes it easier and it's more fun because I can do whatever. Paul [physical education teacher] kinda lets me decide like, you know if there's something hard and I don't really want to do it, he lets me ref or whatever.

Allowing a student to decide what activities they engage in during physical education not only ensures that they participate in activities they enjoy (soccer and frisbee in this case) but simultaneously results in avoiding participation in activities they dislike. I frequently observed James refraining from participating in activities he did not want to partake in, the main consequence being that he experienced limited engagement in physical education:

> A direct consequence of James having control and autonomy over his participation level in physical education resulted in him experiencing a limited choice of activities. I sometimes observed him asking his teacher could he attend another physical education class, giving such reasons as the weather being too wet or too cold or not wanting to play a specific game or activity. More often than not, the teacher gave him permission to leave his own physical education class and attend another one.

Fitzgerald (2005) found similar results in her study on embodied experiences of (dis)ability in physical education and school sport. A key theme identified in Fitzgerald's research was the notion of 'difference' that manifested itself through the activities the students undertook, the location of the activities, as well as the exemptions given to the students. James, like the students in Fitzgerald's study, was happy with not having to participate in the same activities as his peers. To this end, he would often undertake the role of referee or timekeeper either voluntarily or he was often allocated to such a role by the teacher. In one particular class, I noted:

> The teacher stopped the game of badminton to give instruction. James called the teacher over and they briefly spoke. Following this, James wheeled to the top of the court and proceeded to watch his peers play. The teacher told him to umpire the game and he did so for the remainder of the class.

Similar to Fitzgerald's findings, James was happy to comply with different roles to those of his peers as it resulted in him not having to get cold, not having to play outside, or avoiding an activity he did not want to participate in. The level of autonomy and control that James was allowed to exercise appeared to be a strong contributor to his reason for stating that he enjoyed physical education.

Peer support and camaraderie in physical education class

Another key theme that provided insight into James' physical education experiences was the importance of peer support and camaraderie. In interviewing James, I asked how he felt about having peer support in physical education:

Well that's done sometimes, I don't mind. Say one time when we were playing volleyball and it was hard for me to get the ball and so someone just pushed me around to it.

James further stated that he preferred to have a peer assist him in class and to work as part of a team: 'I'd prefer to work with somebody . . . I like team sports cos people can help me out if I need it.'

James stated that having peer support made class easier for him, that he finds the class difficult without it. It was apparent that James' peers provided positive support to him during physical education. This ranged from lifting him up and down steps, helping him set up equipment, handing him equipment that he could not reach and providing camaraderie. I noted:

The class were asked to set up the hall for badminton. James took a net in his lap and was pushed by a peer to help him assemble it. James was laughing with his peers while they were setting up the equipment.

I regularly observed the camaraderie that existed between James and his peers in physical education:

When students were waiting for class to begin, James would regularly be in the middle of a group interacting with peers. They would be talking, laughing and punching each other, with James giving and receiving the same treatment as everybody else. Several of James' teachers commented that James was 'one of the lads', he got on very well with class peers and how important this was for him.

James' physical education teacher also commented on the support and camaraderie he received from class peers:

Did you watch the way he was, I couldn't get over it. I came in [to class], James was there. James was picked on a team and I was watching him. James was playing in goals and you know he moves himself over and back in front of the goals and they were lashing the ball at him . . . but what I saw that day and I thought it was fantastic . . . oh jeepest I was shocked. I was shocked because I had never seen that before now, and afterwards all the talk of the lads was that he should play indoor soccer as a goalie. I mean they were fantastic, those kids are fantastic to him.

Peer support and camaraderie in physical education has been identified in previous research as an important feature for students with disabilities (Goodwin and Watkinson, 2000; Goodwin, 2001). Goodwin and Watkinson (2000) expressed students' experiences of physical education as *good days* and *bad days*. Companionship and peer support were identified as good days in physical education. Goodwin (2001) similarly found peer support as a positive attribute when it was deemed instrumental, consensual and caring. In James' case, the support he received from his peers was closely aligned to these three attributes. It is clear that constructive peer support and companionship positively contribute to how a student with a disability experiences physical education, and should therefore be actively encouraged by physical education teachers. Peer tutoring (pairing students with disabilities with a peer who would support them in class) has been shown to be an effective pedagogical tool in promoting successful inclusion practices in mainstream physical education (Houston-Wilson *et al.*, 1997; Lieberman and Houston-Wilson, 2002). However, Goodwin (2001, 2009) noted that little research has focused on the impact of peer support, partially due to the meritorious quality ascribed to helping others and the assumption that more is better in inclusive instructional settings. In James' context, peer support and camaraderie were important components contributing towards enjoyment of, and participation in, physical education in a mainstream school.

Challenges in presenting the voices of young people with special educational needs

A challenge for disability researchers is to examine the role young people with SEN engage with during the research process. Rose and Shelvin (2004) argue that there has been a discernible transformation in philosophical concepts of childhood during the twentieth century. Young people were traditionally viewed as passive, vulnerable and innocent, and were expected to adhere to the dictum of being seen but not heard. In recent years Irish agencies such as the National Disability Authority and the Children's Research Centre, and international declarations such as the United Nations Convention on the Rights of the Child (United Nations, 1989) have called for an increase in the recognition of the voices of young people with SEN to be included in policy decisions and research impacting on their lives. Specific to research, one may argue that the voices of young people with SEN have largely been ignored within research examining phenomena affecting their lives. Research has largely focused *on them*, as opposed to *with them*.

Research focusing on young people with SEN must give emphasis to children as social and cultural actors where they can meaningfully engage in the research process (NDA, 2006). Fitzgerald (2009, p. 148) adds to this by stating, 'Without insights from young disabled people it is difficult to see how practitioners or researchers can effectively and legitimately advance change within different spheres of life including youth sport.' To this end, researchers must ensure that the rights of young people with SEN are not compromised through research participation and that engagement is empowering, respectful and beneficial to all. Embedded within this is the need to listen to the voices of young people with SEN. Goodwin (2009) further argued that no young person, especially those with a SEN, should be perceived as an object of curiosity or be exploited for research purposes. Researchers employing ethnography, or other phenomenological-related methods, should seek to ensure that students with SEN *want* to engage in research and are not doing so to comply with others. This is particularly important when dealing with young people with intellectual disabilities as they may have a reduced capacity to understand the implications when participating in research.

Another challenge in conducting research on physical education experiences with young people with SEN is the difficulty in encouraging them to communicate candidly. This difficulty arose from my experience of conducting the ethnographic research with James. As previously highlighted, James was not always forthcoming with information when we conversed and this was also true during interviews. James appeared reluctant to answer some of the questions I posed candidly, particularly those focusing on difficulties he experienced with physical education. In relation to questions on his physical education experiences, there were discrepancies between some of his answers and what I observed. An overt example of this involved his inclusion in class, where I asked what the physical education teachers could do to help him participate more. James answered that his teachers do all they can, they try to involve him in everything.

Although James may have perceived this to be the case, as highlighted earlier, this was not observed. It is difficult to know whether James truly perceived this (i.e. that he gets involved in everything or does all he can) or whether he presented me with socially constructed answers where he wanted me to perceive his participation in class as being no different to that of his peers. In relation to James being treated differently to his peers, I noted:

> The school principal informed me that an important aspect to realise was that James wanted to be treated like everybody else, he disliked any inference toward his disability.

This perhaps explains why some difficulty existed with candid communication from James, as he may have perceived me as looking for 'differentness' in his physical education experiences because he had a disability. This challenge is particularly pertinent to the field of disability and physical education, as previous researchers (e.g. Goodwin and Watkinson, 2000) found students with disabilities were aware of their bodies and that other students perceived the bodies of students with disabilities as objects of attention. The nature of physical education is that it focuses on the human body and thus highlights physical aptitude and literacy (Fitzgerald, 2005; Meegan, 2007). Young people with disabilities may feel subjected to stereotypical perceptions of lowered achievement expectations (Griffin and Shevlin, 2007) in physical education and consequently strive to emphasize that they are no different to their peers in how they participate. In James' case, his participation in physical education was, at times, markedly different to that of his peers, notably when he spent classes observing as opposed to participating. Researchers should be mindful of this when conducting physical education research with young people with SEN, and employ research protocols that aim to overcome them providing either socially constructed answers or answers aiming to minimize the impact their disability has on their experiences. Neither of these will provide true reflections of their experiences. Employing ethnography as a research process is one way of addressing this challenge due to the affordance of data triangulation that single research protocols do not permit.

The use of ethnography in seeking to understand the physical education experiences of young people with special educational needs

A key component of ethnographic research is the employment of data triangulation – the use of multiple data collection techniques to reinforce study conclusions (Angrosino, 2007). The present study employed participant observation and semi-structured interviews. Researcher bias is often embedded within qualitative research as, according to Merriam (1998, p. 7), the researcher is 'the primary instrument for data collection and analysis', and, by filtering the data through the researcher's eye and ears, 'interpretations of reality are accessed directly through their observations and interviews' (p. 203). It is not intended to detail the methodological process of these techniques, rather how they contributed to the findings of the study.

The value of ethnography in examining the physical education experiences of young people with SEN lies in the premise that the researcher spends prolonged time in the research environment, observing and listening to the research participants, to gain rich and in-depth insight into their experiences. It is arguable that other forms of research methods, such as interviews and focus groups, do not yield the same level of insight into participants' lives. I propose this as (1) they are limited to one data collection technique, and (2) they do not observe or participate in participants' lives. To illustrate this point I argue that had I employed semi-structured interviews alone, and no observation, it is questionable whether my findings would have been true and accurate representations of James' physical education experiences. I state this because the interviews yielded sometimes limited and conflicting data to what I observed and heard from interviews and informal discussions. Employing ethnography allowed me to recognize this and contextualize James' responses within the broader findings of the study, i.e. compare and contrast his interview responses with observations, teacher interviews and informal conversations. I argue that ethnography is a valuable, and under-used, research method in aiming to understand the physical education experiences of young people with SEN because of the data variety (from multiple techniques) as well as the data richness (from prolonged immersion within the research environment) that it affords. To this end, I encourage researchers interested in examining the physical education experiences of young people with SEN to employ ethnography in aiming to understand this phenomenon.

In relation to employing ethnography, ethnographers must ensure that they carefully monitor their relationship with research participants. It must be acknowledged that this simultaneously links with challenges faced when conducting research with young people with SEN. On reflection, the one question I cannot help but ask is, was James completely comfortable with my presence in his class? The reason I pose this is because I *felt* (I appreciate the subjectivity) that James did not completely engage, or feel fully at ease, with me during some of our informal conversations together. Throughout the study, especially towards the latter stages, I made several unsuccessful attempts to initiate conversation with James, and it was clear on numerous occasions that he did not wish to talk with me. He would either respond with monosyllables or not establish eye contact, and sometimes he would start to wheel his chair away, clearly indicating that he did not want to converse. There are legitimate reasons why he might do this. One: he was a teenager and I was an adult, we had little in common to discuss. Two: perhaps he felt it 'uncool' or was embarrassed to be seen talking with me in front of his friends, as they, and indeed he, may have perceived me as someone who personified the role of a teacher, even though I had no such role. It is important for ethnographers to ensure they do not assume a role that negatively impacts on the research process, even though this may be difficult at times.

Additionally, on reflection, spending a full school year conducting the ethnography study may have been too long a time period. It is arguable that spending this time within a research environment permits you to gain in-depth insight and understanding into your area of research. However, your research participants may become aggravated with you 'being there' for so long and thus may withdraw from the research process by not fully engaging with you during conversations and interviews. As the research progressed, James was not as engaging with me as during the initial research stage. Although James and I had a good relationship throughout the research, spending too long within a research environment *may* adversely affect the researcher and participants' relationship. The key challenge for the ethnographer is to identify when a change in relations between themselves and participants is occurring and move to prevent relationship deterioration by modifying the research process. Examples of this include reducing the amount of time immersed within the research environment or cease observation for a period and then recommence, thereby giving researcher and participants a break from each other. Above all, one needs to establish, and – critically – maintain, a positive relationship between participants and researcher throughout the process while simultaneously remaining immersed within the research environment until data saturation is achieved.

Recommendations for future research practice

The present study employed the observation role of participant-as-observer. Future research could look to adopt alternative roles – for example, observer-as-participant. Practically, this could involve the researcher observing and interviewing students with SEN to ascertain their physical education experiences. The researcher could then assist SEN students in physical education, thereby inadvertently showing the teacher strategies on how to include the student in the class. Subsequent observation and interviews with the student would determine if their physical education experiences had been affected by the introduction of additional teaching strategies through employing the observer-as-participant role. Adopting such a research approach could lead to an examination of whether curriculum negotiation occurs, i.e. whether the physical education teacher aims to modify the curriculum to include students with SEN following the researcher assisting the student. Researchers have called for increased student engagement in curriculum development and implementation (Brooker and Macdonald, 1999; Griffin and Shevlin, 2007; Goodwin, 2009).

Although it is necessary to engage with students with SEN in order to understand their physical education experiences, researchers should be open to alternative methods of examining such experiences. These include using drawings, drama and working with students as co-researchers (Fitzgerald, 2009). Researchers are encouraged to be mindful of adopting research protocols that are supportive and embracing of their participants. In doing so, researchers will empower young people to express their experiences of physical education, through student voice, in a manner that is emancipatory and youth-centred in its approach.

Note

1 'Students with SEN' refers to those students having a restriction in the capacity to participate in and benefit from education on account of an enduring physical, sensory, mental health or learning disability, or any other condition that results in a student learning differently from people who do not have the condition (Education for Persons with Special Educational Needs Act, Government of Ireland, 2004). The term disability is subsumed with SEN. In the present study, James' SEN was having a physical disability. Therefore, the term disability will be used commonly throughout the chapter.

References

American National Research Council (2002) *Scientific Research in Education*. Washington: National Academy Press.

Angrosino, M (2007) 'Doing ethnographic and observational research', in U. Flick (ed.) *The SAGE Qualitative Research Kit*. London: Sage.

Barton, L. (1993) 'Disability, empowerment and physical education', in J. Evans (ed.) *Equality, Education and Physical Education*. London: Falmer Press.

Barton, L. (2009) 'Disability, physical education and sport', in H. Fitzgerald (ed.) *Disability and Youth Sport*. London: Routledge.

Blinde, M.E. and McAllister, S.G. (1998) 'Listening to the voices of students with disabilities', *Journal of Physical Education, Recreation and Dance*, 69: 64–8, in D. Goodwin (2009) 'The voices of students with disabilities. Are they informing inclusive physical education practice?' *Disability and Youth Sport* (pp. 53–75). London: Routledge.

Brooker, R. and Macdonald, D. (1999) '"Did we hear you?" Issues of students voice in a curriculum innovation', *Journal of Curriculum Studies*, 31 (1): 83–97.

Department of Education and Science (1993) *The Junior Cycle Physical Education Curriculum*. Dublin: The Stationery Office.

Enright, E. and O'Sullivan. M. (2007) '"Can I do it in my pyjamas?" Negotiating a physical education curriculum with teenage girls', paper presented at the British Educational Research Association Annual Conference, London, September.

Fitzgerald, H. (2005) 'Still feeling like a spare piece of luggage? Embodied experiences of (dis)ability in physical education and school sport', *Physical Education and Sport Pedagogy*, 10 (1): 41–59.

Fitzgerald, H. (2006) 'Disability and physical education', in D. Kirk, D. Macdonald and M. O'Sullivan (eds) *The Handbook of Physical Education* (pp. 752–766). London: Sage.

Fitzgerald, H. (2009) *Disability and Youth Sport*. London: Routledge.

Fitzgerald, H. and Jobling, A. (2004) 'Student-centred research: working with disabled students', in J. Wright, D. Macdonald and L. Burrows (eds) *Critical Inquiry and Problem Solving in Physical Education* (pp. 75–92). London: Routledge.

Fitzgerald, H., Jobling, A. and Kirk, D. (2003) 'Valuing the voices of young disabled people: exploring experiences of physical activity and sport', *European Journal of Physical Education*, 8 (2): 175–200.

Goodwin, D. (2009) 'The voices of students with disabilities. Are they informing inclusive physical education practice?', in H. Fitzgerald (ed.) *Disability and Youth Sport* (pp. 53–75). London: Routledge.

Goodwin, D.L. (2001) 'The meaning of help in PE: perceptions of students with physical disabilities', *Adapted Physical Activity Quarterly*, 18: 289–303.

Goodwin, D.L. and Watkinson, E.J. (2000) 'Inclusive physical education from the perspective of students with physical disabilities', *Adapted Physical Activity Quarterly*, 17: 144–160.

Government of Ireland (1990) *Building Control Act*. Dublin: The Stationery Office.

Government of Ireland (1993) *Special Education Review Committee Report*. Dublin: The Stationery Office.

Government of Ireland (1996) *A Strategy for Equality: Report of the Commission on the Status of People with Disabilities*. Dublin: The Stationery Office.

Government of Ireland (1998) *Education Act*. Dublin: The Stationery Office.

Government of Ireland (2004) *Education for Persons with Special Educational Needs Act*. Dublin: The Stationery Office.

Government of Ireland (2005) *Disability Act*. Dublin: The Stationery Office.

Griffin, S. and Shevlin, M. (2007) *Responding to Special Educational Needs: An Irish Perspective*. Dublin: Gill & MacMillan.

Houston-Wilson, C., Lieberman, L.J., Horton, M. and Kasser, S. (1997) 'Peer tutoring: a plan for instructing students of all abilities', *Journal of Physical Education, Recreation and Dance*, 68 (6): 39–44.

Hutzler, Y., Fliess, O., Chacham, A. and Van den Auweele, Y. (2002) 'Perspective of children with physical disabilities on inclusion and empowerment: supporting and limiting factors', *Adapted Physical Activity Quarterly*, 19 (3): 300–317.

Jackson, L. (2002) *Freaks, Geeks and Asperger Syndrome: A User Guide to Adolescence*. London: Jessica Kingsley Publishers.

Kristen, L., Patriksson, G. and Fridlund, B. (2003) 'Parents' conceptions of the influences of participation in a sports programme on their children and adolescents with physical disabilities', *European Physical Education Review*, 9 (1): 23–41.

Le Compte, M.D. and Schensul, J.J. (1999) *Analysing and Interpreting Ethnographic Data*. Walnut Creek, CA: Alta Mira Press.

Lieberman, L.J. and Houston-Wilson, C. (2002) *Strategies for Inclusion: A Handbook for Physical Educators*. Champaign, IL: Human Kinetics.

Lindlof, T.R. (2002) *Qualitative Communication Research Methods*. London: Sage.

Marvasti, A.B. (2004) *Qualitative Research in Sociology*. London: Sage.

Meegan, S. (2007) 'Including students with special educational needs in post-primary physical education', unpublished PhD thesis, University of Limerick.

Meegan, S. and MacPhail, A. (2006a) 'Inclusive education: Ireland's education provision for children with special educational needs', *Irish Education Studies*, 25 (1): 53–62.

Meegan, S. and MacPhail, A. (2006b) 'Irish physical educator's attitude toward teaching students with special educational needs', *European Physical Education Review*, 12 (1): 75–97.

Merriam, S.B. (1998) *Qualitative Research and Case Study Applications in Education* (2nd edn). San-Francisco: Jossey-Bass.

Morley, D., Bailey, R., Tan, J. and Cooke, B. (2005) 'Inclusive physical education: teachers' views of meeting special needs and disabilities in physical education', *European Physical Education Review*, 11: 84–107.

National Disability Authority (2005) *Promoting the Participation of People with Disabilities in Physical Education and Sport in Ireland*, Disability Research Series 3. Dublin: National Disability Authority.

National Disability Authority (2006) *Research with Children with Disabilities*, discussion paper. Dublin: National Disability Authority.

Penny, D. (2006) 'Curriculum construction and change', in D. Kirk, D. Macdonald and M. O'Sullivan (eds) *The Handbook of Physical Education* (pp. 566–579). London: Sage.

Place, K. and Hodge, S.R. (2001) 'Social inclusion of students with physical disabilities in general physical education: a behavioural analysis', *Adapted Physical Activity Quarterly*, 18 (9): 304–404.

Rose, R. and Shelvin, M. (2004) 'Encouraging voices: listening to young people who have been marginalised', *Support for Learning*, 19 (4): 155–161.

Sebba, J. and Sachdev, D. (1997) 'What works in inclusive education?', Berkingside: Barnardo's, in N. Frederickson and T. Cline (2002) *Special Educational Needs, Inclusion and Diversity*. Buckingham: Open University Press.

Shavelson, R.J. and Towne, L. (2002) *Scientific Research in Education*. Washington, DC: National Academy Press.

Sherrill, C. (2004) *Adapted Physical Activity, Recreation and Sport: Crossdisciplinary and Lifespan* (6th edn). New York: McGraw-Hill.

Smith, A. (2004) 'The inclusion of pupils with special educational needs in secondary physical education', *Physical Education and Sport Pedagogy*, 9 (1): 37–54.

Sport England (2001) *Disability Survey 2000 – Young People with a Disability and Sport*. London: Sport England.

Suomi, J., Collier, D. and Brown, L. (2003) 'Factors affecting the social experiences of students in elementary physical education classes', *Journal of Teaching in Physical Education*, in D. Goodwin (2009) 'The voices of students with disabilities. Are they informing inclusive physical education practice?', *Disability and Youth Sport* (pp. 53–75). London: Routledge.

United Nations (1989) *Convention on the Rights of the Child*. New York: United Nations.

7 Hypermasculinity in schools
The good, the bad and the ugly

Christopher Hickey

Beneath the common-sense understandings that some boys are sporty and some are not lies a complex suite of identity positions. For those that manage to have their identity confirmed within the powerful sporting discourses that dominate the masculinity landscape, the path to peer acceptance is a clearer one. Conversely, for boys that have their identity diminished by these same discourses, the consequences can be quite dramatic. While physical and athletic prowess are clearly prominent vectors in this sorting process there is a range of other personal and social conditions that impact such trajectories. Built on narrative methodological approaches, this chapter draws on research conducted in a range of settings to describe some of the ways young males understand and enact sporting masculinities. Through a series of research narratives I present the voices of a number of young males as they navigate their identities within and against dominant sporting discourses. To help make sense of the identity practices contained within these narratives a theoretical leaning towards ambivalence will be engaged. Drawing on the work of Foucault, the formation of a masculine sporting identity can be understood as the development of a specific relationship with oneself and with others. Within this framework, sporting identities, like all other identities, are viewed as a process not a state.

Introduction

> The construction of masculinity in sport also illustrates the importance of the institutional setting . . ., when boys start playing competitive sport they are not just learning a game, they are entering an organized institution. (Connell, 2005, p. 35)

While the social practice of sport has grown to include a wide range of pursuits, the combative (hypermasculine) team sports continue to hold a particularly deep traction with young males. In the context of this discussion hypermasculinity can be understood as the performance of extreme or excessive masculine practices. At the start of the twenty-first century competitive, contact, male team sports, namely games of football (be it rugby, soccer, gridiron or Australian Rules) occupy a high public/cultural profile in media-saturated, commercialized social spaces. Whether it is Manchester, Madrid or Melbourne doesn't matter very much. The dominant masculinity is cast against a background of *stoicism, hardness and solidarity*, and personified through games of football. Media, family and peer groups all play their part in constructing strong associations between developing manhood and football. Here, allegiances develop, artefacts multiply, the names of heroes are learned and great feats circulate, as new identities are shaped and negotiated. Whether boys play football or even like football does not necessarily constrain or shield their experience with its discourses. While the attributes of hypermasculinity are not inherently bad, their potential for misappropriation is (often painfully) omnipresent.

Though it is essential to view issues of masculinity as issues of gender, and therefore inseparable from issues of femininity, aspects of contemporary masculine performance clearly warrant specific attention. Foremost here is widespread recognition of the prominence of hypermasculine sporting discourse in the identity practices of mainstream masculinity. Even those that reject this are likely to find themselves measured against it. In the context of schooling the warrant for interrogating masculine subcultures is further advanced by the mainstream educational profiling of boys as *more difficult* than their female counterparts (Newman, Murray and Lussier, 2001; Hickey and Keddie, 2004). Indeed, the channelling of (excess) male energy through physical activity has long been seen as a virtue of the presence of physical education (PE) and sport in the school curriculum. The practice of offering sport and physical activity in schools has its history in promoting the dominant masculinity within English Greater Public Schools in the first half of the nineteenth century. These schools proffered the development of the whole child through active participation in sporting competition (Morris, 1948; Hawkins, 1965). As headmaster of Rugby School in 1828, Dr Thomas Arnold established sport as one of his four key pillars to a balanced boys' education. Many aspects of the way contemporary schools approach their co-curricula programmes continue to have strong lineage to this very philosophy.

Behind the spectre of hypermasculinity, there are many good stories to be told about the young footballers who carry themselves with high distinction and present as good role models. My personal and professional experiences with hypermasculine sporting cultures have been a tapestry of good and bad, disappointment and contentment, disgust and pride, and everything in between. As a participant, father, educator and coach I have had a long and sustained involvement with this culture. At the time of writing this chapter, I am coaching an under-16 Australian Rules football team comprising 21 boys from the local community. Three times a week I spend time with this group of 14- and 15-year-old boys, assisted by a number of mums and dads, as we set about being the best team we can be. The leaders within the team are charged with making this space inclusive and tolerant. Here, acts of violence and aggression are subordinated by friendships and the aspirations of the team. Throughout my involvement in junior football, my experiences with regrettable or distasteful behaviours have been hugely outweighed by positive ones.

Set against my biography is an acute recognition of the problematic (re)production of hypermasculinity in the context of schooling. While hypermasculinity is by no means an absolute or fixed configuration of gender practice, its enactment through football is where many boys learn lessons about how to be *real men* – to get back up after being knocked down, to express themselves physically, to impose themselves forcefully, to mask pain, to expunge weakness and to follow team rules (Messner and Sabo, 1994; Fitzclarence and Hickey, 2001). Guiding my interest here is a concern that social stereotyping constructs participation in combative sports in particular, predetermined ways. The ensuing forms of polarization tend to bracket out other ways of understanding and imagining this issue, wherein the potential to better understand the social drivers associated with the misuse of hypermasculine practices is greatly reduced. The overall effect of the binary con-structs that emerge in the *pro-* and *anti*-football standpoints is to simplify what is a complex set of relationships that are produced by, and produce their own, tensions, contradictions, possibilities and limitations. While I too may have my presupposi-tions to this research, I have been determined to reflexively engage with these, and to deliberately make complex the sorts of assumptions and ideas that I bring to my research into masculinity.

In many ways this chapter is about the tensions and contradictions that drive my research. Drawing on the underpinning precepts of phenomenology, this chapter presents a number of snapshots of lived experiences through the eyes of a number of young males and their engagement with hypermasculine culture. My particular focus here is in the engagements they have alongside hypermasculine sporting dis-courses in the context of schools, and the particular curriculum practices of sport and physical education. Though the methodological parameters do not support unfettered generalization these snapshots are presented as heuristic devices to pro-voke wider discussion and analysis. Though I have not been true to any particular theoretical orientation I have been drawn towards research frameworks that recog-nize the layering of meaning, the potential for contradiction, and the presence of desires and emotions in framing the costs and benefits calculations associated with different gender strategies (Connell and Messerschmidt, 2005). In his critique of *knowledge practices*, Law (2004) argues that so much of the natural, the social and the cultural is, 'vague, diffuse or unspecific, slippery, emotional, ephemeral, elu-sive or indistinct' (p. 2). To this end, I lean towards *ambivalence* in seeking to understand, and potentially assert influence over, the many factors that inform the construction of an ethical masculine identity.

Methodological issues

The methodological foundations of my inquiries into masculinity, sport and educa-tion are best characterized within the paradigmatic lenses of phenomenology. In its broadest sense, phenomenology can be understood as 'a theoretical point of view that advocates the study of direct experience taken at face value' (Cohen, Manion and Morrison, 2000, p. 23). Rooted in the work of Husserl, with subsequent devel-opment from writers such as Heidegger, Gadamer and Merleau-Ponty, the phe-nomenological approach is concerned primarily with seeking to see as others see, and to understand the meanings that others make of their experience. While acknowledging that the researcher is ever present in the research process, phenomenology provokes the use of research methods that privilege the undistorted voices that represent the lived experiences of *real people in real settings*.

Along with the poststructural turn came greater acknowledgement of the place of the researcher in the research process. When I go into schools, community settings or family homes to talk to people about the formation and performance of masculine identities I travel with intellectual and emotional intent. Coffey (1999, cited in Goodson and Sikes, 2001) argues that, 'having no emotional connectedness to the research endeavour, setting or people is indicative of a poorly executed project'. Some writers have gone so far as to suggest that any research involving human lives is inevitably autobiographical and a way of getting to know oneself better (Cole and Knowles, 2001). What is important for me as a researcher, father, educator and coach, is to make a diligent attempt at self-reflexivity, rather than reaching for the unattainable goal of personal and intellectual detachment.

A second methodological aspect of the relationship between researcher and participant is that of power. This issue has been long discussed and debated through the methodological literature. Clearly, in most situations the researcher, as the one who finally represents the data, holds the balance of power. However, three points could be made in relation to this. First, it needs to be acknowledged that the researcher can work only with the experiences and insights that the interviewee contributes. There is almost certainly much that is withheld from the research conversation, either consciously or unconsciously. To the extent that the participant exercises control over what is offered, he or she retains power in the conversation. Second, there are practical strategies that the researcher can undertake to endeavour to ensure that the representation is faithful and accurate (see Crotty, 1998). Third, many contemporary discussions tend to paint power as inherently evil. This is not necessarily the case. Self-acknowledged bias is not inherently malevolent, but needs to divorce itself from hearing the voices of others and depicting them truly.

The research presented in the following section has been gathered using the data-collection methods associated with narrative inquiry. Narrative is an interpretive approach to the social sciences and involves understanding behaviour through collections of anecdotal material (Clandinnin and Connelly, 2000). The anecdotal material gathered is used to focus on how individuals or groups make sense of events and actions in their lives. The research narratives presented here are aggregations of the responses received from boys or groups of boys about their identity practices around hypermasculine codes of football, and the judgements they make about themselves and others. The narrative approach is particularly appropriate to research on the influence of group behaviour. At a cultural level, the stories that people tell about their lives give cohesion to shared beliefs and transmit values (Polkinghorne, 1998). The ways they interpret their experiences carry the values of their culture, by providing insights into the sorts of people they admire and want to be like and those that they want to avoid.

To help make sense of the identity practices contained within the narratives I draw on Foucault's work on how we develop a sense of self. From this perspective the formation of a masculine sporting identity can be understood as the development of a specific relationship to oneself and others (Pringle, 2001, 2005; Markula 2003; Kelly and Hickey, 2008). In a Foucauldian sense there is an ongoing *agonism*, a perpetual struggle over what constitutes such an identity, how it should be made knowable, and who has the responsibility for the management and regulation of different elements of this identity (Foucault, 1983). The analysis used in this theme draws on Foucault's later work on the *care of the self* to identify and analyse how relations of power, forms of regulation and arts of governance – a team, an individual, *yourself* – intersect and interact in ongoing attempts to *make up* (Rose and Miller, 1992) a masculine identity. Mitchell Dean's (1995) concept of *practices of governmental self-formation* owes much to Michel Foucault's (1986, 1988, 2000a, 2000b) ideas about the ways in which we develop a sense of self and the particular characteristics that this self should exhibit.

In the following section I draw on the questions and frameworks that have guided my work in the area of masculinity to highlight some of the drivers that produce certain sensibilities and practices around masculinity. To do so I will describe the influence of different data sets compiled across a number of studies. The themes are by no means comprehensive but rather are framed around the particular focus of this chapter. The three themes I will discuss here are (1) the desire to fit in, (2) the price of not fitting in, and (3) the potential for ethical practice.

Research findings

The desire to fit in

> . . . children get their ideas of how to behave by identifying with a group and taking on its attitudes, behaviors, speech and style of dress and adornment. Most of them do this automatically and willingly: they want to be like their peers. But just in case they have any funny ideas, their peers are quick to remind them of the penalties of being different. School age children, in particular, are merciless in the persecution of the one who is different: the nail that sticks up gets hammered down. (Harris, 1998, p. 169)

It is somewhat ironic that despite the seemingly endless montage of media accounts of sportsmen behaving badly, participation in many codes of football continues to grow. Added to this anomaly is the omnipresence of violence, high risk of injury and sheer physical demand of such games. Within the postmodern condition wherein a greater suite of activity/sporting options are available to young people one could be forgiven for thinking that participation in games of football would be reserved for the few. Auskick is the Australian Football League's (AFL) introductory programme designed to recruit and harness the interest of primary school-aged children between the ages of 5 and 12 years. The Auskick programme has been a huge success, with over 130,000 registered participants in 2008. Knowing that only a tiny minority of these participants will go on to play AFL at the adult level invokes questions about why so many young males, with the support of their parents, are attracted to the game.

Interviews with Auskick participants (children and their parents) provided some interesting insights into the attraction of the programme (Hickey and Fitzclarence, 2004). While individual drivers were many and varied, there was a strong theme around 'being connected'. Indeed, participation in Auskick was widely undertaken as a medium through which young males could access high masculine social capital. Rather than seeing it as a pathway to adult participation in Australian Rules football, many participants were attracted to the allegiances and connections it offered in the here and now. There were numerous comments made by parents that revealed their enthusiasm for Auskick on the grounds that it gave their child an opportunity to be 'part of a male group'. They were keen to make sure that their children would be accepted by their peers and 'fit in'.

> He's not very good at it but I really like to keep him coming. I think it's really good for him. At home he's surrounded by women so to meet up with all these boys is great for him. He does swimming . . . . You don't really get to experience being part of a group. That's important for boys. (Female adult)

> I just think it makes it easier for them at school. My oldest didn't really do much and has always struggled a bit to fit in. With [boy's name] I was really keen to get him involved with the other boys. You always see that the boys that play footy having lots of friends. I don't think he's ever going to be a footballer, but he's enjoying it and I think it's been good for him at school as well. (Female adult)

> It's about belonging and connection. I think they're the sorts of things I'm bringing them here for and what I'd be looking for in a club. It's promoting connection that is so important for our kids. (Female adult)

For their part, most young males also spoke about their friends and peers as key drivers in their participation and enjoyment of Auskick. Being able to identify themselves within or alongside the 'sporty kids' was clearly a badge of honour. In the making of their own identity a number of the boys spoke about how a football identity improves one's peer status and provides opportunities for increased connection.

> I play football at lunchtimes now. I used to not play but now I do. There's 6 kids in my class do Auskick and they're my friends now . . . last year I didn't really play with them . . . doing football is much better. (7-year-old male)

> Everyone at school plays footy so I just play footy too. When I didn't do Auskick I wasn't very good at kicking and marking. I wasn't on any of the teams. Now I'm much better I play footy all at lunchtimes and play[time] . . . When I grow up I want to play AFL. (6-year-old male)

> Footy is the best. Its fun, the players are tough and you can tackle and bump people. We don't do tackles here [at Auskick] and at school some kids cry and sook if you tackle them . . . All my friends play footy. (8-year-old male)

Of course, the relational negotiations these boys forge with themselves and others around their footballing identity require ongoing maintenance.

The price of not fitting in

> I have been beaten, spit on, pushed, jeered at. Food is sometimes thrown at and on me while teachers pretend not to see, people trip me. Jocks knock me down in the hallway. They steal my notes, call me a geek and a fag and a freak, tear up my books, have pissed in my locker twice. They cut my shirt and rip it. They wait for me in the boys' room and beat me up. I have to wait an hour to leave school to make sure they're gone. Mostly, I honestly think, this is because I'm smarter than they are, and they hate that. The really amazing thing is, they are the most popular people in the school while everybody thinks I'm a freak. The teachers slobber all over them. Mostly, the other kids laugh, or walk away and pretend not to see it. The whole school cheers when they play sports. Sometimes, I want very much to kill them. Sometimes, I picture how I'd do it. Wouldn't you? (Michaelis, 2000, p. 13)

In 2002–03 I was involved in a project that explored defining moments in men's lives (Boyer, 2004). Within a methodology that recognized reality as multiple and fluid, and a research design rooted in a narrative epistemology, the project sought to capture the life stories of 16 men. During the interviews the participants were invited, and enticed, to describe incidents or events that had shaped their lives. While each participant's story was intensely individual, the analysis of the data revealed a number of recurring themes. One of these was the prominent existence of PE and sport in the practices and processes associated with defining their identity. Indeed, all 16 men described school incidents where groups of sporting males had banded together to administer abuse of one form or another. For some these stories conveyed very deep and distressing personal reflections while for others their experiences were formed vicariously through observations of the oppression of others. It comes as no surprise that the most frequent victims in their stories were boys that were not resourceful enough to establish an identity that was acceptable with the dominant masculine codes that ruled the schoolyards. It should also be of no great surprise that these codes were powerfully coupled to the culture and practice of hypermasculine sport. Mark's story exemplified the power of this discourse and the difficulty of trying to stand outside of it.

Mark was 12 years old when his life took a dramatic change. At primary school he had always considered himself outside of the 'cool or sporty group', but he had been able to successfully exist alongside them. Mark drew no particular animosity from his peers and though he was generally considered to be one of the more unco-ordinated boys, his academic performance was strong and he had his small group of friends. Mark liked school, and for the most part it seemed that school liked Mark. All that, however, changed during his second week at secondary school. Mark recalled being very nervous about going to secondary school and feeling particularly vulnerable because none of his friends had transited with him from primary school. On the day they took their first PE class Mark remembers feeling particularly alone. In an all-boy setting Mark was allocated to one of four teams for a round-robin basketball competition. While the teacher downplayed the importance of winning, the teams were to play each other once. When the two winners and two losers were pitted against each other in round two it was clear to all that the winner would be the *winner*! During the hour or so that the games took place, Mark recalls having a dreadful time.

> They pretty quickly realised I was hopeless and one kid, who was really good at it, seemed to get a kick out of watching me fumble, drop and miss most of what came my way. He started to deliberately give me difficult passes and then bag me when I stuffed it up. Other kids joined in with him. I remember just wanting to get the hell out of there but I couldn't.

When the end of the class came, Mark remembers feeling a huge sense of relief: 'I just thought, thank god it's over.' Unfortunately for Mark, while the game had stopped, his torture had only just begun. When the class lined up to enter their next lesson Mark recalls being punched several times. 'I can't remember if I cried but I would have been close, I remember being really sad.' From that day a pattern was set whereby Mark would be physically and emotionally violated at school on a daily basis for the next six years. Cast as a 'girl' and 'poofta' by a group of sporty boys, or 'jocks' as he would often refer to them, he quickly learned that there was no place to hide at school. While acts of physical abuse were initially restricted to outside they soon entered classroom settings as well. Mark remembers how particular boys would make sure they sat behind him so that they could poke him in the back with their rulers, punch him and taunt him with names and threats. Somehow none of his teachers seemed to notice the treatment that was being dished out on a daily basis. Occasionally, if a teacher saw one of the boys physically striking Mark he would be called upon to stop. On reflection, Mark is still disappointed that no one intervened on his behalf. Mark concedes that while he may not have 'dobbed them in', he did not actively try to conceal the abuse that was taking place. 'I was hoping they would get caught, but they didn't.'

Mark draws a direct correlation between his experiences as a victim of bullying at school and particular attributes that he carries with him some 15 years later on. Listening to Mark describe the litany of drug treatments he has been prescribed and the array of therapists he has been referred to since school, one can't help but look back on those days and wonder if it could have been different for him.

> Being bullied gave me a distrust and dislike for most people. I am wary of being approached by people. If someone is walking toward me I sort of step to the side because I think they are coming for me. I didn't have a distrust for people when I started school. I wasn't jumpy around people, or nervous. I think that developed very quickly as I stared to have negative social interactions, as in being bullied and disliked – for no reason that I could see.

The potential for ethical practice

> We want people who just aren't going to get into trouble, that respect author-
> ity, that will fit into the team environment and have got a great work ethic.
> They're the things that we want. And I don't think that sort of means they have
> to go and visit hospitals all the time . . . you just don't want them to get into
> trouble, that's all. (Recruiting manager, AFL Club) (Hickey and Kelly, 2009)

In the winter of 2007 I interviewed 12-year-old Brett as part of a study into young
males' understandings of a footballing identity. The study comprised an attitudes
survey and the collection of voices from interviews with a spread of 8–12 year olds.
Brett was one of nine boys that I interviewed as part of my role in the study. Brett's
participation in the study was based on his self-identification as a footballer. In fill-
ing out his background, Brett explained to me that he trained football twice a week,
swam squad two mornings a week, played basketball once a week and played a
football match at the weekend. He was captain of the school football team (though
they didn't play many games) and had recently been selected to try out for the
regional U/13 representative team. Earlier in the year he had won the 100m and
400m running races for his age group at the school athletics carnival. Five minutes
with Brett was long enough to know that through the world of U/13 sports and athletics, he had good social capital.

Additional to his quite precocious sporting prowess, Brett was easy to talk to and
engaging. He spoke about the place of sport in his life with a maturity and reflexivity that seemed to belie his youth. What Brett articulated to me about his sport trig-
gered my attention to a 'voice' that I have had increasing contact with over the past
couple of years. Foremost here was his recognition of the contemporary demands
and expectations placed on elite sportsmen and women. Brett seemed to be attuned
to the sentiment expressed by the above comment of the AFL recruiting manager.
Though he was not precisely sure of how he had come to develop this ethic, Brett
explained that he had learned a lot through the media. He recounted a number of
off-field incidents involving AFL players that had led to recriminations and penal-
ties as the basis of why he understood the emerging demands for elite footballers to
behave well. If such players were understood as role models in Brett's life, it was
only to provide examples of what he would not do!

> I think football clubs look at more than just whether you're a good player these
> days. You still have to be good at football but you have to be a good person too.
> If they think you could let the team down or do stupid things that aren't good
> for the club then they wouldn't pick you . . . I think it's important to do well at
> school and to have a good reputation if you want to be picked in sport.

Brett located his heightened consciousness of the widening social and civic
responsibilities associated with being a footballer to his parents and his football
coach. At a practical level, Brett revealed that his football coach has been active in
presenting messages that 'good footballers' need to be well behaved both on and off
the field.

We have a rule that if you get in trouble at school, not like if you just get told to shut up or something, but if you get in real trouble, you have to tell the coach. He says that we're a team and you have a responsibility to each other and if you do bad at school you let the team down too. One kid got suspended for a week for getting in trouble. I'm not doing that!

I further explored Brett's theories of action through connections between his investment in sport and his understanding of the personal and social responsibilities he felt this carried with it. Canvassing the extent to which Brett's commitment to presenting himself as someone who is thoughtful and responsible, I hypothesized about the extent to which he would be prepared to stand in opposition to his peers, or team-mates. I asked Brett what he would do if he found himself in a situation where there was pressure from his peer group to partake in risk-taking or miscreant behaviours.

> *Brett*:   If my friends and that were stuffing up or I thought they were doing something that wasn't really right, I wouldn't do it.
>
> *Chris*:   So would you try to stop them from doing it, or just remove yourself?
>
> *Brett*:   I guess it depends. I think I would try to stop them if I thought I could or maybe talk to kids that I thought I could stop. It depends if I thought they were going to listen to me. If they were just going to laugh at me or make fun of me because I wasn't joining in, I would just leave.
>
> *Chris*:   So if they were doing something bad, say, and you did end up deciding to just walk away, would you tell anyone about it, like an adult?
>
> *Brett*:   I guess if I thought it was something that was dangerous and that someone could get really hurt by it, I would tell someone. I think I would feel bad if something bad happened and I could have maybe stopped it. It's a bit hard though, 'cause you don't want to be a dobber.

Discussion

Schools are renowned for their inter-group rivalries. Recognition of the important identity struggles that take place in groups is supported by the persistence of sub-cultural groupings labelled as 'jocks', 'nerds', 'freaks', 'geeks' and so on, and a wide range of pejorative ethnic labels (see Walker, 1988; Connell, 1989; MacAnGhill, 1994; Martino, 1999). Such groupings are of course fluid, and individuals move in and out of them according to their deeds, deportments and commitments. Among the most influential of these groups are the codes of unity, entitlement and privilege that can be forged among groups of boys whose identities are strongly aligned with sporting forms of hypermasculinity. Unchecked, these sensibilities have an enormous potential to become abusive (Leftkowitz, 1998). This potential is heightened as the group develops habits and practices that restrain members from acting independently and responsibly. Resultant forms of 'group think' can nurture a culture of unity and the formation of consensus-driven patterns of behaviour wherein individual identities are subordinated to that of the group

(Jenkins, 1998). While this chapter gives further evidence of the destructive potential of such groupness, it also reveals that other possibilities exist.

These narratives, and countless others like them, are reminders that the subcultures that build up around hypermasculine sport can be far from tolerant and inclusive. Viewed as a conduit for exploring the intersection of sport, schooling and masculinity, these narratives exemplify both the concerns and possibilities that exist in this social space. At one level they convey the potency with which the discourses and practices associated with hypermasculine sporting profiles can be garnered to marginalize and alienate. Regardless of whether they are inclined or disinclined towards sport, most young males can expect to have their identity measured off against the culturally dominant forms of sporting masculinity. Those that 'don't make the team' can be rendered very vulnerable in the context of their identity formation. Recognizing the consequences of rejection produces practices of self-formation that actively endorse hypermasculine performance. This is undertaken through the active formation of a particular set of relationships with self and others, as evidenced in the explanations for why so many young males are attracted to participate in AFL Auskick. As a (albeit transitional) conduit to accessing hypermasculinity, young males, and their parents, view Auskick as a place where they can become active agents in the formation of identity. As such, the construction of a masculine identity must be seen as a process, not a state.

Within this process exists a very fine line between the productive and destructive enactment of the attributes and deportments associated with hypermasculine performance (Fitzclarence, Hickey and Nyland, 2007). For their part, schools must recognize the important role that they play in supporting hypermasculine cultures. Indeed, the thing that binds the narratives presented in this chapter is their connection with schools. While schools may not be the primary site of where understandings of hypermasculinity are framed, there is no doubt that their presence in these spaces is significant. Foremost here, the voices presented in the three narratives are those of schoolboys who, for better or worse, were negotiating processes that were framing their identity against their notions of masculine performance. Given what is at stake for students who have their identities subordinated or alienated by these discourses, it is incumbent on schools to monitor their enactment. As those most directly charged with overseeing these discourses, it is particularly important that sport and PE teachers play an active role in monitoring the practices and sensibilities that are formed around hypermasculine sporting discourses.

Regardless of what your individual views of football are, there can be no doubting the pull it has on young males. Elsewhere I have commented on the capacity of football to hold the attention and interest of young males who are otherwise disconnected and uninterested in schools and other adult-mediated experiences (Hickey, Fitzclarence and Matthews, 2000). This chapter helps to further expound the lure young males have, as they look to establish a secure place within the confines of a hypermasculine sporting identity. Though the methodological precepts do not support unfettered generalization the narratives presented here can be instructive on a number of fronts. Foremost, they convey the complex and fluid nature of sporting masculine identities and some of the different ways these are accessed and curtailed. Drawing on Foucault's later work, it is useful to understand the deeds and sensitivities that boys partake in within and alongside hypermasculinity as part of them actively developing and performing their 'sense of self' (Foucault, 2000a). From this perspective the formation of a masculine sporting identity can be understood as the development of a specific relationship to oneself and others.

Implications for practice

Listening to the meanings young people give to their identity-creating practices is integral to making sense of, and ultimately influencing, their self–other relationships. The narrative approaches employed in this chapter have sought to facilitate an examination of how individuals construct their experiences in relation to their peer group. Recognizing the situatedness of meaning allows for a more thorough analysis of identity within a given environment. Thus, the process of mapping individual experience onto cultural or social systems allows us to better understand the drivers behind particular meanings and actions. Rather than seeing identity as a personal pursuit, I embrace methodological approaches which recognize that 'people weave life experiences into coherent stories, or narratives, in ways that reconstruct images of themselves and the groups or communities with which they affiliate' (Lightfoot, 1997, p. 2). As such, identity is seen as a process wherein individuals are creating and establishing a sense of self that is tied to specific cultures, communities and groups. To this end, it is important to locate the actions of individuals within the 'symbolic forms, communicative practices, and shared idioms of culture' (Lightfoot, 1997, p. 8). If as both researchers and educators we are more attuned to both the benefits and pitfalls of particular identity positions then we will be better placed to influence the practical environment. At the heart of this is the uptake of more ambivalent theoretical standpoints and tools.

Operating within a complex and sometimes competing set of social codes and practices, young people's engagement in sport and PE must involve a measure of critical interrogation and reflection. Such offerings need to resonate with the practices of self-formation beyond the formal and structured settings. To help them become aware that a responsible participation in sport and PE is about more than being able to run, throw, kick and catch, the pressure is on to produce learning frameworks that cultivate a measure of social and ethical reflexivity. Emanating from this chapter is a call for the provision of both the personal resources and institutional support to help reconcile the competing demands of fitting in and conforming with the need for more independent, ethical and moral forms of masculine sporting identity. Embedded in this is the need for a pedagogical framework through which young males can locate and articulate alternative ways of being and doing. This is foundational in the development of more tolerant and responsible engagements with hypermasculine sporting discourses.

Underpinning my use of narrative methodologies is a desire to foster communication with young people in ways that are mutually generative and supportive. Where young people feel, for whatever reason, that communication about an issue or event is not warranted or worthwhile with a particular audience (namely, their parents and teachers), it is reasonable that they will conceal the information. They may seek opportunities to discuss such issues or events in more supportive environments (among friends) or simply choose not to talk about them at all. The latter is a very easy option for someone, who may be feeling anxious or vulnerable, to take. The less they are afforded opportunities to talk about their understandings and experiences, the less likely they are to expose them to critique. The process of sharing and externalizing narratives harbours the potential to make personal experiences and understandings the object of scrutiny and analysis (Epston and White, 1992). The externalizing process involves turning subjective understandings into more objectified perspectives. In the process the participants are able to unravel, across time, the basis on which they, and others, make particular choices and engage in particular behaviours. To this end, the narrative method encourages the generation of alternatives or counter-narratives in the identity-construction practices of self and others.

A key plank in this agenda is the need for PE and sport teachers to act more strategically to engage with and monitor the pervasiveness of groupness in hypermasculine sporting cultures. In practical terms this requires a pedagogic shift that involves PE teachers and sports coaches working more purposefully with young males to broaden the parameters for self-formation with the legitimate and desired uptake of such an identity. As curriculum practices in schools, PE and sport offer a unique social space for laying the foundation of more tolerant and inclusive forms of sporting masculinity. My interest here is in exploring how different knowledge practices, such as storytelling, can find a space in the governmentalized knowledge practices that structure how we understand and shape hypermasculine identities. Schools are particularly well placed to influence the identity practices that are forged around hypermasculine sporting discourse from a very early age. While it is not without its tensions, this process is clearly not something that should be left to chance. PE teachers, sports coaches, parents and other significant adults can play important roles in forging productive alignments between young people's participation in hypermasculine sports and the promotion of group cultures that are socially responsible and tolerant.

References

Boyer D. (2004) 'Defining moments in men's lives', unpublished doctoral thesis. Deakin University, Geelong, Australia.

Clandinin, D. and Connelly, F. (2000) *Narrative Inquiry: Experience and Story in Qualitative Research*. San Francisco: Jossey-Bass.

Cohen, L., Manion, L. and Morrison, K. (2000) *Research Methods in Education*. London: Routledge Falmer.

Cole, A. and Knowles, G. (eds) (2001) *Lives in Context: The Art of Life History Research*. Walnut Creek, CA: Alta Mira Press.

Connell, R. (1989) 'Cool guys, swots and whimps: the interplay of masculinity and education', *Oxford Review of Education*, 15 (3): 291–303.

Connell, R. (2005) *Masculinities* (2nd edn). Crows Nest, NSW: Allen & Unwin.

Connell, R. and Messerschmidt, J. (2005) 'Hegemonic masculinity: rethinking the concept', *Gender & Society*, 19 (6): 829–859.

Crotty, M. (1998) *The Foundations of Social Research: Meaning and Perspective in the Research Process*. St Leonards: Allen & Unwin.

Dean, M. (1995) 'Governing the unemployed self in an active society', *Economy and Society*, 24 (4): 559–583.

Epston, D. and White, M. (1992) *Experience, Contradiction, Narrative and Imagination: Selected Papers of David Epston and Michael White, 1989–1991*. Adelaide: Dulwich Centre Publications.

Fitzclarence, L. and Hickey, C. (2001) '"Real footballers don't eat quiche": old narratives in new times', *Men and Masculinities*, 4 (2): 118–139.

Fitzclarence, L., Hickey, C. and Nyland, B. (2007) 'The thin line between pleasure and pain: implications for educating young males involved in sport', in K. Davidson and B. Frank (eds) *Masculinities and Schooling: International Practices and Perspectives*. Canada: The Althouse Press.

Foucault, M. (1983) 'The subject and power', in H. Dreyfus and P. Robinow (eds) *Michel Foucault: Beyond Structuralism and Hermeneutics* (pp. 208–226). Chicago, IL: University of Chicago Press.

Foucault, M. (1986) *The Care of the Self*. New York: Pantheon.

Foucault, M. (1988) 'Technologies of the self', in L. Martin, H. Gutman and P. Hutton (eds) *Technologies of the Self: A Seminar with Michel Foucault*. Massachusetts: University of Massachusetts Press.

Foucault, M. (2000a) 'The ethics of the concern for self as a practice of freedom', in P. Rabinow (ed.) *Ethics: Subjectivity and Truth*, by Michel Foucault. London: Penguin.

Foucault, M. (2000b) 'Subjectivity and truth', in P. Rabinow (ed.) *Ethics: Subjectivity and Truth*, by Michel Foucault. London: Penguin.

Goodson, I. and Sikes, P. (2001) *Life History Research in Educational Settings: Learning from Lives*. Buckingham: Open University Press.

Harris, J.R. (1998) *The Nurture Assumption*. New York: The Free Press.

Hawkins, T. (1965) *The Queensland Great Public Schools*. Sydney: Jacaranda.

Hickey, C. and Fitzclarence, L. (2004) '"I like football when it doesn't hurt": factors influencing participation in, and beyond, AFL Auskick', *ACHPER Healthy Lifestyles Journal*, 51 (4): 7–12.

Hickey, C. and Keddie, A. (2004) 'Teaching without class: the limits to pedagogies of separation', *Australian Educational Researcher*, 31 (1): 57–77.

Hickey, C. and Kelly, P. (2009) '"We'll only recruit public school boys in the future": issues of risk management in talent identification and professional development in the AFL', in J. Saunders, C. Hickey and W. Maschette (eds) *People, Participation and Performance: Contributions of Professional Practice in Sport and Physical Education*. Melbourne: ACU.

Hickey, C., Fitzclarence, L. and Matthews, R. (eds) (2000) *Where the Boys Are: Gender, Sport and Education*. Geelong: Deakin University Press.

Jenkins, H. (1998) 'Introduction: childhood innocence and other modern myths', in H. Jenkins (ed.) *The Children's Culture Reader*. New York: New York University Press.

Kelly, P. and Hickey, C. (2008) *The Struggle for the Body, Mind and Soul of AFL Footballers*. Melbourne: Australian Scholarly Press.

Law, J. (2004) *After Method: Mess in Social Science Research*. London: Routledge.

Leftkowitz, B. (1998) *Our Guys. The Glen Ridge Rape and the Secret Life of the Perfect Suburb*. Berkeley, CA: University of California Press.

Lightfoot, C. (1997) *The Culture of Adolescent Risk-Taking*. New York: The Guilford Press.

MacAnGhill, M. (1994) *The Making of Men. Masculinities, Sexualities and Schooling*. Buckingham: Open University Press.

Markula, P. (2003) 'Technologies of the self: sport, feminism and Foucault', *Sociology of Sport Journal*, 20 (2): 87–107.

Martino, W. (1999) '"Cool boys", "party animals", "squids" and "poofters": interrogating the dynamics and politics of adolescent masculinities in school', *British Journal of the Sociology of Education*, 20 (2): 239–263.

Messner, M. and Sabo, D. (1994) *Sex, Violence and Power in Sports: Rethinking Masculinity*. Freedom, CA: Crossing Press.

Michaelis, K. (2000) 'From injustice to indifference: the politics of school violence', paper presented at the Annual Meeting of the American Educational Research Association. New Orleans, Louisiana, 24–28 April.

Morris, W. (1948) *Sons of Magnus*. Brisbane: William Brooks & Co.

Newman, R., Murray, B. and Lussier, C. (2001) 'Confrontation with aggressive peers at school: student's reluctance to seek help from the teacher', *Journal of Educational Psychology*, 93 (2): 398–410.

Polkinghorne, D. (1998) *Narrative Knowing and the Human Sciences*. Albany: State University of New York Press.

Pringle, R. (2001) 'Competing discourses: narratives of a fragmented self, manliness and rugby union', *International Review for the Sociology of Sport*, 36 (6): 425–439.

Pringle, R. (2005) 'Doing the damage? An examination of masculinities and men's rugby experiences of pain, fear and pleasure', unpublished doctoral thesis, University of Waikato, New Zealand.

Rose, N. and Miller, P. (1992) 'Political power beyond the state: problematics of government', *British Journal of Sociology*, 43 (2): 173–205.

Walker, J. (1988) *Louts and Legends. Male Youth Culture in an Inner City School*. Sydney: Allen & Unwin.

8 Looking back, looking sideways

Adult perspectives about student experiences of queerness in Canadian physical education

Heather Sykes

> *Q:* What images come to your mind when you think of physical education?
> *Scout:* Torture.
> *Q:* Torture . . .

Many students have alienating or embarrassing experiences in physical education that deter them from developing confidence in their physical ability. Often these embarrassing or alienating moments in physical education arise from discrimination based on sexual orientation, gender expression and body shape/size. This chapter focuses on the experiences of students who were marginalized during physical education because of their sexual or gender identity, or the size and appearance of their body. Theoretically, the chapter explores how discourses about the body in physical education, many of which are taken for granted, contribute to particular forms of ableism, heterosexism and body discrimination within students' experiences of schooling.

The purpose of this book is to hear and learn from the voices of youth who are subjected to, and also finding ways to resist, the normalizing pressures of school physical education. There is immediacy, indeed an urgency, to do activist research with youth who are currently being harmed by school practices. Yet, this chapter seeks to supplement this action-orientated approach by introducing reflective and retrospective voices of adults in order to identify some continuing and changing patterns of discrimination in physical education. Thus, I hope to contribute to the conversation about youth voices by listening to how some adults struggle to *make sense of* their experiences after they had left school. Of course, I want to avoid overvaluing 'adult' knowledge that, yet again, risks overriding and silencing the voices of youth. Rather, I hope that by offering some experiences of adults who were, themselves, marginalized as students and frequently had extremely negative experiences in physical education, conversations and reminiscences about power and oppression across generations will open up. Thus, this chapter focuses on adults *looking back* on their physical education experiences as a supplement to, and invitation to dialogue about, the present experiences of youth caught in the system right now.

To a certain extent, looking back on people's experience forms an important part of any interview. The term 'experience' refers to, on the one hand, a type of knowing accumulated through direct, personal involvement and, on the other hand, how this personal way of knowing accumulates with the passage of time. Different approaches to qualitative interview-based research utilize both meanings of the term experience. So, an interviewer might try to capture how students *are* experiencing their current situation within a school, with a particular physical education teacher, and as a student. Many versions of participatory action-orientated research seek to turn up the volume, and hopefully mobilize, based on the immediate experiences of people in marginalized, oppressive social contexts. The political and epistemological premise of this type of activist research is to challenge and improve the life circumstances of research participants during the course of the research itself. Another interviewer might seek to find out about the longer-term impact of physical education classes and teachers, and gather information about how life at school forms just one part of a person's overall life experience. This interviewing approach seeks to document, and also challenge, the very ground of possibility upon which particular groups of students come to be regarded as less than, as different, as marginal in physical education. This type of research, informed more by poststructural politics of contesting oppressive discourses, engages in longer-term struggles over who gets to define, and who finds ways to resist, the process of positioning some groups of students as Other. Adult retrospective accounts of schooling can provide information about the social and political context of their education; personal sense making about past experiences; and assess the impact of education on later life.

Student experiences of queerness in Canadian physical education

This chapter also focuses on adults *looking sideways* at physical education – that is, the chapter highlights people with non-mainstream and critical perspectives about physical education. It attempts to include perspectives about physical education that, too often, remain on the margins and beyond the conversations about best practices, curriculum reform and new directions for physical education.

Discrimination based on sexuality, gender expression and bodily appearance is a regular occurrence in schools. The 2001 National School Climate Survey reported that 68 per cent of lesbian, gay, bisexual and transgender (LGBT) students felt unsafe in US schools because of their sexual orientation, and 89 per cent of transgender students felt unsafe because of their gender expression (GLSEN, 2001). Many LGBT youth of colour report being harassed because of *both* their sexual orientation and their race/ethnicity (GLSEN, 2003). Gender expression is also a source of discrimination. Within the Toronto Board of Education, boys who are perceived as feminine and girls who are regarded as being too masculine reported harassment more frequently than 'feminine' lesbians and 'masculine' gay boys because the former group had gender self-presentations that differed from heterosexual norms (Rice and Russell, 2002). In physical education, middle and high schools students experience homophobic and heterosexist behaviours on a daily basis (Morrow and Gill, 2003). Schools still regard students with physical disabilities as having 'deficit' bodies rather than possessing valuable knowledge about how to live with physical abilities and disabilities, strengths and weaknesses (Wendell, 1996; Clare, 1999; Pharr, 1999). Minority youth, especially girls, experience varying degrees of estrangement or disembodiment in physical education lessons (Williams and Bendelow, 1998) and the majority of women in the United States reported being dissatisfied with the size and shape of their bodies (Cash, Winstead and Janda, 1986; Cash and Henry, 1995); 50 per cent of adolescent women in Canada report feeling they are too fat (Rice and Russell, 2002) while women who were fat in adolescence completed fewer years in school (Gortmaker *et al.*, 1993). A recent study of 2279 girls in southern Ontario reported almost one-third of girls who are of healthy weight are currently dieting because they believe they are too fat (Jones *et al.*, 2001).

In physical education contexts, it has been clearly shown that heterosexism and homophobia negatively impact the experiences of many students and teachers (Dewar, 1990; Griffin and Genasci, 1992; Sparkes, 1992, 1994; Sparkes and Templin, 1992; Squires and Sparkes, 1996; Epstein and Johnson, 1998; Clarke, 2001; Kirk, 2001). There are an increasing number of physical education studies into marginalized femininities (Chepyator-Thomson and Ennis, 1997; Wright, 1996b; Ennis, 1999), masculinities (Hickey, Fitzclarence and Matthews, 1998; Gard and Meyenn, 2000; Skelton, 2000; Gard, 2001) and their relationality (Wright, 1996a; Kirk, 1999; Paechter, 2001; Penney, 2002). In disabilities studies, Karen DePauw (2000) noted that, while race and gender issues have been studied from a sociocultural perspective in physical education, issues of disability have been regarded exclusively as a biological category. She called for 'an examination of the assumptions about disability, the body and physical activity' (p. 358). These studies focus on how students are excluded on the basis of a single identity or social issue – as 'lesbians' *or* people with disabilities *or* marginalized boys. This single-issue approach has been subject to scholarly criticism. 'Marginalization' examines how these processes of exclusion and inclusion intersect across different social locations. This approach emerged in response to challenges within the gay/lesbian movements raised by bisexual, transsexual and transgender people and within black movements by biracial and multiracial people (Adams, Bell and Griffin, 1997; Bell, 1997). The study reported in this chapter was designed to draw together these lines of research into marginalized sexual identities, disability and body-based discrimination.

Looking backwards, looking sideways

The focus of the research described in this chapter is the marginalization of students from physical education on the basis of sexuality, gender, physical dis/ability and body shape/size. This chapter discusses an ongoing study about the impact of heterosexism, transphobia, ableism and body-based discrimination in Canadian physical education on the formation of students' embodied subjectivities. The purpose of the study was to understand how the normative and discriminatory aspects of these body discourses about sexuality, gender, disability and body shape/size influenced students' sense of embodiment, bodily satisfaction and participation in physical activity. The research builds upon earlier feminist poststructural research into the social construction of lesbian, and to a lesser extent gay and bisexual, identities of students and teachers in physical education and sport contexts to examine the intersections between multiple forms of marginalization that negatively impact a wider range of students.

The research is informed by sub-fields in critical sociology, sexuality and gender studies including feminist poststructuralism, queer theory, trans theory, crip theory and feminist fat theory (Sykes, 2009). These postmodern, critical theories about embodiment provide a framework for understanding how normative discourses about the body affect students in physical education contexts. Specifically, the theoretical framework uses the concepts of *queerness* and *marginalization*. Marginalization is used to conceptualize intersections between heterosexism, ableism and body size/shape discrimination within physical education. Queerness is used in this research to refer to non-normative sexualities, genders, abilities and body shapes/sizes. Used together, the concepts of queerness and marginalization provide a way to *look sideways* at the assumptions and discourses underlying taken-for-granted ideas about bodies in physical education. This chapter illustrates how queer categories of bodies in physical education are not discrete but produced through similar logics – such as visibility, degeneracy and miscegenation (seeing is believing, fears about development, change and mixing) (Seitler, 2004).

The study explored these issues via semi-structured, qualitative interviews with 39 adults who self-identified as a sexual minority, gender minority, having a physical disability and/or having a socially undervalued body shape/size.

Members of the research team contacted participants initially by using their personal contacts followed by a limited snowball technique. Each member of the research team had personal, activist or professional involvement in one or more of the marginalized groups that provided crucial access to these populations. Most people interviewed were located in the greater Toronto area, although a small number of participants were based in other Canadian and US locations.

As mentioned earlier, one advantage of interviewing adults is the potential to gather retrospective data about their experiences as students, and how the meanings of their experiences change over time (Middleton, 1998). The following excerpt from Kiki's interview illustrates the richness of *looking backwards* onto the impact of schooling.

> *Kiki:*   I'm trying to really think of how I made sense of it. I don't know if I did. I may have you know really kind of felt myself to be you know unlucky and of course it sort of gave me a bad feeling about myself. Like, why do I have to be this way? Why do I have to be different? Why can't I just be flat-chested like all the other girls?
>
> There's a sense of kind of being sexualized by other kids and by adults. That had a certain impact on me. I had a hard time becoming

comfortable with my sexuality because it was almost defined for me at a very young age by other people . . . Because of my appearance, right? 'Oh, she has big boobs' and thinking that I'm this way or that way. Just making assumptions about me.

So, I kind of feel like after analysing it, being older, just realizing how it was kind of sexualizing me at a young age, when I wasn't even thinking about sex or ready to have sex. So that made me very insecure and questioning about my own sexuality.

Kiki began this narrative by thinking, 'how I made sense of it' and asking several questions about why her breasts were perceived to be 'different' from those of other girls. She goes on to explain how, during the time she went to school, people made assumptions based on her body shape that were 'sexualizing me at a young age' which, over time, resulted in her being insecure and questioning about her sexuality. This narrative shows how adult retrospective accounts can sometimes offer detailed, personal theorizing about the impact of body-based assumptions and discourses that circulate in schools and physical education.

The individual interviews, which were semi-structured, were audio-taped and transcribed verbatim using a protocol developed by Mishler (1991, 1995). Interview topics included individuals' memories of physical education, confidence in physical abilities and feelings about their body, the impact of physical education teachers, and how physical education might learn from participants' experiences of marginalization. Participants were requested to choose their own pseudonym, and researchers subsequently inserted pseudonyms for the real names of all other people and places. Interviewees were invited to verify and edit their own interview transcript.

In the first stages of data analysis, members of the research team independently inserted comments and numerical codes onto the transcripts according to the interview topics. The interviews were numerically coded and sorted using word-processing software (La Pelle, 2004) into themes and sub-themes relating to each of the broad interview topics. Within these themes, Kvale's (1995) condensation and interpretation approaches were then used to provide more detailed analyses. This chapter draws on the themes 'Memories of Physical Education', which is divided into sub-codes, negative memories, positive memories or mixed memories, and the code 'Experiences of Discrimination in Physical Education', with the sub-codes of fat phobia, homophobia, transphobia and ableism.

Discourses of queerness in Canadian physical education

The following analysis illustrates how discourses of heterosexism, transphobia, ableism and fat phobia overlap and mutually influence students' memories of physical education and their embodied subjectivities. The analysis depicts how bodily discourses intersected in participants' narratives about discrimination. Participants' memories illustrate how discourses of disability, gender, sexuality, body size and racialization are entwined in physical education – sometimes explicitly, and other times in more intricate ways. Like any qualitative analysis, the following analysis of intersecting discourses about queer bodies is by no means exhaustive. It can only represent some major forms of normalization and discrimination that take place in physical education. Nevertheless, I hope the following themes illustrate how different forms of embodied subjectivity are produced through a matrix of complex, sociocultural power relations that, persistently, work to marginalize students who embody various forms of queerness.

Discourses of athleticism, able-bodiedness and body size

Athleticism is an overarching discourse about the body in physical education. The idea of 'athleticism' may seem obvious, innocuous even, given that the teleology of physical education is so frequently assumed to be the development of a physical body that is athletic, skilful and capable of moving *citius, altius, foritus*. For instance, Maybelline (pseudonym) described himself as a Native American gay man, and remembers experiencing homophobic harassment during physical education.

> *Maybelline:*   There was days when you'd only get couple of comments, and there was times when there'd be more. There were times when most people wouldn't show up and I actually enjoyed going to class because not everybody made fun of me, just certain individuals. It's usually the popular jocks who do it . . .

Maybelline suggested that students who are perceived as 'gay' or 'nerdy' or 'fat' are harassed because they are perceived not to be athletic.

> *Maybelline:*   . . . It's usually the popular jocks who do it. Like, there's always a gay kid in the class, and there's always a nerd, and there's always a fat kid. I was the gay kid. I think, honest to god, I think I was the only one in that class of 30 boys that was. It was a weird feeling.

Maybelline distinguished the 'popular jocks' – who exemplify athleticism – from the 'gay kid', the 'nerdy kid' and the 'fat kid'. This indicates how an athletic body is differentiated from gay, nerd and fat bodies.

In able-bodied culture, an athletic body and disabled body is also regarded as mutually exclusive. Discourses about motor skill, athleticism and sporting ability still rely on constructing disabled and differently abled bodies as 'less than' athletic.

> *Johnathon:*   The thing about disability in gym class, well I mean, the gym is a really ableist kind of place, so the only disability stuff that would come up would be derogatory things about disability. Like are you handicapped? Like when you speak about bodies in gym class, it's really through ableist language.

The mainstream discourse of athleticism actually depends upon, we could say it leans upon, disabled bodies and, yet, these assumptions about disability and physical activity (DePauw, 2000) *debilitate* so many bodies.

Body size is another discourse that is used in oppressive ways to distinguish athletic and unathletic bodies. One of the key body size discourses circulating within contemporary physical education equates being fat with being unhealthy and/or unfit. The inaccurate conflation between fatness and being unhealthy or unfit is a foundational discourse of fat phobia.

> *Q:*   What were they trying to teach you? And did you learn what they were trying to teach you?
>
> *Karen:*   I really don't know what they were trying, like what the objective was of phys ed. You know, the purported intention, I think, was to just let the kids have healthier bodies, and that would in turn increase their abilities in the classroom. Um, but, I don't necessarily think that's what really happened, or what the hidden agenda was.
>
> *Q:*   What do you think the hidden agenda was?
>
> *Karen:*   I think even back then there was definitely this fat phobic attitude, and, I, I think that a large part of it was just trying to eradicate the fatness of the kids. Cause I was in elementary school in the late 70s and early 80s, and, and, you know I think that that was probably around the time where, where it was really being noticed that the kids were being more sedentary. And so they . . . I think that that was . . . that phys ed. was sort of used to combat that.

Karen recalled how body size and fat phobia were part of physical education in the 1970–80s, which is important when considering how 'obesity epidemic' discourses continue to be extremely pervasive and harmful in current physical education (Gard and Wright, 2005; Duncan, 2008; Sykes and McPhail, 2008).

Intersecting discourses of queerness

Analysed in this way, discourses of homophobia, binary gender, sexuality, ableism and fat phobia can show how students are discriminated against on the basis of a single identity or social issue – as lesbian or gay *or* as living with a disability *or* a student who is overweight or fat. This single-issue approach can be strategically useful in certain political and educational reforms but only to a limited extent. Distinct and separate subject positions such 'gay', 'disabled' and 'fat' beg the question how the underlying assumptions and tropes about heterosexuality, ableism and obesity coalesce to support the taken-for-granted discourse of athleticism and 'popular jock'. What is so often ignored are the ways in which 'gay', 'disabled' and 'fat' are derived from common, underlying tropes about bodily difference and, furthermore, how they interact to mutually reinforce the normative ideal of athleticism. Thus, I am suggesting that the apparently obvious notion of an 'athletic body' produces, and indeed relies upon, an array of non-athletic constructions about how bodies move. When interpreted through the concept of marginalization and theory of queerness, the logic that classifies 'gay', 'disabled' and 'fat' bodies as non-athletic becomes puzzling rather than obvious. This requires a closer analysis of how normative discourses about gender, sexuality, racialization and disability amalgamate to ostracize the experiences of particular students within physical education contexts. This is where looking sideways through the concepts of marginalization and queerness can further the analysis. The next section illustrates some of the ways in which bodily discourses articulate with one another to produce various 'queer bodies' in physical education.

Athleticism and racialized masculinity

Throughout the history of physical education, one of the most prominent and overarching discourses about gender has equated masculinity with being athletic. However, this hegemonic idea about masculinity is underpinned by racialized discourses about body size and gay male sexuality. Two Asian gay men, Adam and Kevin, recalled how racialized notions about their body size were an integral aspect of the homophobia they experienced in physical education.

Adam (pseudonym), who described himself as a gay/queer South Asian/ Pakistani man, remembered feeling self-conscious, alienated and ashamed in physical education. He dreaded physical education classes:

> *Adam:*   Well I felt very alienated. I felt that I had no choice, you know, that it was school and that I had to do it. Of course I got a little scared that I wouldn't be able to do certain things. I also felt ashamed because I felt that I wasn't able to do many things in PE.

Lack of choice and feeling unsuccessful in many activities were the main reasons why Adam remembers physical education in negative terms. He never felt confident, physically or emotionally; rather, he recalled how physical education made him feel 'not good enough, not fit enough, not fast enough'.

> *Adam:*   You were made to feel that if you aren't the way that they wanted you to be – which is I guess masculine – that you were somehow less of a person.

Adam felt that not being good in physical education was linked to not being 'properly' masculine. Whenever this hegemonic association between being masculine and being athletic is evoked, it eclipses other gendered ways of being athletic. It also obscures other bodily discourses – such as body size, race, sexuality and dis/ability – in order to produce and maintain the singular discourse that being athletic is to be masculine.

For Adam, being Asian meant the idea had been 'instilled' in him that sport was more about speed and talent, rather than strength and big body size.

Adam: It was instilled in me that [athletics] is one area that really my people were never, you know being an Asian, will never be good at. I think also that has to do with our culture . . . that maybe in this South Asian culture, you know the gym? Recently it's become the biggest thing but it wasn't. It was never something . . . bigger bodies and sports had to do more with your talent than your strength. It had to do more with your speed, not so much your body size or your height, for example. So yeah, in my middle school and high school experience, I remember that the best people any team were the Black and the White, and you had the occasional Spanish person . . . but you know I don't remember ever seeing any kind of role model that was Asian.

Thus, in Adam's experience, Asian masculinity was associated with shorter and small body sizes producing athleticism of speed and talent, which is coupled to being less 'masculine' and 'less of a person'. Kevin, who also identified as gay, experienced a somewhat similar form of social exclusion during physical education, despite being considered tall.

Kevin: I was Asian and I wore glasses, I was small. Well, I was pretty tall back then too, but still, I was considered sort of in the lower end of the hierarchy in terms of who's more popular and who's less popular. I was in the less popular group. I was with, I was friends with this other guy who was, well . . . he was somewhat effeminate so he got made fun of a lot, and so we kind of got along pretty well because we were both picked on a lot.

As gay youth, both Adam and Kevin had to negotiate these stereotypical discourses about South Asian male bodies, which positioned them outside the 'popular group', as other to the 'popular jock', and their bodies as 'less' athletic. This is one illustration of how discourses about body size are laminated onto Orientalist tropes about Asian gay male sexuality (Eng, 2001).

Ableism and fat phobia

The following narrative illustrates how discourses about the fat female body, as always already not athletic, meshed with ableist expectations about which types of physical activity were valued in physical education. Starburst, who identified as a white, queer, fat woman, lives with a heart condition for which she had a 'medical exemption' from physical education although she wryly explained how, during high school, 'I decided to voluntarily withhold my medical exemption, because there they had an indoor swimming pool, and I really liked swimming.' She enjoyed swimming because, in part, she felt being fat enabled her to become skilful in the water.

Starburst: But I liked the swimming pool, and I learned to swim. And because physical size didn't come into it, as a matter of fact, I think I was a better swimmer because I was very buoyant because of the fat. I really liked it, and I was good at it, so I didn't feel any of the negativity towards it. Then I was able to do other things too. I was able to garner a little bit of skill. I took archery, and nothing mattered there, because it wasn't something where you had to run or jump or whatever. I was good at it, because I had decent strength and a good eye for the target. And I did golfing, because they had a golf course there and a golf pro who taught us golfing. I was never good at it, but it didn't really matter whether or not you were good at it. You just sort of went at your own speed and your own pace. I found it interesting. So that was a slightly better experience, except [physical education] still had the health component to it that was just as bad as it had been in Greenville. They still weighed you. They still talked about food. And because then you were dealing with high school, they started to actually train the girls in how to feed their families and how to look after their families. They worked a little home economics into it as well.

Starburst recollected being able to participate and enjoy swimming. She focused on the phenomenological aspects of being in the water, how her buoyancy enabled her to develop her swimming skills. Starburst developed some confidence in the manipulative, accuracy activities of golf and archery, where she could 'go at her own pace' and 'nothing mattered'. The way Starburst valued particular activities starts to reveal an overlap between the erroneous, fat-phobic assumption that fat bodies are less mobile and the able-bodied, lack of appreciation for varying qualities of locomotor movements with prostheses or different sensory inputs. In most areas of physical education, however, Starburst rarely felt physically confident.

> *Starburst:*   Of course nobody ever wanted me on their team, no matter what. Even on the swimming team, because I was slow. I was not a physically fit person ... I always felt that I couldn't make the same kind of contribution than I could other places, and I didn't feel successful there at all.

'Slow' swimming wasn't valued within the physical education context, regardless of the meaning it held for Starburst. In Starburst's experience, the notion of her fat body swimming slowly, lazily even, challenged the meritocratic, competitive notion of swimming that was taken for granted as normal and worthwhile.

Thus discourses about fatness and disability entwined to leave Starburst repeatedly feeling inferior in physical education. This resonates with Johnathon's perspective that 'sport constantly has to be disciplined, how you're performing'. Such a notion of physical education valorizes and, over time, normalizes types of physical activity produced through self-discipline and performance – a profoundly ableist construction of worthwhile physical movement. Scout was a competitive gymnast whose experiences reveal another connection between discourses of body size and ableism. She described how fat phobia and hyper-discipline of the body operate together, almost seamlessly, in gymnastics.

> *Scout:* When it came to organized activities at high school, like gymnastics, it was just really, really controlling. You're going through all of these routines and they're forcing your body to do things – not what it's meant to do. You're pounding your body and your joints and it's very painful. If you have like most of the minuscule amount of body fat, you need to get rid of that. I'm in no way fat [*laughs*], I am now but not then. So, it's really twisted, and it's really compulsory.

As a gymnast, Scout 'could run really fast and tumble and go 10 feet in the air and land' and yet couldn't do well on the national fitness test because 'I couldn't do 18 push-ups or run a mile.'

> *Scout:* It was really bizarre because you're made to feel inferior you because you can't do this. And on this other scale you're one of the best. It's twisted, it's backwards.

Heterosexuality and body size/shape

Heteronormativity was another discourse that framed Starburst's possibilities for doing gender and sexuality, to the degree that becoming queer 'just didn't exist' in her experience of physical education at school.

> *Q:* You identify as queer on the demographics form, did that play into your physical education experiences at all?
>
> *Starburst:* Not at all. I was totally unaware. I just considered myself a girl, and I didn't question it beyond that. I liked boys. I had my flirtations. I never felt attracted to girls. But I mean there was no opportunity for even thinking about it, because it just didn't exist in my world. There would have been such strong social sanctions that if there were other feelings towards other girls or other women, you would have put them away pretty fast, because you would have faced social ostracization.

Thus, Starburst had to negotiate numerous marginalized subject positions as 'medically exempt', as 'fat', as 'girl', as 'heterosexual', which laminated onto each other throughout physical education. Cumulatively, these intersecting bodily discourses resulted in Starburst remembering 'how passive it all was, and how I really disliked it, and how I dreaded [physical education] as the period approached'.

Kiki went further, to link the potential for social exclusion if same-sex feelings towards other girls were expressed in physical education with the visual judgements made by girls about each other's body size in the changing rooms.

Kiki: Definitely, well in terms of I guess gender and sexuality . . . I kind of remember there's always kind of talk. Now that you mention it thinking about how the sexuality is present in physical education. There are always, like if you think about let's say sports, and when we're playing sports and guys are calling guys fags, and girls are calling girls lesbians because of their certain physical like attributes, or if you're good at sports then you're a dyke, and if you're not then you're gay, and that kind of thing. And in the change room especially girls are very judgmental, and I remember I was very insecure also about thinking it's not even in front of men but also in front of women being exposed, for my body to be exposed to women because I was so insecure about my body and my sexuality. So in that sense –

   . . . I think I felt like very tip-toey with my sexuality. I felt like I was always I guess being judged and being looked at, and I just felt like very, like it just turned me very inward, and I wasn't able to really explore my sexual side with men or women. I just felt very very closed off, because of, because of like you know being kind of an outsider in that sense being different in a sense. It was like I was you know the kid that people could make fun of or always make fun of. So for girls whether they were feeling jealous or just like something else, like you know I think because I had super big breasts it was like kind of a symbol that I was overly sexual. So whether it was with the women or men, like I was always you know kind of accused of being, of you know wanting to be sexual with people whether it be you know girls or boys. And because I hid my sexuality, then other kids decided to determine that I was either gay or not interested in men or whatever. So there was always labels that came out of it.

As an adult Kiki identifies as bisexual, but her memories of schooling give a nuanced account of how categorizing body size is profoundly enmeshed with normalizing heterosexuality. Conversely, it becomes clearer how bodily differences that cannot be readily categorized jeopardize the logic of heteronormativity that is so pervasive in physical education spaces.

The imbrications of sexual and gender categories with body size differences was also evident in the experiences of some gay men. Jason and James, both gay men, emphasized the judgemental visual scrutiny they experienced when getting changed for swimming and making their way into the water. In contrast to Starburst's positive memories about swimming, they both found that fat phobia made the process of getting changed for swimming and being seen naked excruciatingly difficult. As Jason stated, 'you're the most vulnerable there. You're in your swim suit. You're practically naked . . .'.

Jason: Especially during swimming, I hated it even like so much more because I was overweight. Not to most people's standards, but I felt that I was overweight. I would compare myself to other people in the class. There were people in my class who were divers and swimmers and had that *complete athletic build*. There was no fat on their bodies.

For Jason, the extreme scrutiny of fatness on his body during swimming lessons in physical education continues in the fat phobia of the urban gay male culture of Toronto, colloquially referred to as 'Church Street':

> *Jason:* And then once I came to Church Street and started hanging out with people who weren't exactly the best for me, it got worse because of the comments that were made. And it's like you have to be flawless.

He offered the following explanation as to why fat phobia flourishes in some contemporary gay male cultures:

> *Jason:* I took things so much more critical because I always felt that I had to be that much better. I still feel that now, because I am an adolescent gay male. I feel I have to be that much better than the norm because I'm not part of that. I'm not automatically accepted.

James' explanation was more accidental but, perhaps, no less profound because of this.

> *James:* I figured it was mostly about the skinny gay, I mean skinny guy, not necessarily gay. Interesting Freudian slip! Schools are brutal places where any type of difference is not only noticed but belittled. Different people are hounded into conformity. If someone is different because he or she does not conform easily according to appropriate gender norms, then he or she is also subject to scrutiny regarding sexuality. That is, a masculine-looking girl is labeled a dyke, whether she is one or not and a feminine-looking, skinny guy is labeled a fag, whether he is one or not. So, 'skinny gay' is a most apt Freudian slip here, I think.

Binary gender discourse

Another taken-for-granted discourse is that of the 'gender binary', meaning that gender consists of two mutually exclusive binary categories: male and female or masculine and feminine. One effect of the 'gender binary' discourse is to construct any intersexed bodies, transgender identities and non-normative gender expressions as transgressive, exceptional, abnormal or problematic. Several people in the project identified as trans, intersex or gender queer. For instance, Alan's gender identity – which he described as being both feminine and masculine at different points when he was growing up – was partly defined in relation to the discourse of masculine athleticism (roughhousing, sport):

> *Alan:* I always had a bit of a gender dysphoria when I was younger . . . When I was a little boy, my masculinity was really assaulted by everyone else around me. I was constantly reminded, told, chastised, belittled on my masculinity. 'You act like a girl. You look like a girl. You talk like a girl. You're friends with the girls. You hang out with the girls.' So I learned from a very early age, there was something inherently wrong with my body. That was strong. I didn't understand why am I not a girl. Had I been a girl, my interests, my playmates, and my lack of interest in roughhousing with other boys through sport, wouldn't have been chastised. There would have been lots of room for me to explore what I wanted to explore, which were considered feminine, you know? It's no surprise now that I worry about my masculinity at 25.

There was little to no room for Alan to make sense of, or be supported in, doing gender differently. Other students reported being overtly harassed for not performing their gender according to binary categories. Temperance identified her gender as bio-femme and her sexuality as queer. Here she recalled harassment aimed at herself for being a fat student, a boy for his body size, and another student for being either intersexed or having an ambiguous gender expression:

> *Temperance:* I remember a small little kid named Andrew who was teased about being small. Um, so basically all white, mostly female, I'm the only fat kid. I don't remember gender issues until high school. There was a rumor that there was a kid at the other school who was, uh, OK I'm going to say this in grade 9 language, half boy and half girl. And I remember, I mean her name was Susan, and she, she I remember being singled out and taunted and harassed, and just really put through the wringer. They used to call her Sus*it*. And, and all these vicious rumors. I mean I'm thinking about all of these elaborate rumors that were started to somehow, um, to somehow talk about how she would, you know, be, male and female. I didn't know her, but I remember that being a very big deal in high school.

Scout had physical disabilities, as an adult, and identified herself as mixed race, white trash. Scout described her sexuality as 'queer for lack of a better word, like gender-lesbian' and her gender/sex as 'intersexed but you would suppose I was a woman'.

> *Q:* You mentioned one of the images of physical education is torture. Are there any other images that come to your mind when you think of physical education?
>
> *Scout:* Elitism . . . occlusion . . . bullying . . . For the most part, that's what physical education was, you know, white, beach, California girl!

So, this analysis began with Maybelline's memories about 'popular jocks' and concludes with Scout's recollection about the 'white, beach, California girl'. The 'popular jock' and 'white beach girl' exemplify the highly normative notions about an 'athletic body' in physical education.

Conclusion

The aim of this study has been to look sideways, to see how these taken-for-granted notions of the 'athletic' body rely on the marginalization of multiple forms of queerness. Looking backwards, via adults' memories of physical education, has revealed some articulations between fat phobia, binary gender, compulsory heterosexuality and able-bodied movement.

The experiences of Scout, Starburst and Johnathon reveal how the very notion of athleticism requires a distinction between athletic and non-athletic bodies that is, implicitly, produced by constructing disability and fatness as always already less athletic. Thus, the discourses that fat and disabled bodies are not mobile, athletic or healthy serve, albeit in an uneasy and unacknowledged relation, to bolster the hegemonic discourse that conflates athleticism with masculinity. The racialization of Kevin's and Adam's bodies through particular ideas about Asianness suggests how normative assumptions about whiteness and fatness reinforce pejorative ideas about gay male body size; assumptions that, again, work together to reinforce the superficial discourse that equates masculinity with athleticism. Starburst's and Kiki's narratives go on to reveal how compulsory heterosexuality is often based on rigid assumptions about the size and athletic ability of bodies – assumptions that are readily enforced given the high visibility of bodies in physical education spaces. In other instances, as Scout and Temperance recalled, the indeterminacy of sex or sexuality worked alongside anxieties about the mobility, and ultimately morbidity, of the body to produce the need for clear identity categories and stable identifications. Queer sexualities and non-binary gender identities all served to threaten the normative logic of gender, sex and sexuality that was repeatedly taken for granted in the physical education contexts of the people we interviewed. This normative logic – the 'popular jock' and the 'white beach girl' – was given meaning, indeed depended upon, rigid ideals about how bodies should move and their appearance.

These taken-for-granted notions about athletic bodies, and the forms of queerness they depend upon, are not without history. The binary categories of male and female, like categories of homosexuality, have been mutually produced by and productive of westernized, scientific discourses about racial categories, dis/abilities, physical appearance and anatomies (Seitler, 2004). While a full historical analysis is beyond the scope of this chapter, both methodologically and theoretically, I conclude by briefly mentioning revisionist histories of sex, sexology and queerness (c.f. Bland and Doan, 1998) that could extend the line of inquiry offered in this chapter. Historically, binary gender categories have been (re)produced to stave off concerns about human development, change and mixing; specifically, indeterminate forms of sex, sexuality and gender, and also fears about interracial desire and miscegenation (Prosser, 1998; Somerville, 2000). Western scientific discourses associated both homosexuality and gender indeterminacy with a lack of human evolution, as a developmental abnormality or primitive phase or inversion. These ideas emerged in conjunction with eugenic scientific ideas about racial hierarchies. The western scientific imagination, influenced by these underlying ideas about evolution and biology, produced a discourse about human evolution that culminated with stable sexual difference between males and females, and white European racial supremacy. These nineteenth-century scientific anxieties about human classification continue to provide foundations for contemporary discourses that marginalize intersex, transsexual and transgender subjectivities. Indeed, the sexological historical production of homosexuality and transsexuality is interdependent with multiple categories of perverse, abnormal and freakish bodies (Seitler, 2004). Racialization through Orientalist ideas about the Other, Sara Ahmed (2007) suggests, is part of the process upon which whiteness relies to distance and distinguish itself. 'Whiteness', Ahmed writes, 'becomes what is "here," a line from which the world unfolds, which also makes what is "there" on "the other side"' (p. 121). Furthermore, whiteness *and* heterosexuality both lie at the absent centre (Frankenburg, 1993) of the gendered discourse that proclaims that masculine gender *is* athletic.

Thus, race, gender, ability and sexuality, along with many other non-normative bodily forms and practices 'interact dynamically in a process of mutual reinforcement, for the very existence of the one confirms the perversity and "peculiarity" of the other' (Seitler, 2004, p. 47). Contemporary forms of ableism, heterosexism and body discrimination in physical education continue to be haunted, and strangely sustained, by these troubling histories of perversity and peculiarity. This continues to create situations in which so many students who embody some form of queerness have to engage in difficult emotional and embodied negotiations to cope with what Scout described as the 'elitism, occlusion and bullying' in physical education.

Acknowledgements

I extend my deepest gratitude to all the people who shared their perspectives and experiences during interviews for this project. I would like to also acknowledge the invaluable contributions made by all members of the SSHRC Queer Bodies Research Team, who were Tonya Callaghan, Shaindl Diamond, Tammy George, Deborah McPhail, Vanessa Russell and Ricky Varghese. This project has been funded by the Social Sciences and Humanities Research Council of Canada.

References

Adams, M., Bell, L.A. and Griffin, P. (1997) *Teaching for Diversity and Social Justice: A Sourcebook*. New York: Routledge.
Ahmed, S. (2007) *Queer Phenomenology: Orientations, Objects, Others*. Durham, NC: Duke University Press.
Bell, L. A. (1997) 'Theoretical foundations for social justice education', in M. Adams, L.A. Bell and P. Griffin (eds) *Teaching for Diversity and Social Justice: A Sourcebook* (pp. 3–29). New York: Routledge.

Bland, L. and Doan, L. (1998) *Sexology in Culture: Labeling Bodies and Desires*. Chicago, IL: University of Chicago Press.

Cash, T. and Henry, P. (1995) 'Women's body images: the results of a national survey in the United States', *Sex Roles*, 33: 19–28.

Cash, T., Winstead, B. and Janda, L. (1986) 'Body image survey report: the great American shape-up', *Psychology Today*, April: 30–37.

Chepyator-Thomson, J.R. and Ennis, C. (1997) 'Reproduction and resistance to the culture of femininity and masculinity in secondary school physical education', *Research Quarterly for Exercise and Sport*, 68 (1): 89–99.

Clare, E. (1999) *Exile and Pride: Disability, Queerness and Liberation*. Cambridge, MA: South End Press.

Clarke, G. (2001) 'Difference matters: sexuality and physical education', paper presented at the British Educational Research Association Conference, Leeds, 13–15 September.

DePauw, K. (2000) 'Sociocultural context of disability: implications for scientific inquiry and professional preparation', *Quest*, 52 (4): 358–368.

Dewar, A. (1990) 'Oppression and privilege in physical education: struggles in the negotiation of gender in a university program', in R. Tinning (ed.) *Physical Education, Curriculum and Culture: Critical Issues in the Contemporary Crisis*. Philadelphia, PA: Falmer.

Duncan, M. (2008) 'Special Issue: the social construction of fat – "The personal is political"', *Sociology of Sport*, 25 (1): 1–6.

Eng, D. (2001) *Racial Castration: Managing Masculinity in Asian America*. Durham, NC: Duke University Press.

Ennis, C. (1999) 'Creating a culturally relevant curriculum for disengaged girls', *Sport, Education and Society*, 4 (1): 31–50.

Epstein, D. and Johnson, R. (1998) *Schooling Sexualities*. Buckingham: Open University Press.

Frankenburg, R. (1993) *White Women, Race Matters: The Social Construction of Whiteness*. Minnesota, MN: University of Minnesota Press.

Gard, M. (2001) 'Dancing around the "problem" of boys and dance', *Discourse: Studies in the Cultural Politics of Education*, 22 (2): 213–225.

Gard, M. and Meyenn, R. (2000) 'Boys, bodies, pleasure and pain: interrogating contact sports in schools', *Sport, Education and Society*, 5 (1): 19–34.

Gard, M. and Wright, J. (2005) *The Obesity Epidemic: Science, Morality and Ideology*. New York: Routledge.

GLSEN (2001) *The 2001 National School Climate Survey: Lesbian, Gay, Bisexual and Transgender Students and their Experiences in Schools*. New York: Gay Lesbian Straight Educators Network.

GLSEN (2003) *Findings from the 2003 National School Climate Survey: School-Related Experiences of LGBT Youth of Color*. New York: Gay Lesbian Straight Educators Network.

Gortmaker, S., Must, A., Perrin, J., Sobol, A. and Dietz, W. (1993) 'Social and economic consequences of overweight among adolescents and young adults', *New England Journal of Medicine*, 329: 1008–1012.

Griffin, P. and Genasci, J. (1992) 'Addressing homophobia in physical education: responsibilities for teachers and researchers', in M. Messner and D. Sabo (eds) *Sport, Men, and the Gender Order: Critical Feminist Perspectives*. Champaign, IL: Human Kinetics.

Hickey, C., Fitzclarence, L. and Matthews, R. (1998) *Where the Boys Are: Masculinity, Sport and Education*. Geelong, Australia: Deakin University Press.

Jones, J., Bennett, S., Olmsted, M., Lawson, M. and Rodin, G. (2001) 'Disordered eating attitudes and behaviours in teenaged girls: a school-based study', *Canadian Medical Association Journal*, 165 (5).

Kirk, D. (1999) 'Physical culture, physical education and relational analysis', *Sport, Education and Society*, 4 (1): 63–73.

Kirk, D. (2001) 'Schooling bodies through physical education: insights from social epistemology and curriculum history', *Studies in the Philosophy of Education*, 20 (6): 475–487.

Kvale, S. (1995) *InterViews: An Introduction to Qualitative Research Interviewing*. Thousand Oaks, CA: Sage.

La Pelle, N. (2004) 'Simplifying qualitative data analysis using general purpose software tools', *Field Methods*, 16 (1): 85–108.

Middleton, S. (1998) *Disciplining Sexuality: Foucault, Life Histories, and Education*. New York: Teachers College.

Mishler, E. (1991) 'Representing discourse: the rhetoric of transcription', *Journal of Narrative and Life History*, 1 (4): 255–280.

Mishler, E. (1995) 'Models of narrative analysis: a typology', *Journal of Narrative and Life History*, 5 (2): 87–123.

Morrow, R. and Gill, D. (2003) 'Perceptions of homophobia and heterosexism in physical education', *Research Quarterly for Exercise and Sport*, 74 (2): 205–214.

Paechter, C. (2001) 'Power, bodies and identity: how different forms of physical education construct varying forms of masculinity and femininity in schools', paper presented at the British Educational Research Association Annual Conference, Leeds, England, September.

Penney, D. (2002) *Gender and Physical Education: Contemporary Issues and Future Directions*. London: Routledge.

Pharr, S. (1999) 'Foreword', in E. Clare, *Exile and Pride: Disability, Queerness and Liberation* (pp. vii–ix). Cambridge, MA: South End Press.

Prosser, J. (1998) 'Transsexuals and transsexologists', in L. Bland and L. Doan (eds) *Sexology in Culture: Labeling Bodies and Desires* (pp. 116–131). Chicago, IL: University of Chicago Press.

Rice, C. and Russell, V. (2002) *Embodying Equity: Body Image as an Equity Issue*. Toronto, ON: Green Dragon Press.

Seitler, D. (2004) 'Queer physiognomies: or, how many ways can we do the history of sexuality?', *Criticism*, 46 (1): 71–102.

Skelton, C. (2000) '"A passion for football": dominant masculinities and primary schooling', *Sport, Education and Society*, 5 (1): 5–18.

Somerville, S. (2000) *Queering the Color Line*. Durham, NC: Duke University Press.

Sparkes, A. (1992) *Research in Physical Education and Sport: Exploring Alternative Visions*. Washington, DC: Falmer.

Sparkes, A. (1994) 'Self, silence and invisibility as a beginning teacher: a life history of lesbian experience', *British Journal of Sociology of Education*, 15 (1): 93–118.

Sparkes, A. and Templin, T. (1992) 'Life histories and physical education teachers: exploring the meaning of marginality', in A. Sparkes (ed.) *Research in Physical Education and Sport: Exploring Alternative Visions* (pp. 118–145). Philadelphia, PA: Falmer.

Squires, S. and Sparkes, A. (1996) 'Circles of silence: sexual identity in physical education and sport', *Sport, Education and Society*, 1 (1): 77–101.

Sykes, H. (2009) 'The qBody Project: from lesbians in physical education to queer bodies in/out of school', *Journal of Lesbian Studies*, 13 (3): 238–254.

Sykes, H. and McPhail, D. (2008) 'Unbearable lessons: contesting fat phobia in physical education', *Sociology of Sport*, 25 (1): 66–96.

Wendell, S. (1996) *The Rejected Body: Feminist Philosophical Reflections on Disability*. New York: Routledge.

Williams, S. and Bendelow, G. (1998) *The Lived Body: Sociological Themes, Embodied Issues*. New York: Routledge.

Wright, J. (1996a) 'The construction of complementarity in physical education', *Gender and Education*, 8 (1): 61–80.

Wright, J. (1996b) 'Mapping discourses of physical education: articulating a female tradition', *Journal of Curriculum Studies*, 28 (3): 331–351.

Part III

Theoretical frames and methodological approaches

9 Push play every day

New Zealand children's constructions of health and physical activity

Lisette Burrows

Introduction

In New Zealand, as is the case elsewhere, healthy eating and exercise messages pervade both popular culture and professional contexts. Within schools, new regulations specify the amount of quality physical activity children must receive (Ministry of Education, 2006; Sport and Recreation New Zealand, 2007) and dictate the kinds of foods and beverages that may be sold and/or brought into the school environment (Ministry of Education, 2007). Curriculum materials emphasize healthy eating and exercise as vehicles for the achievement of health (Ministry of Education 1999a, 1999b) and, increasingly, outside agencies are volunteering or selling their nutrition and physical activity initiatives (e.g. Jump Jam; Jump Rope for Heart) to the school market (Macdonald, Hay and Williams, 2008). As Miha and Rich (2008) and Holloway and Valentine (2003) have noted, when it comes to health-related messages, the boundaries between school and community contexts are also increasingly permeable. Popular culture meets schooling via internet youth sites, reality television and an ever expanding range of health promotion and social marketing campaigns. Each of these sites offers children knowledge and practices that together comprise the discursive resources they have available to draw on to make sense of the nature and role of physical activity, physical education and sport in their lives.

In this chapter, I advance a twin agenda of sharing insights from a New Zealand study that examines how children are making sense of the plethora of health and physical activity imperatives that infuse their lives, while simultaneously endeavouring to show how poststructural theoretical resources may usefully inform our understanding of children's engagement with these imperatives. I begin by briefly discussing an emergent body of international research that investigates how children and young people themselves understand physical activity and health in the context of their daily lives. What characterizes this cadre of studies is a genuine attempt to engage with what children themselves do and feel in relation to health and physical activity. This is an approach that differs from the large-scale quantitative work that has predominantly contoured the policies and initiatives created for children (e.g. James and Prout 1990; Mayall 1998; Smith 1999; Holloway and Valentine, 2000).

In Canada, a growing body of research has interrogated young people's constructions of health and fitness, drawing on focus groups, 'draw and write' techniques and individual interview methods (e.g. Seely, 2002; Rail, 2004, 2009; Shea, 2006). Despite the diverse communities these researchers have worked with (e.g. Francophone youth, youth with disabilities and Newfoundland youth), food consumption, exercise behaviour and 'weight' were overwhelmingly the key things students articulated as indicators of 'health' *and* 'fitness'. Schools were regularly identified as important sites for acquiring information about physical activity and health, although many young people in each of these cohorts were certainly cognizant of the plethora of media health and body messages circulating in their particular sociocultural contexts. Interestingly, despite the saturation of young people's contexts with healthist and individualist discourses of health and fitness (Crawford 1980; Kirk and Colquhoun 1989), evidence of students' capacity to disrupt these and to recognize the limitations of regarding a 'healthy' person as one who necessarily looks good, is a 'normal' weight, runs a lot and subscribes to a prescriptive 'healthy' diet, emerged in each of these studies.

In Australia, the Life Activity Project (Wright and Macdonald, 2001–2006), has an ongoing commitment to understanding the place and meaning of health and physical activity in young people's lives, and studies conducted under this rubric have generated significant understandings of this in relation to variously located children and young people (see Chapter 2 in this volume). Macdonald *et al.*'s (2005) research with young Australian children points to the pivotal role of 'fun' in children's experiences of physical activity, their – albeit superficial – understanding of links between sport and healthy lifestyles, and the importance of everyday 'play' as a site for pleasures derived from free and spontaneous engagement with others. Studies exploring the role of physical activity in older students' lives, too, yield compelling insights regarding the ways adolescents conflate health with fitness and pervasively link physical activity to 'work' on the shape and weight of their bodies (Wright, MacDonald and Groom, 2003; Wright, O'Flynn and Macdonald, 2006). Further, ongoing work by Leahy and Harwood (2006) is beginning to illustrate that meanings for physical activity and engagement in it are significantly contoured by cultural and spatial location material constraints and class, pointing to the importance of non-universalist accounts of what physical activity might mean or 'do' for all children everywhere.

MacDougall, Schiller and Darbyshire's (2004) focus-group work with 204 Australian children aged 4–12 years yields considerable insight regarding the meanings children attribute to concepts like 'sport', 'play', 'physical activity', 'exercise' and 'fitness'. As they attest, 'the meaning of "play" was immediately recognizable in all focus groups as different from sport, physical activity and fitness' (MacDougall *et al.*, 2004, p. 379). For the participants, descriptors associated with play included '"fun", "spontaneity", "interactions with friends", "not too competitive" and "not too aggressive"' (MacDougall *et al.*, 2004, p. 380), whereas those associated with exercise and fitness were largely confined to things like 'running around', power-walking, muscle building, gym circuits and weight-lifting. The responses to the prompt 'play' also evoked a sense of neighbourhood and community, while those provided in relation to sport, physical activity and/or fitness generally did not. The researchers concluded that mixing images of play and sport with young children might be counterproductive, given the more open, child-centred meanings they advanced for play.

Perhaps the most interesting finding in this study is the relative lack of association between physical activity (in any of its forms) and health that was drawn by participants. The children did not spontaneously refer to health benefits of physical activity and, indeed, required substantive prompting to draw any links between the two. As MacDougall *et al.* (2004, p. 384) concluded, 'it is thus unlikely that strategies heavily based on health arguments would have high recognition or engagement' with children in years 4 or 8. The standout conclusion from their work is their view that 'children bring to the discourse about physical activity some ideas that challenge the views adults hold about children' (p. 369).

In the United Kingdom, Smith and Parr's (2007) research exploring young people's views on the nature and purposes of school-based physical education, yields interesting insights pertaining to the current study (see Chapter 4 in this volume for the views of young people in the United States on the purpose of physical education). The importance of fun, enjoyment and sociality to young people's experience of and perceptions of physical education was strongly foregrounded in this work, as was the case in Macdonald *et al.*'s (2005) study. Together with the notion of physical education as cathartic release – that is, a welcome break from the rigours of academic work – the 15–16 year olds in their study also offered justifications for physical education based on its health-promoting properties and its assistance in the development of game- and sport-related skills. Interestingly, in contrast to the above-mentioned studies, Smith and Parr (2007) conclude that the notion that physical education can play a role in improving the health status of students was evidenced at a 'surface' level in student responses, yet rarely expressed in their lived experiences of physical education – a conclusion further supported in the work of Harris (1994) and Williams and Woodhouse (1996).

Prior work that colleagues and I have done with National Education Monitoring Project data affords some insight into young New Zealanders' perceptions of health and fitness (e.g. Burrows, Wright and Jungersen-Smith, 2002; Burrows and Wright, 2004a, 2004b; Wright and Burrows, 2004; Burrows and Wright, 2007). Some of the key conclusions emerging from that work included the fact that many students equate 'being healthy' with 'being fit' and being fit with 'looking good', and that student understandings about health and fitness change between year 4 (8–9 years old) and year 8 (11–12 years old), with students at year 8 offering more holistic, expanded understandings and demonstrating more awareness of the consequences of specific behaviours for health and fitness. 'Being healthy' for a majority of students meant, eating 'right', being clean, not smoking and not being overweight; being 'fit', for the majority of students, meant being able to run, being 'not fat' and having a 'better life'. Most students regarded health and fitness as states of being that were dependent on 'the individual' and many students, especially at year 8, suggested that if you are not fit, you are not healthy and therefore you are lazy and/or weak – that is, links between achieving health and being a 'good' and/or 'moral' person were drawn. Very few responses suggested that becoming healthy and/or fit was a pleasurable activity. Rather, students recited lists of what a person 'should' do to become healthy or fit. *Don't* was a frequent verb used by students – for example, 'don't eat *any* fat', 'don't eat lollies' and don't watch television'. Finally, a clear link was drawn between fitness and 'non-fatness' by a majority of students.

In summary, it would seem that the empirical work reviewed has produced some remarkably consistent findings. Dominant discourses of health that emphasize individual responsibility for health, the primacy of eating and moving as behaviours for achieving health, and the importance of body weight and size as indicators of a healthy person are shared at least across some groups of young people in Canada, Australia and New Zealand, and represented – at least, at 'surface' level – in the testimony of Smith and Parr's (2007) UK students.

A discursive understanding of New Zealand students' understandings of health and physical activity

In this section, I suggest that a poststructural analysis of qualitative data affords one way of beginning to understand the amalgam of health and physical activity messages the aforementioned research suggests young people currently engage with. This approach is certainly not a novel one. Indeed, latterly, several physical education researchers have grounded their enquiry in poststructuralist commitments. O'Flynn (2004), for example, uses Foucault's 'technologies of the self' as a lens through which to examine the operation of health and physical activity discourses in the constitution of young women's subjectivities in schools. Knez (2007) has deployed Foucauldian theory to understand the construction of young Muslim women's subjectivities in relation to physical culture and education. Wright and Macdonald's (2001–2006) work with diverse Australian cohorts of young people illustrates well the utility of qualitative health and physical activity investigations drawing on poststructural perspectives, and Atencio's (2006) ethnographic work with young people from 'diverse "racial", "ethnic" and diasporic backgrounds' (p. vii) draws extensively on poststructural analysis. Further, Rail (2009) and colleagues' qualitative work with young people in Canada makes ready use of poststructuralist-inspired methodologies and analytic tools. The current chapter contributes to this body of scholarship, endeavouring to illuminate how and why poststructuralist concepts are both useful and timely tools through which to interrogate student understandings of health and physical activity, while simultaneously sharing the findings of a New Zealand study that interrogates the ways health imperatives are taken up in two primary school contexts. In particular, I argue that drawing on Foucauldian concepts can help us to understand the complex ways in which power and knowledge operate to produce conditions of possibility for 'being' healthy and/or 'doing' health in any particular context.

To illustrate this proposition I draw on interviews conducted with 24 children aged 9–10 (12 boys and 12 girls) from two different primary schools in New Zealand, together with the responses of 70 students across both schools, to a health survey conducted in 2007. I regard both the interview commentaries and the survey responses as examples of 'texts' that do not necessarily yield the 'truth' of what children experience of physical culture. Rather, their talk serves to illuminate the discursive resources children have available to draw on and the ways they position themselves as 'healthy' (or not) subjects in relation to these. The term 'discourse' is crucial here. Variously defined by different scholars, Stephen Ball (1990, p. 2) suggests that 'discourses are about what can be said and thought, but also who can speak, when and with what authority'. This definition points to the role discourses play in constituting both meaning and subjects. As I have already indicated, there are particular features of the contemporary 'health' context in New Zealand that inevitably contour the kinds of resources, both material and conceptual, that children have access to. Reading children's texts alongside and against these is therefore integral to my analytic strategy.

Subjectivity is another poststructuralist notion that guides choice of questions, research cohorts and the interview methods deployed. In poststructuralist-inspired inquiry, identity is traded for the notion, subjectivity, in an effort to elaborate the multiple, fluid and shifting 'selves' that are constituted in and through discourse. That is, rather than viewing children and young people as fixed or essential identities, who they are and what they may become are regarded *in relation* to the language and social practices that surround them. Thus, interview questions are designed to extend our understanding of *why* a child thinks about physical activity in a particular way, *what* might have influenced his/her perception or experience and *how* each child has come to understand their self in *relation* to broader discourses at work in any given context (e.g. discourses of fitness and sport). For example, if a child declares that eating five portions of fruit per day will render them slim, as researcher, I would want to know how a child has come to regard this maxim as 'truth' and how this truth impacts on her capacity to regard herself as healthy (or not).

The particular way in which Foucault (1990) conceived of power and its relationship to knowledge also influences the way I 'read' the children's texts and how I interrogate the environments within which they are produced. For Foucault (1980), power and knowledge always imply one another. He contends that 'we are forced to produce the truth of power that our society demands, of which it has need, in order to function . . . Power never ceases its interrogation, its inquisition, its registration of truth: it institutionalizes, professionalises and rewards its pursuit' (Foucault 1980, p. 93). Power, in this account, infiltrates all social relations and creates ways of viewing the world that legitimize certain knowledge and practices. In the context of the current study, conceptualizing power–knowledge in this way orientates me towards attending to the ways in which children are both 'constituted and regulated by institutions of disciplinary power' (Burman, 1991, p. 142), but also towards investigating how children themselves participate in the manufacture of relations of power and control. How do children resist, re-work and/or embrace orthodox knowledge about physical activity? What possibilities for thinking and doing physical activity emerge in the children's talk? How do dominant discourses 'shape up' (Gore 1993) children in diverse ways? My interest, then, is not so much

in who holds power but rather, following Gore (1995), in how children are constituted as particular kinds of beings by power–knowledge relations in the realm of
physical culture (see also Chapter 3 in this volume).

In choosing the cohorts of students for interview, a diverse mix of genders, ethnicities and social-class positioning was sought. Moreover students were drawn
from two distinctly different school locations in an effort to ensure that the texts
analysed did not privilege one particular 'kind' of school student (e.g. the middle-
class student so often prioritized in educational research). Toroa School is a school
located in a low socio-economic area, drawing predominantly Pasifika (Samoan in
particular) and Maori children, while 6 km away from Toroa is Merivale, a school
with a high socio-economic index, encompassing children from predominantly
(although not exclusively) non-indigenous New Zealand families. Interviews were
conducted in pairs (either at school or in the context of after-school recreation programmes) for a duration of 30 minutes to an hour. Informed by the poststructuralist
notions of discourse, power and the subject, questions on both the survey and the
interviews were orientated towards understanding what children think about their
own and others' health, what resources they draw on to formulate these understandings and how contemporary health imperatives, largely attuned to obesity
concerns, may (or may not) be contouring the ways they come to understand their
'selves' as healthy young people. Ethnographic observations of children in classrooms and playgrounds, collation of school-based learning resources, interviews
with teachers and pictorial representations of the two spaces were used to glean a
richer understanding of the nuances of each school environment and the health
imperatives each supported.

In the following section, I draw on interview and survey responses to questions
interrogating how young people understand the concept 'health', to illustrate some
of the ways health discourse works to shape up students in particular ways. In the
section after that I investigate some of the resources young people draw on to make
sense of the role and nature of physical activity in their lives, and their positioning
as healthy (or not) citizens. Finally, I explore some of the research and policy
implications evident throughout this poststructuralist-inspired analysis.

Shaping up through health and physical activity

In a context replete with messages about 'healthy lifestyles' (Fullagar, 2002;
Burrows and Wright, 2007) and, in particular, the contribution of physical activity
towards these, it is no surprise to find that all of the children, across both school
sites, clearly linked deliberate physical activity to the achievement of 'health'. In a
Foucauldian sense, it appears that the annexing of two ostensibly distinct discourses has produced a discursive formation that delimits the range of possible
responses children could or would offer to the question 'how would you know if a
person is healthy?' The statement, 'weight, how fit they are, what they have in their
lunch boxes' encapsulates the tenor of many of the students' answers to this generic
question – that is, most children committed to unequivocal causal links between
health and physical activity, nutrition and weight/shape. When asked how they felt

about their *own* health, responses like 'excited . . .'cause I'm actually fit and actually really healthy' (Mary), 'pretty good because you can run a lot faster . . .' (Michael) and 'good because I play heaps of sports' (Jess) were typical, pointing to the ways in which discourses (like those of health and fitness) create opportunities for children to recognize themselves as healthy (or not) subjects.

A coupling of health with fitness discourse also renders certain social practices more viable and desirable than others, a point illustrated clearly in the responses of children to the question 'What are the most important things that someone could do to keep healthy?' Here physical activity – described variously as exercise, fitness, sports or 'being active' – predominated in students' responses. As Mary declares, 'Walk like down the street or up the street or round the block and play with your friends so you can keep fit . . .'. For Michael, 'don't eat too much lollies and do a lot of exercise', and for Emily, 'you should get at least one hour exercise in your day'. Further, even those children who already declared themselves to be 'healthy' were aware that more physical activity would be necessary in order to retain or improve that health status (e.g. 'get more exercise', 'I would like to play more sports', 'do some more running around and more sports'). Two-thirds of the children surveyed across both schools had thought about doing more exercise, and in most cases had deliberately set out to engage in more. Their reasons for doing so ranged from illness prevention, improving strength and fitness to a concern to change the weight, shape or size of their body, and indeed their lifestyle per se. Their justifications included:

> 'because I was starting to grow bigger'
> 'Sometimes I don't really exercise and it feels like I'm getting fatter'
> 'because I feel fat'
> 'I got on the scales – wow'
> 'cause when I come home I eat a lot of junk food and just watch tv or go on the computer'
> 'I get puffed easily'

As the testimony of Marc (below) suggests, working out how much exercise is needed is not necessarily a straightforward matter, yet as with many of the children in this study, the assumption that weight gain is an important impetus for action is clear in his ponderings:

Interviewer:	How do you know Marc if you're doing enough exercise?
Marc:	Um I don't really quite know but I think I'm doing just a tiny bit little less exercise than I should.
Interviewer:	Yeah, what makes you think that?
Marc:	Um because I've put on a bit more weight.

For the small percentage of children who did *not* think they needed to exercise more than they did currently, rationales were similarly annexed to perceptions of their current weight together with eating and fitness practices. For example:

'because I am fit'
'because I have the right weight'
'because I look skinny'
'I am not overweight so I don't [need to exercise]'
'Think I'm eating right'

This propensity to regard physical activity as a weight-management strategy, which in turn will yield a slimmer and thereby healthier 'self', is a familiar refrain and one regularly rehearsed by children in other research with young people in New Zealand and abroad (Burrows and Wright, 2004a, 2004b; Rail, 2004; Atencio, 2006; Burrows, Wright and McCormack, in press). The certain links between weight, physical activity and health drawn in the children's testimony is perhaps not surprising given the ready associations drawn between them in both public health promotion strategies and within formal school-based pedagogies (Evans *et al.*, 2005; Gard and Wright, 2005). Nevertheless the sheer volume of responses of this nature, supplied often in relation to questions that ostensibly have nothing to do with weight, is worthy of note, especially given the certainty with which these associations are often made, and the relative youth of our participants. Further, given the Health and Physical Education in the New Zealand Curriculum's (Ministry of Education, 1999c) emphasis on a holistic notion of health – one that embraces social, cognitive, emotional and spiritual constituents of health alongside the 'physical' – these ready associations between physical activity and body shape, size and weight are interesting. It would seem that, as was the case in earlier New Zealand-based studies (e.g. Burrows and Wright, 2004a, 2004b; Burrows, Wright and McCormack, 2007), children are primarily regarding health as a corporeal matter, something to be 'read off' the body via assessing its changing dimensions and weight (Bordo 1993; Shilling 1993; Lupton 1995).

The quantity as well as the quality of movement engaged in was also signalled by many children across both cohorts as an important factor in evaluating the health-enhancement potential of specific physical activities. Children were clearly cognizant that 'more' is better, that exercise that makes you 'puff' is best, and running was overwhelmingly valued as a health-enhancing activity, despite its reputation as a somewhat exhausting and unpleasurable thing to do (Lineham, 2003; MacDougall *et al.*, 2004; Macdonald *et al.*, 2005; Smith and Parr, 2007). Dancing, for some of the girls, was 'fun' but not necessarily assigned health-promoting properties, while running as far and fast as one can, was. Children at Merivale School, in particular, were keen to recite often lengthy lists of the kinds of physical activities they pursued both within school time and outside of it. Indeed, despite their often prolific engagement in activities ranging from hip-hop, swimming and dancing, to organized sports like cricket, rugby, netball and soccer outside of school hours, they were still constantly reflecting on their need to do 'more'. This clear engagement in self-monitoring of 'activity levels', desire to adjust their practices in light of their understanding that 'lots' of exercise is required is interesting, particularly when read alongside popular understandings of young people as a cohort who 'live in the present', fail to consider future consequences of current practices and are generally incapable of imagining future ill health (Wyn and White 1997; Skelton and Valentine 1998). What Foucault (1990) has referred to as 'technologies of the self' are illustrated here – that is, children appear to be surveilling their own and others' behaviour, evaluating their current state and applying prescriptive practices in pursuit of a healthier and presumed happier 'self'.

In attempting to understand why a young person may wish to engage in such practices, student commentary on the links between body shape and physical activity is germane. For, example, when asked what advice they would give to an overweight friend, the children almost invariably suggested 'exercise'. Their advice included the following:

'Just um get exercise for like 20 minutes or something'
'You should at least get one hour of exercise into your day'
'... Um they could "Push Play" [NZ physical activity initiative] for 30 minutes'
'Um to get active . . .'
'Go for a jog'

Further, Cara's testimony points to the pivotal influence families can have in establishing relationships between weight/shape and exercise:

Interviewer:	OK, um do you hear people in your family talking about shapes, about peoples shape or weight? Yeah, what sorts of things might they talk about?
Cara:	Um my Nana she told um my sister Leah to um go for a jog, to be healthy run.
Interviewer:	Yeah, and is that because of her shape?
Cara:	Yeah and I went with her.

A genuine sense of fear at becoming 'fat' (Aphramor, 2005; Murray, 2008) characterizes many of the children's responses, born of awareness that many debilitating physical *and* emotional outcomes accompany a 'fat' status. As many sociologists have noted, abjection can be a powerful motivator, something foregrounded in Molly and Rachel's comments about 'sad', 'fat' and unhealthy people below:

Interviewer:	If you're really if you're unhealthy how do you reckon it feels?
Molly:	Um bad.
Interviewer:	Bad yeah what ___.
Molly:	Sad.
Interviewer:	You feel sad?
Molly:	Because you could um like you might be overweighted and you'll get too fat.
Interviewer:	Right, and what would happen then?
Molly:	Um . . .
Rachel:	Then you'll explode!

> *Interviewer*:   Explode . . . So if you were overweight or too big or whatever and you're like, that makes you unhealthy?
> *Rachel*:   Yeah.
> *Interviewer*:   Yeah, and how do you think it would make you feel?
> *Molly*:   Bad about the things we eat and not doing fitness.

The children in the study not only understand that some body shapes and sizes are indicative of better health than others, but also that a fat body impacts on one's general sense of happiness, outlook on life and especially on one's capacity to 'fit in', to be part of social groupings and activities that are valued in children's culture. Indeed, for most of the children, being big was equated with reduced capacity to be active and this, in turn, linked to concerns around social acceptance (Fox, 2000; Smith and Parr, 2007).

Mary and Jane, for example, offer extended commentary on what it must feel like for children who fail to 'move their bodies about'.

> *Interviewer*:   How do you think they would feel [if they didn't move much]?
> *Mary*:   Really lazy.
> *Jane*:   They'd feel like they're stuck in one place. They wouldn't be able to, they wouldn't know much about fitness and they can't run that far and as fast . . . if kids they play with are running around having fun playing a game and they're trying to keep up and they won't be able to . . .
> *Interviewer*:   OK I see so they won't be able to take part in things as far as they could OK.
> *Jane*:   And people wouldn't really like them for that 'cause they think they're slow so yeah that's how some people at our school feel. If people are slow they don't pick them on their team.

As Mary and Jane's commentary illustrates, with the presumed inactivity linked to fatness comes a host of potentially debilitating social consequences: not being picked for a team, not being able to 'join' in, missing out on fun and being disliked by peers. Their own observations of others experiencing this social exclusion, perhaps coupled with the regular portrayal of inactive children in this way in social marketing and in school-based resources, has contoured these children's understanding that the capacity and inclination to 'move' is crucial to an acceptable life as a kid both within and outside school. It is in this kind of context that children who are unable or unwilling to move in health-contributing ways can readily be regarded by others and their 'selves' as marginal.

An environment fuelled by a concern about fat and a certainty that fat and physical activity are inextricably linked, also permits ordinary 'objects' as well as subjects to be re-cast as symbols of ill health. In the next section, I demonstrate how an everyday furniture item has, in a health-saturated context, become imbued with meanings that would be unthinkable or knowable in different times or contexts.

Get off the couch and push play

In New Zealand, as is the case elsewhere, the phrase 'couch potato' is regularly recited in popular (Hitti, 2005) and professional mediums as a symbolic referent to an avowedly sedentary, lazy, potato-munching subject – the kind of subject that health-promotion efforts are focused on remediating. The children in our study displayed a ready familiarity with the couch potato, using the phrase to describe unhealthful behaviour and also drawing on it when thinking about how they would get a healthy exercise message across to others. Both the repetitive use of the 'couch' as metaphor for ill health and the ease with which the couch was linked to other presumed un-healthful practices was striking across the commentary of children in both contexts. 'Don't be a couch potato,' declares Mary when asked what she has learned about health at her school. According to Jane, schools should make children exercise because 'some people only do nothing and they just sit on the couch at home doing nothing and they've got to keep them fit'. Making a television health advertisement, for Erin, would involve asking the audience, 'which would you rather do? – sit around on a couch or run round and eat healthy things?' and, for Mere, overweight kids would find sport hard 'because you wouldn't know how to do it properly if you're just used to sitting on a couch changing channels, eating popcorn or McDonald's'. In so saying, evidence of playful engagement with the miscreant 'couch' is found in at least one of the children's practices. Kayla, for example, describes a class lesson where they had to write about what sports they like and 'why they are healthy and stuff'. She says, 'there's this guy in my class and he wrote, "I like sitting on the couch watching TV" [*laughs*]'.

The impact of the 'couch potato' metaphor on these children's conceptualizations of physical activity powerfully illustrates one of the ways in which discourse works. As Howarth and Stavrakakis (2000, p. 3) suggest, discourses are social and political constructions that establish 'a system of relations between different objects and practices, while providing (subject) positions with which social agents can identify' – that is, repeated iterations of the couch-potato slogan in both professional (e.g. Sport and Recreation New Zealand) and popular mediums (e.g. through social marketing campaigns, parental talk, in popular magazine articles) ascribe the message a currency, a 'truth' status that is produced and enacted despite evidence to the contrary. For example, while many of the children in our study were adamant that their television watching and so-called sedentary leisure did not preclude *also* being engaged in regular physical activity (e.g. 'you can do both'), the same children were nevertheless ready and able to describe 'couch-sitting' as an errant behaviour, both 'evidence' of a non-regard for one's health and also as the inevitable outcome of failing to exercise in the prescribed doses. As Jane declares:

> I do hip hop, netball, swimming and all this stuff and then some people only do nothing and they just sit on the couch at home doing nothing and they've got to keep them fit.

The propensity to negatively evaluate the practices of others was widely reiterated by students, particularly those from Merivale School, many of whom were engaged in multiple out-of-school physical activities. It would seem that, even when students don't necessarily feel the 'get off the couch' message applies to them, they are nevertheless ready and willing to urge errant others to comply. Once again, this is illustrative not only of the way discourse works, how it is exchanged in any given community of practice, but also of a tendency for dominant discourses to not only be taken up in disciplinary mode by the self, but to contour how one comes to regard and treat others whose practices do not comply with the normalizing regimes implicated in any specific discursive framework – in this case, the 'couch sitters'.

We do not need to look far for further evidence of the ways catchy slogans like 'couch potato' potentially configure children's dispositions and practices in relation to physical activity. 'Push Play', a government physical activity campaign that has saturated television and print media in New Zealand since the early 1990s, has also clearly entered the consciousness of many of the young people in our study. The Push Play message is that children need to 'push play' every day by engaging in at least 60 minutes of physical activity. Frequent references to 'Push Play' were made in relation to questions about what people can do to improve their health (e.g. 'you can just do things like push play') and where health messages come from (e.g. 'like that "push play" advert'). When assessing the veracity of the push-play message, children readily pointed to the saturation of their school and community contexts with 'Push Play'. Put simply, the message is 'everywhere' so it *must* be true.

Ethnographic observations in the Toroa School's community attest that, indeed, Push-Play messages are highly visible, displayed in posters on classroom walls, featured in weekly news magazines supplying the area, splashed on T-shirts that local touch rugby players wear, and painted on the sides of trucks and billboards in the area. Together with these daily reminders of the need to push play, intensive social marketing campaigns aired on free-to-air television feature lifestyle ambassadors (Mission-On, 2006) showing how they 'push play' every day, and children's television programmes sponsored by New Zealand's Mission-On initiative afford children more 'tips' on how to get active. As the children attest, there are also 'collectable' Mission-On cards available free to children who want ideas about how to accumulate the 60 minutes per day recommended dose of physical activity. As Jane says, 'they have that Mission-On one and it's these like little cards that you get at sports shops. And you can take them home and you can um choose like which one you want to do; so it's got like activities that doesn't involve TV, but it involves like your friends and stuff'. Further, at Merivale School, children recalled that BJ Bear, a man dressed up in a bear suit, visited to talk 'about Push Play and what you can do'. As Mary puts it, 'he showed us what things aren't really getting fit in Push Play like sitting on the couch watching TV'.

While on the one hand, the children's awareness of push-play imperatives can be regarded as a resounding success for health-promotion campaigns in that children know what to push play means and are ready and willing to enact its imperatives, on the other hand, there are several potentially disturbing aspects to this ready capacity to accept the push-play message as 'true' and worthy of spreading to all they know. First, as discussed earlier, is the tendency for some of the students to understand the push-play message as one that is particularly directed towards fat people who need to 'lose weight'. Second is the certainty with which they express their perspectives that simply 'pushing play' will effect major changes in the health status of all those who do it, and third is the ready association children draw between 'seeing' something on television, for example, and assuming, therefore, that it must be 'true'. Despite the World Health Organization's (2005) backing of the notion that 60 minutes of exercise per day is sufficient to promote 'health', there are many from both within and outside biomedical science who have questioned the causal links ascribed between specific amounts of exercise and the achievement of health (e.g. Campos, 2004; Gard and Wright, 2005; Campos *et al.*, 2006). Further, while the notion that everyday activity 'counts' in the push-play recipe (e.g. walking to school, playing with friends) is perhaps comforting to those who are pondering where their 60 minutes will come from, as our study's children's testimony suggests, one of the unintended yet readily resulting impacts of taking Push Play to 'heart' is the way ordinary, pleasurable and playful activities can potentially become annexed to a mission to get healthy and/or thin. Children were eager to explain the innumerable ways in which they pushed play every day. Bouncing on the trampoline in the back yard, riding their bikes, playing with balls, running around the house and simply playing with friends were each regarded as potential push-play activities. At Toroa School, each lunchtime children formed a long jogging line, meandering their way around the school, with children dropping off or joining the 'snake' whenever they pleased. Their response to the research assistant's query about what it was they were doing, was 'We're just doing our push play, miss!'

As more and more everyday activities are annexed both in children's minds and in the formal enunciation of the message on television campaigns, the likelihood that any and all forms of active leisure are conceived of as 'Push Play' moments escalates. Indeed, in 2008, the latest television advertisement for Push Play has groups of young children staging a 'krump-off' with adults in an effort to promote the notion that kids need 60 minutes per day and adults just 30 minutes. Krumping is a creative, free-flowing activity where young people invent and display 'moves' in a hip-hop-like dance style. To date, in New Zealand at least, it is something that has been largely adopted by young people, and particularly by young Pasifika youth. As is the case with many constituents of youth culture, it would seem that krumping has been drawn from the margins to the big screen in an effort to recruit more young people to the Push Play 'way'. While it is unsurprising that Push Play advertisement creators would wish to draw on images it imagined that youth would identify with (Hirschhorn Donahue, Haskins and Nightingale, 2008), in so doing krumping as 'cultural practice' in effect is diluted, re-envisaged as yet another way to push play every day.

Conclusion

Throughout this chapter I have endeavoured to show how poststructural resources can assist in researching young people's engagement with physical activity and health imperatives. Analyses of their responses to questions about health, together with the analyses of Push Play and the metaphoric 'couch', would suggest that children are clearly cognizant of and taking up in various ways the imperatives to 'get active' for the sake of their health, yet by what criteria should we measure the success of a health-promotion campaign like SPARC's 'Push Play'? From a policy perspective, it would seem apposite to consider the oft unintended consequences of well-intentioned initiatives for those at their centre. Understanding how simplistic and widely promulgated messages like 'Push Play every day' can be, and are, taken up by children and young people is a first step. Being cognizant of the potential such campaigns afford for increasing levels of body and health surveillance among young people, and designing programmes that foreground the pleasure of movement rather than the need to monitor it is another. Recognizing that a simple message does not guarantee a monolithic response is also important. As I have endeavoured to illustrate throughout this chapter, subjectivities are slippery customers. Children are positioned differently in relation to existing knowledge. For some, the kinds of messages instantiated in government or school campaigns produce a recognition of 'self' as 'normal'. For others the messages produce a dis-ease, a discomfort with self or others and a desire to engage in self-surveillance and monitoring that may not necessarily enhance their 'health'.

For many of the children whose testimony is reported in this chapter, physical activity – preferably of a kind that makes you 'puff' – is not only being conceived of as a non-negotiable constituent of a healthy lifestyle, but also as a moral obligation. As others have noted, in relation to adult fitness and health imperatives (Crawford, 1980; Kirk and Colquhoun, 1989), the incitement to 'move' is generated not simply by a desire to be healthy, but also can be construed as an understandable response to an environment saturated with messages that represent exercise and 'healthy' eating as an individual responsibility – something that is inextricably linked to being a 'good' citizen, one who, through personal behaviour, benefits the public good (Fullagar, 2002). While the children in our study may not necessarily understand the nuances of this argument, they are clearly ready, willing and able to try their best to live out exercise imperatives in their day-to-day lives. In an Althusserian sense they have been 'hailed' by the imperative to 'move', despite the fact that, for many of them (particularly those from Toroa School), their efforts to become the healthful subject envisaged as ideal does not necessarily produce the desired effects. Further, while not specifically discussed within the chapter, the ways gender, class and ethnicity contour children's capacity to engage with such messages, and the effects of doing so, warrant further analysis. These issues are discussed in chapters by Lee and Oliver (Chapters 2 and 3, respectively) in this volume.

Accessing what children and young people think, know and do in relation to physical activity is no easy matter, and the research methods employed in the study reported here do not necessarily enable all children to convey their understandings in the ways they would like to. Particularly when interviews are conducted, as they were in this case, within a school environment, the potential for children to regard the interview experience and/or survey as some kind of 'test' multiplies. Further aural and/or written responses clearly afford more possibilities for children with a wider repertoire of language to express themselves than those who prefer to express themselves via other routes (e.g. drawing or photography). While insights regarding familial practices and the cultural contexts within which physical activity takes place were offered throughout interviews, richer understandings of the specific contexts that contour children's engagement with physical activity and health imperatives could arguably be discerned through additional interviews and/or ethnographic work in families and communities. Despite these cautionary notes, I suggest that, as 'texts', the transcripts of interviews with the young people afford considerable insights about the discursive context within which children enact health and physical activity practices, and the ways dominant discourses frame the possibilities for envisioning themselves as 'healthy'. The fact that the majority of students interviewed articulated remarkably similar meanings perhaps tells us more about the magnitude of health and physical activity messages currently circulating than it does about what children 'really' think and do in their daily lives. In so saying, from a poststructural point of view, there *is* no essential truth to be discovered. Rather, truth is constructed and unstable, and the task is one of unravelling the multiple ways in which it is produced, its effects and the ways subjectivities are enabled and/or constrained in relation to it.

References

Aphramor, L. (2005) 'Is a weight-centred health framework salutogenic? Some thoughts on unhinging certain dietary ideologies', *Social Theory and Health*, 3 (4): 315–340.

Atencio, M. (2006) '"Crunk", "cracking", and "choreographies": the place and meaning of health and physical activity in the lives of young people from culturally diverse urban neighbourhoods', unpublished thesis, University of Wollongong.

Ball, S.J. (ed.) (1990) *Foucault and Education: Disciplines and Knowledge*. London: Routledge.

Bordo, S. (1993) *Unbearable Weight: Feminism, Western Culture, and the Body*. Berkeley, CA: University of California Press.

Burman, E. (1991) 'Power, gender and developmental psychology', *Feminism & Psychology*, 1 (1): 141–153.

Burrows, L. and Wright, J. (2004a) 'The good life: New Zealand children's perspectives of health and self', *Sport, Education and Society*, 9 (2): 193–205.

Burrows, L. and Wright, J. (2004b) '"Being healthy": Young New Zealanders' ideas about health', *Childrenz Issues*, 8 (1): 7–12.

Burrows, L. and Wright, J. (2007) 'Prescribing practices: shaping healthy children in schools', *International Journal of Children's Rights*, 15 (1): 83–98.

Burrows, L., Wright, J. and Jungersen-Smith, J. (2002) '"Measure your belly". New Zealand children's constructions of health and fitness', *Journal of Teaching in Physical Education*, 22 (1): 20–38.

Burrows, L., Wright, J. and McCormack, J. (2007) *New Zealand Children's Constructions of Health and Fitness: Probe Study Research Report*. Wellington: Ministry of Education.

Burrows, L., Wright, J. and McCormack, J. (in press) 'Dosing up on food and physical activity: New Zealand children's ideas about health', *Health Education Journal*.

Campos, P. (2004) *The Obesity Myth: Why America's Obsession With Weight is Hazardous to Your Health*. New York: Gotham Books.

Campos, P., Saguy, A., Ernsberger, P., Oliver, E. and Gaesser, G. (2006) 'The epidemiology of overweight and obesity: public health crisis or moral panic?', *International Journal of Epidemiology*, 35 (1): 55–60.

Crawford, R. (1980) 'Healthism and the medicalisation of everyday life', *International Journal of Health Services*, 10: 365–388.

Evans, J., Rich, E., Allwood, R. and Davies, B. (2005) 'Fat fabrications', *British Journal of Physical Education*, 36 (4), Winter: 18–21.

Foucault, M. (1980) *Power/Knowledge: Selected Interviews and Other Writings 1972–1977*. London: Harvester.

Foucault. M. (1990) *The History of Sexuality. Vol. I. An Introduction*. New York: Vintage.

Fox, K. (2000) 'The effects of exercise on self-perceptions and self-esteem', in S. Biddle, K. Fox and S. Boutcher (eds) *Physical Activity and Psychological Well-being*. London: Routledge.

Fullagar, S. (2002) 'Governing the healthy body: discourses of leisure and lifestyle within Australian health policy', *Health*, 6: 69–84.

Gard, M. and Wright, J. (2005) *The Obesity Epidemic: Science, Ideology and Morality*. London: Routledge.

Gore, J. (1993) *The Struggle for Pedagogies: Critical and Feminist Discourses as Regimes of Truth*. New York: Routledge.

Gore, J. (1995) 'On the continuity of power relations in pedagogy', *International Studies in Sociology of Education*, 5 (2): 165–188.

Harris, J. (1994) 'Young people's perceptions of health, fitness and exercise: implications for the teaching of health related exercise', *Physical Education Review*, 17: 143–151.

Hirschhorn Donahue, E., Haskins, R. and Nightingale, M. (2008) 'Using the media to promote adolescent well-being', *The Future of Children*, Policy Brief, Spring. Online. Available at: www.futureofchildren.org (accessed 27 January 2010).

Hitti, M. (2005) 'Couch potato kids pack on the pounds'. Online. Available at: http://www.webmd.com/fitness-exercise/news/20050913/couch-potato-kids-pack-on-pounds (accessed 3 September 2008).

Holloway, S. and Valentine, G. (eds) (2000) *Children's Geographies: Living, Playing, Learning*. London: Routledge.

Holloway, S. and Valentine, G. (2003) *CyberKids: Children and the Information Age*. London: Falmer Routledge.

Howarth, D. and Stavrakakis, Y. (2000) 'Introducing discourse theory and political analysis', in D.R. Howarth, J.A. Noval and Y. Stavrakakis (eds) *Discourse Theory and Political Analysis: Identities, Hegemonies and Social Change*. Manchester: Manchester University Press.

James, A. and Prout, A. (eds) (1990) *Constructing and Reconstructing Childhood: Contemporary Issues in the Sociological Study of Childhood*. London: The Falmer Press.

Kirk, D. and Colquhoun, D. (1989) 'Healthism and daily physical education', *British Journal of Sociology of Education*, 10 (4): 417–434.

Knez, K. (2007) 'The meaning and place of physical activity in the lives of young Muslim women', unpublished thesis, University of Queensland.

Leahy, D. and Harwood, V. (2006) 'Physical activity inequalities, fluidity and the dilemma of "activity" in the lives of young people living in rural areas', paper presented at AIESEP World Congress, Jyvskyla, Finland, July.

Lineham, C. (2003) 'The voices of our non-participants', in B. Ross and L. Burrows (eds) *It*

Takes Two Feet: Physical Education and Health Teaching in New Zealand. Palmerston North: Dunmore.

Lupton, D. (1995) *The Imperative of Health: Public Health and the Regulated Body*. London: Sage.

Macdonald, D., Hay, P. and Williams, B. (2008) 'Neoliberal times and physical education', in L. Burrows (ed.) *Physically Educating for the Future*, 41 (3): 6–13. Wellington: Physical Education New Zealand.

Macdonald, D., Rodger, S., Abbot, R., Ziviani, J. and Jones, J. (2005) '"I could do with a pair of wings": perspectives on physical activity, bodies and health from young Australian children', *Sport Education and Society*, 10 (2): 195–209.

MacDougall, C., Schiller, W. and Darbyshire, P. (2004) 'We have to live in the future', *Early Child Development and Care*, 174: 369–387.

Mayall, B. (1998) 'Towards a sociology of child health', *Sociology of Health & Illness*, 20: 269–288.

Miha, A. and Rich, E. (2008) *The Medicalization of Cyberspace*. London: Routledge.

Ministry of Education (1999a) *Healthy People Eat Healthy Food: Food and Nutrition, Years 1–3*. Wellington: Learning Media.

Ministry of Education (1999b) *Choice Food: Food and Nutrition Years 7–8: The Curriculum in Action Series*. Wellington: Learning Media.

Ministry of Education (1999c) *Health and Physical Education in the New Zealand Curriculum*. Wellington: Learning Media.

Ministry of Education (2006) *The National Administration Guidelines*. Online. Available at: http://www.minedu.govt.nz/educationSectors/Schools/PolicyAndStrategy/PlanningRep ortingRelevantLegislationNEGSAndNAGS/TheNationalAdministrationGuidelinesNA Gs.aspx (accessed 6 September 2008).

Ministry of Education (2007) *The New Zealand Curriculum*. Wellington: Learning Media.

Mission-On (2006) Online. Available at: http://www.sparc.org.nz/news/mission-on (accessed 12 April, 2007).

Murray, S. (2008) '"Pathologizing fatness": obesity, authority and popular culture', *Sociology of Sport Journal*, 25 (1): 7–21.

O'Flynn, G. (2004) 'Young women's meanings of health and physical activity: the body, schooling, and the discursive constitution of gendered and classed subjectivities', unpublished PhD thesis, University of Wollongong.

Rail, G. (2004) 'De/re/constructions of fitness and health among Canada's youth: closing the imperial eye and increasing our understanding of marginalized subjectivities', paper presented at ACHPER National/International Conference, Wollongong, July.

Rail, G. (2009) 'Canadian youth's discursive constructions of health in the context of obesity discourse', in J. Wright and V. Harwood (eds) *Biopolitics and the 'Obesity Epidemic': Governing Bodies*. London: Routledge.

Seely, M. (2002) 'Un/healthy, un/fit, dis/abled: constructions of health and fitness among adolescents with mobility impairments', unpublished thesis, University of Ottawa.

Shea, J. (2006) '"An apple a day keeps the doctor away": immigrant youth in St John's, Newfoundland and Labrador and their constructions of health and fitness', unpublished thesis, Memorial University of Newfoundland.

Shilling, C. (1993) *The Body and Social Theory*. London: Sage.

Skelton, T. and Valentine, G. (eds) (1998) *Cool Places: Geographies of Youth Cultures*. London: Routledge.

Smith, A. (1999) 'Children's rights: an overview', in A.B. Smith, M. Gollop, K. Marshall and K. Nairn (eds) *Advocating for Children: International Perspectives on Children's Rights*. Dunedin: University of Otago Press.

Smith, A. and Parr, M. (2007) 'Young people's views on the nature and purposes of physical education: a sociological analysis', *Sport, Education and Society*, 12 (1): 37–58.

Sport and Recreation New Zealand (2007) *Physical Activity Guidelines for Children and Young People*. Wellington: Sport and Recreation New Zealand.

Williams, A. and Woodhouse, J. (1996) 'Delivering the discourse – urban adolescents' perceptions of physical education', *Sport, Education and Society*, 1: 201–213.

World Health Organization (2005) 'Why move for health?' Online. Available at: http://www.who.int/moveforhealth/en/ (accessed 6 September 2008).

Wright, J. and Burrows, L. (2004) '"Being healthy": the discursive construction of health in New Zealand children's responses to the national education monitoring project', *Discourse*, 25 (2): 211–230.

Wright, J. and Macdonald, D. (2001–2006) *Life Activity Project*. Australian Research Council funded project, University of Wollongong and University of Queensland.

Wright, J., Macdonald, D. and Groom, L. (2003) 'Physical activity and young people: beyond participation', *Sport Education and Society*, 8 (1): 17–34.

Wright, J.E., O'Flynn, G. and Macdonald, D. (2006) 'Being fit and looking healthy: young women's and men's constructions of health and fitness', *Sex Roles – A Journal of Research*, 54 (9–10): 1–15.

Wyn, J. and White, R. (1997) *Rethinking Youth*. St Leonards: Allen & Unwin.

10 'Carving a new order of experience'[1] *with* young people in physical education

Participatory Action Research as a pedagogy of possibility

Eimear Enright and Mary O'Sullivan

Introduction

It is June 13th 2008, a bright, warm, much appreciated, summer's day in Ireland. The school holidays have begun and three teenage girls have chosen to attend the Physical Education, Physical Activity and Youth Sport (PE-PAYS) Annual Forum.[2] Dressed in their black and luminous pink, self-designed, club hoodies, they are standing in front of a crowd of 20 or so people, sharing their experiences as activist researchers, designers and participants in The Pres Girls' Physical Activity Club (The Pres Girls, Enright and O'Sullivan, 2008). They are nervous but they speak honestly and passionately. They have not learned off by heart what they are saying; rather they speak from their hearts and their recent memories. The crowd are engaged, hanging on the girls' words, and at times laughing appropriately at the incredible honesty of what they are hearing. One of the girls has earlier led a two-hour hip-hop dance workshop for interested physical education teachers and health promotion professionals. Afterwards the girls talk quickly and excitedly about their experience: 'the buzz' they got from being listened to by so many people; the photographer who had told them their poster was visually the best at the conference; how they felt everyone understood their presentation because '[they] didn't use big, confusing words like "motivational climate" like the other presenters' (all adult researchers) and '[they] were just [them]selves'. One of the girls, Daniella, did not speak during the presentation as she had planned to. 'I was just too nervous. My heart was hopping,' she explains. Levi and Zara tell her that they were glad she was there with them to support them, whether she said anything or not. Later she comes into her own, fielding questions from interested teachers and researchers. 'I'm speaking up there the next time,' she resolves. After their initial excitement dissipates, a brief silence follows. Levi then asks: 'Do you think now that they've heard us talking about it they'll try to make their PE classes better and get their students to help them make PE better and make clubs with them and all?' Levi cares about other students' experiences. She wants to know her work, her investment, will make a positive difference in the lives of other students. 'I hope so Levi,' Eimear replies. (Adapted from field notes, p. 112)

Student voice 'describes the many ways in which youth actively participate in the school decisions that shape their lives and the lives of their peers' (Mitra, 2007, p. 727). The student voice movement supports a shift in the status of students in school from passive objects to active participants (Hodgkin, 1998). Daniella, Levi and Zara, the students introduced in the narrative above, embody this shift. They have become advocates for a student voice initiative, which engaged them as designers and evaluators of their physical education curriculum and an after-school physical activity club in their community (Enright and O'Sullivan, 2007; The Pres Girls, Enright and O'Sullivan, 2008).

For them student voice means:

> Listening to us and helping us express ourselves, and letting us make real decisions, and the teachers hearing us and working with us to make PE and sports and stuff better for everyone. . . . And that's what it's all about, us making PE classes that we want to be in, and that are good fun and that we learn interesting, and useful things in. (Daniella, student researcher)

Student voice is, as Daniella suggests, about more than just listening to students; it is about listening to students with the intent of responding to what we hear (Fielding, 2004; Cook-Sather, 2007). Responding appropriately to what we hear requires that students' voices 'need to not only be heard, but also engaged, reconciled and argued with' (Hargreaves, 1994, p. 251). We need therefore to create safe, democratic spaces where teachers and students can come together, 'discover what they recognize together and appreciate in common' (Greene, 1995, p. 39), and work towards increased student engagement and subsequently deeper and more relevant student learning.

This chapter is an attempt to stimulate a rethinking of how student voice is conceptualized and enacted in physical education research and teaching. It is an effort to promote an appreciation of young people as curious, thoughtful, social agents who have the desire and capacity to imagine more engaging and meaningful physical education and physical activity experiences, and to create the changes they wish to see in their worlds. Our primary aim in writing this chapter is to challenge physical education teachers and researchers to work with students to trouble the boundaries of what's possible in physical education, imagine what is possible, and work towards what could be (Lather, 1991; Fine, 1992; Greene, 1995; Oliver *et al.*, 2009).

One approach to such a re-imagining is to focus on Participatory Action Research (PAR) as a theoretical construct, a research methodology and a pedagogical framework. Participatory Action Research in this context constitutes a 'pedagogy of possibility' (Giroux and Simon, 1989; Freire, 1994; McLaren, 1999). The ability of PAR to promote the creation of more educationally meaningful and socially relevant learning experiences for all students in physical education is evidenced with reference to four recent PAR-orientated projects in physical education (Enright and O'Sullivan, 2008; Fisette, 2008; McMahon, 2007; Oliver, Hamzeh and McCaughtry, 2009; Oliver and Hamzeh, 2010). It is our hope that learning from these efforts will 'light the slow fuse of possibility' (Dickinson, 1960, quoted in Greene, 1997), encouraging more teachers and researchers to challenge existing boundaries of experience in educating students in and through physical education.

The chapter begins with some theoretical foregrounding on the emergence of student voice. We then position PAR as a framework to support student voice-orientated work in physical education, and chart three phases of student engagement: naming inequities; broadening horizons; and change-agency. Some of the challenges and benefits associated with supporting a PAR pedagogy are then discussed, and implications for all who seek to engage with student voice in physical education are presented.

Silenced voices

The traditional positioning of students as passive recipients of teaching renders them as 'blank slates', 'beneficiaries', 'consumers', 'conformists' and 'subordinate subjects' (Thiessen, 2007), supporting the popular aphorism 'children should be seen and not heard'. The student voice agenda challenges these traditional images of youth, daring all those who work with young people in schools to support students in taking an active, meaningful role in decision making related to their learning. 'Meaningful student involvement' has been defined as 'the process of engaging the knowledge, experience and perspectives of students in every facet of the educational process, for the purpose of strengthening their commitment to education, community and democracy' (Fletcher, 2004, p. 4). Definitions of student voice and involvement, such as that proposed by Fletcher (2004), support schools where students are engaged as 'teachers, education researchers, school planners, classroom evaluators, system-wide school decision makers, and education advocates' (p. 4).

This type of educational imperative has been knocking on the door of physical education for quite some time. Physical education researchers have persistently highlighted the marginality of student voices in curriculum-making practices in physical education (Dyson, 1995; Brooker and MacDonald, 1999; Macdonald, 2003; Penney, 2006). A decade ago, Brooker and Macdonald (1999) asserted that '[w]hile curriculum supposedly exists to serve the interests of learners, their preferences, if sought at all, are marginalized and their voices are mostly silent in curriculum making' (p. 84). More recently Macdonald (2003) observed:

> While the literature in the curriculum field recognizes the difficulty in creating meaningful curriculum change within current school structures, the majority of innovations and analyses are blind to the bigger and more significant questions surrounding change: Who are the young people in schools, and what, where and how do they learn? (p. 147)

This blindness has particular significance for physical education – a subject that is greatly mediated by the media, and the interests and culture of its students (Tinning and Fitzclarence, 1992; Brooker and Macdonald, 1999). Critiques of curriculum reform efforts suggest that selecting and constructing a physical education curriculum that connects and speaks to the heterogeneity of young people is near impossible, if the voices of the young people the curriculum seeks to connect with are absent from the construction process (Penney and Evans, 1999; Macdonald, 2003; Glasby and Macdonald, 2004; Penney, 2006). Penney (2006) contends that 'the starting point for more and innovative research has to be new conceptualizations of curriculum . . . Such conceptualizations will rightly refocus attention on students but also prompt more involvement of them in both curriculum development and research in physical education' (p. 576). It has also been suggested that curricula for the agentic student, curricula that harness student interest and potential, be created through negotiation (Boomer, 1992; Shor, 1992, 1996; Brooker and Macdonald, 1999; Greene, 2000; Glasby and Macdonald, 2004). While there exist numerous possibilities for curriculum negotiation and shared curriculum decision making with students in physical education, it is difficult to find reported examples of such practices.

Students' roles in research and the corresponding critique of these roles by the research community have followed a similar trajectory to that of the literature relating to students' marginal positioning within curriculum development. Christensen and Prout (2002) identify four perspectives on children in research: the child as object; the child as subject; the child as social actor; and an emerging approach that positions children as participants and co-researchers. Historically, educational researchers have positioned students as objects, using, for example, limited-response questionnaires and statistical analysis to conduct research *on* students (Erickson and Shultz, 1992). This perspective and these methods fail to recognize students as experts on their own lives, fracture student experience, and do not acknowledge student subjectivities or agency. The publication of a monograph on student voice in 1995 by the *Journal of Teaching in Physical Education* marked a methodological shift in physical education research, towards an understanding of students as research subjects (Graham, 1995). In line with this shift, in the last decade there has been a multitude of studies that focus on students' perspectives of their physical education experiences (for example, Carlson, 1995; Dyson, 1995, 2001, 2002; Hopple and Graham, 1995; Pope and Grant, 1996; Cothran and Ennis, 1999; Hastie, 2000; Burrows, Wright and Jungersen-Smith, 2002; Hunter, 2002; Kinchin and O'Sullivan, 1999; Azzarito, Solomon and Harrison, 2006). Much has been learned from listening to student perspectives. For example, we now know that students often perceive only a vague rationale for their physical education curriculum, and often do not find physical education relevant (Cothran and Ennis, 1999). We also know that affording students greater roles and responsibilities within the learning context (Hastie, 1998; Ennis, 1999), providing opportunities for their critical interpretation, challenge and resistance of dominant and often harmful discourses of the body (Oliver and Lalik, 2001), and facilitating students in interrogating and making meaningful connections between school-based physical education and contemporary physical culture (Kinchin and O'Sullivan, 1999), can work to facilitate student engagement and deepen student learning. We can surmise, therefore, that it is not disengaged students that are always the problem but often the pedagogical contexts within which they are expected to participate, and the curricula with which they are instructed to engage (Wright, 1996; Ennis *et al.*, 1997; Flintoff and Scraton, 2005; Sandford and Rich, 2006).

We have clearly learned a lot from listening to student perspectives and, while it is very necessary, listening alone is not sufficient if we hope to challenge current curriculum-making practices or promote a change in the status of students within schools or within educational research (Brooker and Macdonald, 1999; Rudduck, 2007). In the general education literature the methodologies that frame and support students' roles within research are becoming increasingly sophisticated and diverse (Thiessen, 2007). There is an evolving appreciation of students' potential roles in research as 'co-researchers', 'co-constructors of knowledge', 'collaborators', 'researchers', 'advisors', 'co-interpreters', 'inquirers', 'architects', 'activists', 'advocates' and 'evaluators' (Thiessen and Cook-Sather, 2007). Within physical education research we are also now beginning to see this shift, particularly among feminist critical scholars (Enright and O'Sullivan, 2007, 2008; Hamzeh, 2007; Fisette, 2008; Oliver *et al.*, 2009; Oliver and Hamzeh, 2010).

Recognizing students as active agents, researchers and curriculum makers necessitates the construction of an entirely different set of relationships to the ones that currently characterize how many teachers and students *do* physical education, and indeed education generally. The potential of PAR as a critical pedagogical tool, which can support negotiated curricular practices and forge more democratic relationships between teachers and students, has received support (Udas, 1998). So, too, has the potential PAR 'offers as a means by which marginalized students, teachers and university researchers can work collaboratively towards positive outcomes for participants and their schools' (Bland and Atweh, 2007, p. 337).

Participatory Action Research

We have framed the research reviewed in this chapter as PAR. We might have borrowed from various perspectives presented by physical education and non-physical education scholars, and framed our pedagogical efforts as critical democratic pedagogy for self and social change (Shor, 1992), feminist critical pedagogy (Oliver and Lalik, 2001), empowering education (Shor, 1992), poststructural pedagogy (Wright, 2003), postmodern physical education (Macdonald, 2003), democratic education (Beane, 1997), coherent curricula (Ennis, 2003), curriculum co-construction, power sharing, co-governance, authentic assessment, integrated curricula (Glasby and Macdonald, 2004), or negotiated curricula (Boomer *et al.*, 1992; Shor, 1996; Glasby and Macdonald, 2004). Similarly the research efforts described within this chapter might have been articulated as feminist activist research (Fine, 1992), socially critical research (Devis-Devis, 2006), praxis-orientated research (Lather, 1991), emancipatory social research (Lather, 1992) or poststructural feminist research (Nilges, 2006). The work cited in this chapter does reflect principles inherent in all of these research and pedagogical frames.

We chose PAR, however, as it foregrounds collective action, a principle that, considering our understanding of student voice and our belief that students who have become 'collaboratively disengaged' (Chaplain, 1996) need to be collaboratively re-engaged, we viewed as particularly important. Like Shor (1992), we believe that 'knowledge is power only for those who can use it to change their social conditions' (p. 6). PAR supports this belief representing 'an epistemology that assumes knowledge is rooted in social relations and most powerful when produced collaboratively through action' (Fine *et al.*, 2001, p. 173). PAR sees people 'co-creating their reality through participation; through their experience; their imagination and intuition, their thinking and their action' (Reason, 1998, p. 262). It has a double objective, first, 'to produce knowledge and action directly useful to a group of people' and, second, 'to empower people at a deeper level through the process of constructing and using their knowledge' (Nieuwenhuys, 2004, p. 210).

Participatory Action Research acknowledges that the researched possess critical social knowledge, and repositions them as participants in and architects of research (Torre and Fine, 2006), thereby promoting a higher level of participation than action research. PAR is explicitly political premised on the notion that marginalized people can transform their realities through education, research, action and reflection. Udas (1998) contends 'Participatory Action Research must be aimed toward social justice, involve critical reflection on practice, question assumptions on which practice is predicated, and promote collaborative collective action' (p. 606). We draw on four physical education PAR studies as exemplars of this approach to student voice. A brief introduction to each of these studies is presented here. We do not have the scope in this chapter to go into detail on the students' contribution to the PAR process, nor do we have the space to introduce you to each of the student researchers. We do however make an effort, in the sections that follow, to allow you to enter as fully into the spirit and practicalities of the research journeys as we can.

Enright and O'Sullivan (2007, 2008) carried out a three-year PAR project with disengaged students in an all-girl, urban, post-primary school in Ireland. The aim of the project was to work with the students to understand and transform their self-identified barriers to in-school physical education engagement and their out-of-school physical activity participation. The PAR project was initially focused on the engagement of one class of teenage (aged 15–19 years) girls as physical education curriculum designers and evaluators (Enright and O'Sullivan, 2007). The project extended to a further two classes and to the design and evaluation of an after-school physical education club in the second year (The Pres Girls, Enright and O'Sullivan, 2008), thereby challenging formal physical education learning boundaries.

Adopting curriculum negotiation as a theoretical framework, McMahon's (2007) study sought to engage one co-ed class of 5th class primary school students (aged 10–11 years) in the process of physical education curriculum negotiation. The purpose of the study was to understand students' views of their involvement in curriculum negotiation, and how it affected their ownership of and investment in their physical education curriculum. Her ten-week study involved students in a process of curriculum negotiation with the researcher/teacher in which together they determined the purpose, content, aims, teaching methods and assessment of a curriculum. Unlike the other three PAR studies (Enright and O'Sullivan, 2007,

2008; Fisette, 2008; Oliver *et al.*, 2009; Oliver and Hamzeh, 2010) profiled in this chapter, all of McMahon's (2007) students self-identified as enjoying physical education prior to her study.

A strong Participatory Action Research theme underpins much of Oliver and Lalik's work (Oliver and Lalik, 2000, 2001, 2004a, 2004b). For the purpose of this chapter we will focus on Oliver and colleagues' most recent research (Oliver *et al.*, 2009; Oliver and Hamzeh, 2010), the purpose of which was to (a) understand 5th grade (aged 9–10 years) girls' self-identified barriers to physical activity, and (b) work with the girls to design and practise strategies for publicizing and changing the barriers they identified (2009). Oliver *et al.*'s participants were all identified by their teachers as unenthusiastic physical education participants prior to her study.

Fisette's (2008) study engaged a group of seven teenage (aged 13–16 years) girls in undertaking their own exploratory physical education projects. This group was selected with the help of their physical education teacher as a representative sample of their physical education class, and included students with low and high levels of engagement in physical education. The girls formulated their own projects to further their knowledge on a topic or issue in physical education that was significant for them. For example, one group chose embarrassment in physical education as their focus of inquiry. Through her work with the girls Fisette (2008) sought to understand (a) how adolescent girls perceive and feel about their bodies while they engage in physical education, and (b) how they navigate ways to feel comfortable within their own bodies and the physical education environment.

Naming inequities

Shor (1992) proposes that '[f]inding a generative theme, that is a theme generated from student conditions that is problematic enough to inspire students to do intellectual work, can produce a wealth of student expression' (p. 5). Physical education is a subject that is particularly problematic for many students (more girls than boys) and as such is ripe for intellectual work. Fine *et al.* (2007) contend that 'young people, who witness injustice in schools, are willing to research the capillaries of inequity, and work hard to redesign school structures, policies and practices' (p. 806). For years scholars have documented blatant, insidious and persistent injustices inherent in physical education practices. These injustices relate to gender (Flintoff and Scraton, 2006; Gard, 2006), sexuality (Clarke, 2006), social class (Evans, 2006), ability (Fitzgerald, 2006), and race and ethnicity (Harrison and Belcher, 2006). More recently, the intersection of these social structures has received attention (Azzarito and Solmon, 2005; Oliver, Chapter 3 in this volume). Students have been perpetrators, subjects and witnesses of these intersecting inequities, and are therefore uniquely positioned to name and change dysfunctional, inequitable physical education practices, and they are as Fine *et al.* (2007) suggest, and as our four profiled PAR studies (Enright and O'Sullivan, 2007, 2008; McMahon, 2007; Fisette, 2008; Oliver *et al.*, 2009; Oliver and Hamzeh, 2010) reveal, 'willing' change agents.

Each of the PAR studies reported on in this chapter began with the selection of one or more generative themes. Participatory methods were used to open up dialogue and begin to engage students in critical inquiry in all cases. Participatory methods are those that facilitate participants in finding their own language to articulate what they know; methods that help participants put words to their ideas and share their understandings of their worlds. These methods work to facilitate students thinking 'in light of local knowledge' first, and generating what Clifford Geertz (1983) calls a 'feeling for immediacies' (cited in Greene, 1995, p. 68). The participatory methods used in the four profiled PAR studies included photography (Enright and O'Sullivan, 2008; Oliver *et al.*, 2009; Oliver and Hamzeh, 2010), development of personal biographies (Enright and O'Sullivan, 2008; Fisette, 2008; Oliver *et al.*, 2009; Oliver and Hamzeh, 2010), free writing, body drawing, journal writing (Fisette, 2008), student drawings (McMahon, 2007), posters sessions (Enright and O'Sullivan, 2007; Fisette, 2008), and physical activity timelines (Enright and O'Sullivan, 2008).

The participants in Enright and O'Sullivan's (2007) study identified their first generative theme as 'lack of voice and choice', with students being particularly critical of the hierarchical and institutional power embodied by teachers and principals: 'the teachers make all the decisions and the principal and they never listen to us' (Kelly). The only decisions the girls perceived they made in physical education were: 'to participate' (Debra), 'put in effort and try or to mooch' (Kelly) and 'to bring in gear or not' (Shelly). By making these decisions, the girls refused to be passive recipients of the physical education teachers' formal and unilateral authority. In fact through these decisions they actively constructed their disengagement from physical education and physical activity. The girls felt that boys were far better catered for, in terms of sports and physical activity provision in their communities, highlighting how lack of voice and choice in relation to physical activity options extended beyond school boundaries. The second generative theme to emerge for the participants was 'stupid physical education'. All of the girls were critical to some extent regarding the choice of activities offered to them through their physical education curriculum. While some just wanted a little more variety, others rejected all of the activities they had experienced in physical education, 'for three years all we've ever done is basketball, rugby-rounders or soccer and that's it, stupid and boring madness' (Kelly). This perspective is not surprising considering that the nature of the activities offered through their post-primary physical education experiences were incredibly consistent. Their physical education curriculum had mirrored the traditional multi-activity sport model, privileging competitive team sport over other forms of physical activity (Ennis, 1999).

For Fisette's (2008) participants, 'gender issues' and 'class/curriculum design' in physical education were selected initially by one of her student groups as the two themes they wanted to investigate. They dropped the theme of class/curriculum design once they realized how complex and time consuming it was going to be to focus on gender issues alone. The girls in this group struggled particularly with what they perceived as male dominance in physical education. Her second group of students decided on 'how you feel in physical education' as their generative theme, believing that this theme encompassed both their key questions/concerns: what influences girls' participation and what makes them embarrassed in physical education. These girls were particularly critical of the public, performance aspect of physical education, and feared their bodies and their performance being watched and judged by other classmates.

Oliver and colleagues (Oliver *et al.*, 2009; Oliver and Hamzeh, 2010) worked with two groups of 9–10-year-old girls. For the first group the generative theme was 'girly girl' and how being a 'girly girl' hindered the girls' physical activity and physical education engagement. For the second group the primary physical activity barrier and the theme selected by the participants for further study and potential transformation was 'the boys won't let us play'.

McMahon's (2007) co-ed group of students expressed a unanimous rejection of their limited involvement in decision making in physical education. 'Making decisions in physical education' therefore constituted the generative theme, which inspired her students' intellectual work.

Broadening horizons

Maxine Greene (1995) wrote:

> Only when the given or the taken-for-granted is subject to questioning, only when we take various, sometimes unfamiliar perspectives on it, does it show itself as what it is – contingent on many interpretations, many vantage points, unified (if at all) by conformity or by unexamined common sense. Once we can see our givens as contingencies, then we may have the opportunity to posit alternative ways of living and valuing and to make choices. (p. 23)

In order to facilitate students in seeing the 'givens' in physical education as 'contingencies' and better positioning them to imagine alternatives, efforts need to be made in a physical education PAR pedagogy to introduce 'unfamiliar perspectives' and thereby broaden student horizons. Horizon activities help students develop two types of language, that of critique and that of possibility (Giroux, 1997; Lalik and Oliver, 2005).

For the participants in Enright and O'Sullivan's (2008) study, taster classes of alternative physical activities, based on participant suggestions, were used to broaden the participants' frame of reference on potential content in physical education. During these taster classes both content and pedagogical strategies were varied and, after each class, participants were encouraged to reflect critically on the activities, and on how the lesson was delivered and assessed. This was facilitated by Eimear and Róisín, who engaged participants in discussion around some key questions every week. These key questions included: What was the purpose of this class? What did you learn? What helped you to learn? What made it difficult to learn? How did you (or could you) show that you learned something? How could we improve the class to maximize learning?

Similarly, students in McMahon's (2007) study were first engaged in a Sport Education unit where they had the opportunity to experience increased roles and responsibilities. The Sport Education experience challenged their conceptions of what could constitute a physical education curriculum, therefore increasing their appreciation of curricular possibilities. Oliver and colleagues (Oliver *et al.*, 2009; Oliver and Hamzeh, 2010) used sporting goods magazines to broaden students' horizons regarding their engagement in physical activity. Oliver asked the girls to identify equipment in the magazines that they might like to use in the pursuit of physical activity.

Change-agency

In each of the four profiled PAR studies these horizon activities expanded the dialogue between students, teachers and researchers, and opened up new vistas within which a critique of existing physical education and physical activity practices and the imagining of physical education alternatives could take shape. That the students had begun to understand and critically engage with their realities, and to imagine alternatives, was not enough however. A PAR pedagogy is orientated to 'change-agency' (Shor, 1992). Change-agency 'means learning and acting for the democratic transformation of self and society . . . people tak[ing] responsibility for rethinking and changing the conditions they are in' (p. 190). Students who participate in a physical education PAR pedagogy are facilitated in 'taking responsibility for rethinking and changing' their physical education and physical activity experiences. This may be through direct involvement in curriculum re-conceptualization (McMahon, 2007; Enright and O'Sullivan, 2008; Oliver *et al.*, 2009), or advocacy for the benefits of physical activity in the form of creating newsletters and writing for local newspapers (Fisette, 2008), school presentations (Oliver *et al.*, 2009; Oliver and Hamzeh, 2010), public performances (McMahon, 2007), research conference presentations (The Pres Girls, Enright and O'Sullivan, 2008) or media interviews (The Pres Girls, Enright and O'Sullivan, 2008). In all of these examples, students' voices were 'authorized' (Cook-Sather, 2002). Drawing from Heilbrum (1988), Cook-Sather (2002) defines authorizing as 'the ability to take one's place in whatever discourse is essential to action and the right to have one's part matter' (p. 3). By appreciating students' knowledge and capacity to imagine more engaging and meaningful physical education and physical activity experiences, and to create the changes they wish to see in their worlds, the above studies serve as examples of authorizing student voice in physical education.

Supporting a PAR pedagogy

Roles

To authorize student perspective 'those invested with authority must confront the power dynamics inside and outside our classrooms [that make] democratic dialogue impossible' (Ellsworth, 1989, p. 107). Gore (1992) suggests 'we must use our power in an attempt (that might not be successful) to help others exercise power' (p. 59). Teachers and researchers who work within a PAR pedagogy are what Aronowitz and Giroux (1985) called 'transformative intellectuals'. They facilitate students in their development as change agents. As adult allies they foster students' capacities to critique and transform that which is dysfunctional in their education, in this case their physical education experiences.

Rudduck reminds us 'we should not underestimate the degree of challenge student voice can present to both experienced and new teachers' (2007, p. 607). Teachers and schools need to be supported in 'giving up some control and handing it over to students' (Smyth, 2007, p. 655). Working in democratic ways with students, recognizing their authority and agency as curriculum designers and co-researchers requires an identity shift and role redefinition, not just in relation to students' roles but also for all those who seek to facilitate students' engagement with the process. Oldfather (1995) supports this assertion, suggesting that 'learning from student voices . . . requires major shifts on the part of teachers, students, and researchers in ways of thinking and feeling about the issues of knowledge, language, power and self' (p. 87). Positioning physical education as the focus of the PAR curriculum constituted a significant conceptual shift, for all involved in the profiled PAR studies, with regards to what constituted teaching and learning in physical education, and what constituted teacher and student roles and responsibilities. Both the subject reconceptualization and the role redefinitions sometimes met with resistance.

In the beginning, a minority of Enright and O'Sullivan's (2008) students proposed that student involvement in decision making would constitute a '*waste of time*', time that, they argued, could be spent on activity as, after all, '*this is PE isn't it?*' Student and teacher role re-definition was also met with some opposition, with one student articulating her dissatisfaction quite clearly: '*That should be your job shouldn't it? So what are you going to be doing, if we're doing your job [designing the curriculum]?*' (Debra). Debra understandably voiced resistance when initially introduced to PAR. Students like Debra have had years of practice of being told exactly what to do. They are used to being managed and directed. Sharing responsibility for their learning is often something completely new to them and something that they understandably may find quite frustrating initially.

Róisín, the teacher in Enright and O'Sullivan's (2007) study, experienced similar challenges negotiating her new facilitator identity, citing a conflict between '*doing what teachers are expected to, are supposed to do*' and '*trying to work with and respect students' voices and choices*'. Rudduck (2006) suggests that moving 'from a familiar and safe position of power to a relationship that is more collaborative, open, responsive, and consultative' results in a 'temporary destabilising period of change' for teachers (p. 607). There are traditional ways of being a teacher. Deviating from tradition and negotiating this 'temporary destabilising period of change', requires courage on the part of the teacher, and is a difficult and complex departure without institutional and collegial support. A colleague observing one of Enright and O'Sullivan's (2007) lessons commented disapprovingly that at times it looked as if '*the students were running the show*'. The irony that '*students running the show*', in terms of student-led curriculum reform, was exactly what we were striving for, escaped her.

Inclusion

The research reviewed in this chapter sought to open up the distinct and contradictory voices of each of the student participants. The researchers were mindful of 'ventriloquating' others' voices (Bakhtin, 1981). We were mindful, however, not just because of our potentially problematic positioning as ventriloquists, speaking through the voices of the students, but also because of the likelihood of the student participants speaking themselves through the voices of others. Efforts were made to avoid losing individual voices to group mimicry, as is sometimes the case when one works with peer groups.

It is a difficult task to credit all voices, and to capture and work with the contradictions of competing voices. McMahon (2007), for example, reported gender-based inequalities regarding who participated in decision making, with one of her female students initially citing the physical education decision makers as '*all boys and the teacher*' (Beky). Interestingly when dance was selected by her students as the focus of their negotiated curricular unit, roles were reversed to the point where one of her male students commented that, in the negotiated unit, '*[The girls] kind of ruled over us*' (Mitch).

Fisette (2008) highlights the distinct personalities of her participants with, for example, Lilly being described as gregarious and outspoken, versus Dot who was very quiet and kept to herself. This is a reality in any group of students and is one of the greatest challenges associated with facilitating a physical education PAR pedagogy. Enright and O'Sullivan (2007, 2008) found that while the majority of participants were more than confident and willing to speak their minds in the group context some were very reluctant to speak out and contribute to group discussions about research and curriculum decision making processes. It took one of the girls, Grace, five months to feel confident participating in group conversations. During this period she was more than happy to engage in the PAR tasks and showed a clear desire to be part of the PAR process, on one occasion even requesting that Eimear interview her individually about the PAR process and the changes she would like to effect. Grace, more than any other student, highlighted for us the necessity to be pedagogically sensitive to the silenced voices in the classes we work with. She shared that she did not feel comfortable contributing in the group because sometimes it took her a little longer to think about what she wanted to say than the other girls and the conversation moved too quickly for her, and she was afraid that she 'didn't have the right things to say then at the right time'. There is also clearly a lesson to be learned here with regard to research design. If our research had been of a shorter duration, we might never have come to hear the voices of the reluctant/resistant/shy/marginalized participants such as Grace. Inspired by an appreciation of the absolute necessity of hearing students like Grace and Dot, Macbeath *et al.* (2003) remind us of the dangers of further disenfranchizing those students who arguably have the most to gain from student voice-orientated work:

> There is evidence that those pupils who are most articulate in the language of the school are both more likely to shape the decisions of their peers and to be

'heard' by teachers – leaving others, ironically, feeling disenfranchized in an initiative specifically designed to empower them. What we have to remember is that consultation processes can sometimes reflect rather than challenge existing divisive practices in schools. (Macbeath *et al.*, 2003, p. 42)

All students' voices deserve attention: contesting voices, coherent voices, loud and articulate voices, and particularly those that are muted. It is the responsibility of those who work to support any PAR process to engage all students in dialogue. This can take considerable time and patience, and has implications also for research design (i.e. time spent working with students to allow for and assess impact on all students).

Another important voice, which should not be allowed to be usurped in our effort to attend to student voice is that of the teacher. Bragg (2007) asserts, 'There are clear contradictions in insisting on listening to pupil voice when teacher voice has been undermined' (p. 670). It is arguably impossible for teachers to listen to student voice if their voices have been muted. If teachers are to take on new patterns of interaction and new pedagogies, they will need others (principals, students, staff) to support and listen to them. To undertake student voice-orientated work confidently and wholeheartedly in the first place 'teachers need to feel that they have a voice, that they are listened to, and that their views matter' (Rudduck, 2007, p. 600).

School structures/cultures and sustainability

Mitra (2007) reminds us that 'often the institutional and normative features of schooling prevent substantial student power', suggesting that a supportive school context is key to enabling and sustaining student voice-orientated change efforts (p. 742). It is important that teachers and students feel supported in pursuing awakening curricular experiences. It is equally important that efforts are made at creating structures that support the sustainability and extension of student voice-orientated initiatives. Kathy Armour has raised a significant and challenging question for those who engage in participatory ways with students: 'Who nurtures the shoots?' (personal communication, 17 June 2008). Outside and beyond our student-led reform efforts, how, if at all, are students' increasing curiosity, self-confidence, self-efficacy, motivation and love of learning nurtured? Equally important is that the teachers' foray into and sustainability of their new role is nurtured. Strategic efforts need to be made to 'break the crusts of conventionalized and routine consciousness within schools' (Dewey, 1954, cited in Greene, 1993, p. 211) and kindle the flames that a PAR pedagogy has ignited.

Establishing and investing in long-term relationships with student participants is necessary for all adult allies who wish to support a PAR pedagogy. Bland and Atweh (2007) remind us that 'it takes time for students to adjust to the novelty of having their voices respected in meaningful collaboration with adults' (p. 344). Teachers need to be willing to invest this time, because developing meaningful collaborative relationships with students will take longer than telling students exactly what to do. Researchers, too, need to commit their time, as PAR is arguably more demanding than conventional educational research designs. It takes time 'to touch teachers and reach students', but that is what educational research is or at least should be about (Armour, 2006, p. 470). Experience tells us that physical education teachers and researchers have heart, and care deeply about student experience and learning. PAR is one avenue through which teachers and researchers can channel their 'ethic of caring' (Noddings, 1984) in a way that 'challenges young people to imagine a better world and to try out ways of making it so' (Beane, 1998, p. 11).

Benefits for students, teachers and researchers

Students

The benefits of engaging with students through a PAR pedagogy far outweigh the challenges for teachers and students alike. Student voice initiatives in schools have had a positive impact on curriculum, teaching and learning, assessment practices and student–teacher relationships (Soo Hoo, 1993; Fielding, 2004), leading to enhanced student outcomes and school climate (Mitra, 2004). There is a wealth of research in the general education literature that documents the potential benefits of student voice efforts for the students involved. At a classroom level student participation in educational decision making has been documented as resulting in increased student engagement and academic achievement (Oldfather, 1995; Rudduck and Flutter, 2000); greater student attachment to schooling (Newman, 1981); increased sense of agency, autonomy, competency, belonging, empowerment and concern for others (Oldfather, 1995; Mitra, 2004, 2007; Rudduck, 2007); increased self-confidence and commitment to learning (Soo Hoo, 1993; Rudduck, 2007); and the development of students' problem-solving, public-speaking, negotiation and listening skills (Mitra, 2007).

The benefits noted by students in our profiled studies included: increased opportunities to be physically active (Enright and O'Sullivan, 2007; The Pres Girls, Enright and O'Sullivan, 2008; Oliver *et al.*, 2009; Oliver and Hamzeh, 2010); opportunities to name and challenge inequities students identify around physical activity provision and participation (Enright and O'Sullivan, 2007; Fisette, 2008; The Pres Girls, Enright and O'Sullivan, 2008; Oliver *et al.*, 2009; Oliver and Hamzeh, 2010); opportunities to effect real change (Enright and O'Sullivan, 2007; Fisette, 2008; The Pres Girls, Enright and O'Sullivan, 2008; Oliver *et al.*, 2009; Oliver and Hamzeh, 2010) and ownership over physical activity practices (Enright and O'Sullivan, 2007; McMahon, 2007; The Pres Girls, Enright and O'Sullivan, 2008).

All of the students in the profiled PAR studies were encouraged to be critical analysts of the communities and societies in which they live. Students therefore began to expose the structures that constructed their relationship with education, physical education, physical activity and, importantly, between themselves and others, collectively developing an understanding of issues that were real to them. The opportunity to name and challenge the inequities around and barriers to their physical education and physical activity participation, as well as the opportunity to effect real change was ultimately received excitedly and respectfully by the student researchers. This took time. They felt ownership over their physical activity practices. Through this process they also became researchers of teaching and learning. Debra, one of Enright and O'Sullivan's (2007) participants, clearly highlights an important benefit she attached to the PAR curriculum:

> We learned about learning . . . and about teaching PE and about the things you have to think about when you're teaching . . . and as well how you know that you've learned something that's important too.

Part of what Debra alludes to here is meta-learning, 'a process of always monitoring the assumptions, hidden rules, and expectations of formal and informal educational processes' (Kincheloe, 2007, p. 758). In this sense a PAR pedagogy represents an awakening curriculum (Greene, 1993, p. 220).

Teachers

Many of the benefits students accrue from their engagement in student voice activities are also benefits for teachers, but there are also many additional benefits for teachers who engage in student voice work. Flutter (2007) highlights what she calls a simple and profound rationale for teachers to engage with student voice:

> It affords teachers an opportunity to refocus their attention on what really matters – learners and how they learn best. The cornerstone of teacher development lies in extending teachers' knowledge and understanding to enable them to practise their art more effectively: pupil voice strategies are one way in which teachers can go about extending their knowledge and understanding, through investigation. (p. 345)

Engaging with student voice has the capacity to raise significant and challenging professional questions for physical educators. Oliver and colleagues (Oliver *et al.*, 2009) contend, 'When girls are given the opportunity to critically study barriers to their physical activity, researchers and teachers can begin to see beyond the dominant discourse' (p. 108). Once the girls in their study had made their physical education teacher aware of the problems they were having being active at recess, the physical education teacher began to pay more attention to the dynamics between boys and girls during recess. Seeing the dominant discourse is not enough however. Teachers do need to be willing to 'review familiar beliefs and practices that have provided or that provide the promise of security and stability' (Rudduck, 2007, p. 607), but they also need to work together with their students to understand and challenge dominant, often harmful, physical activity and physical education discourses. The physical education teacher in Oliver and colleagues' (Oliver *et al.*, 2009) study went this extra step, by playing an active role in supporting girls' physical activity during recess and encouraging others to do so. Róisín, the teacher in Enright and O'Sullivan's (2007, 2008) research, highlighted the impact her attempt to respond to the students had on her teaching and her extra-curricular scheduling:

I'm definitely going to incorporate more choice, less competitive team games and for extra-curricular I want to help coordinate the club they have designed because otherwise all they'd really have is basketball. You get sick of fighting with them all the time. I want them to be active and what I've learned from this experience is that they will be when we listen to them and give them more ownership over their experiences. I think it's a lot about ownership. This is something I have started to do already with my other classes as well.

Researchers

Educational researchers, too, have much to gain from recognizing student voice and agency within a PAR framework. Morrow and Richards (1996) contend that 'the biggest ethical challenge for researchers working with children is the disparities in power and status between adults and children' (p. 98). They suggest 'Using methods which are non-invasive, non-confrontational and participatory, and which encourage children to interpret their own data, might be one step forward in diminishing the ethical problems of imbalanced power relationships between researchers and researched at the point of data collection and interpretation' (Morrow and Richards, 1996, p. 100). Participatory research is without doubt a time- and thought-intensive design for researchers. Educational researchers who espouse empowerment of students in their own learning, however, have a responsibility to support students in achieving their goals and in helping them to change the system in ways highlighted by their engagement in a critique of their worlds. PAR facilitates researchers in developing an understanding of the meaning of students' lives and social worlds as understood by the students themselves.

Conclusion

While there is much hope in this chapter, there is also an acknowledgement of the complexities involved in pursuing critical, collaborative, activist research with youth. A PAR pedagogy is an informed, methodologically rigorous, productive process that requires extensive facilitation. There are many questions that emerge from this chapter that should be seriously considered by all adult allies who hope to facilitate students' participation in a PAR pedagogy: Who frames the research? Who names the problem? Who is considered expert? How are participants selected? Which students are heard? Whose voices are privileged? Whose voices are ignored, marginalized or silenced? Do we make a conscious effort to seek out the silences, the outliers, the dissidents, and the privileged? Is the teacher's voice heard? What is the role of the teacher's voice in a PAR pedagogy? How do we listen to student voice? What kind of strategies do we use to help students articulate their feelings, understandings, ideas and hopes? Whose language is privileged and whose is marginalized? Whose knowledge is privileged and whose is marginalized? How do we create a safe space where students can debate with each other and with adult allies, and feel confident taking multiple, sometimes opposing, sometimes contradictory positions? How do we work to help students contextualize their understanding and experiences? Do we hold high expectations for all students? How do we respond to what students say? How, where and by whom is change conceptualized and enacted? How does the school, community, social, cultural context challenge, distort or support our student voice-orientated initiatives? How are teachers who facilitate a PAR pedagogy supported in terms of time, space, resources, emotional and intellectual support? Is consent a one-off event or is it renegotiated as the research proceeds? Is student voice actively promoted in how other subjects, the school, the community etc. are organized? Who is given the opportunity to listen to what students have to say?

Although many of these questions have been considered in this chapter, they remain significant questions that should be considered by anyone who wishes to support a physical education PAR pedagogy. The answers to these questions will determine the degree and nature of student participation, student voice, student choice and student engagement in any PAR pedagogy, and impact the relevance and depth of student learning.

Physical education teachers and researchers need to have the courage and conviction to explore with their students the nature of curriculum content and the strategies for delivering content that would engage students more meaningfully in physical education and physical activity outside of school, as well as developing awareness and advocacy for their voice in their educational experiences. Young people, when provided with guidance, encouragement and support, can and will rise to the challenge and take ownership of their learning, and doing so can be a positive, energizing and exciting experience for both teacher and student. However, the transition to 'carving a new order of experience' in physical education will challenge students and teachers, and both need support in persevering beyond the transition and the novelty of initial excitement.

Implications

A PAR pedagogy is a profoundly practical response to student disengagement, one of the greatest professional challenges that many contemporary physical educators face (Enright and O'Sullivan, 2007). One implication of this work is the need for professional development of teachers with opportunities to see and hear how others have negotiated curriculum and the challenges and benefits for them and their students. Another implication is the need for the process of student voice-orientated work to be studied more carefully. We need to work harder to understand how adult allies and schools can facilitate sharing decision making with students. We also need to work to understand the key impacts of such negotiations on student learning, and what is perhaps gained and lost in learning in and through a PAR pedagogy. Perhaps this chapter might be a catalyst to others to engage in this exciting and important research agenda.

Notes

1 Quotation originally crafted by Maxine Greene and drawn upon more recently by Rudduck and Flutter (2000).

2 The PE-PAYS (Physical Education, Physical Activity and Youth Sport) Forum is a research conference hosted annually by the PE-PAYS Research Centre at the University of Limerick. Further information on the PE-PAYS Research Centre is available at www.ul.ie/pepays.

References

Armour, K. (2006) 'The way to a teacher's heart: narrative research in physical education', in D. Kirk, D. Macdonald and M. O'Sullivan (eds) *Handbook of Physical Education* (pp. 467–486). London: Sage.

Aronowitz, S. and Giroux, H. (1985) *Education Under Siege*. South Hadley, MA: Bergin & Garvey.

Azzarito, L. and Solomon, M. (2005) 'A reconceptualization of physical education: the intersection of gender/race/social class', *Sport, Education and Society*, 10: 25–47.

Azzarito, L., Solmon, M.A. and Harrison, L. (2006) '". . . if I had a choice, I would . . .": A feminist poststructural perspective on girls in physical education', *Research Quarterly for Exercise and Sport*, 77 (2): 222–239.

Bakhtin, M. (1981) *The Dialogical Imagination* (ed. M. Holquist). Austin: University of Texas Press.

Beane, J.A. (1997) *Curriculum Integration: Designing the Core of Democratic Education*. Williston: Teachers College Press.

Beane, J.A. (1998) 'Reclaiming a democratic purpose for education', *Educational Leadership*, 56 (2): 8–11.

Bland, D. and Atweh, B. (2007) 'Students as researchers: engaging students' voices in PAR', *Educational Action Research*, 15 (3): 337–349.

Boomer, C. (1992) 'Negotiating the curriculum', in C. Boomer, N. Lester, C. Onore and J. Cook (eds) *Negotiating the Curriculum: Educating for the 21st Century*. London: The Falmer Press.

Boomer, G., Lester, N., Onore, C. and Cook, J. (eds) (1992) *Negotiating the Curriculum: Educating for the 21st Century*. London: The Falmer Press.

Bragg, S. (2007) '"It's not about systems, it's about relationships": building a listening culture in a primary school', in D. Thiessen and A. Cook-Sather (eds) *International Handbook of Student Experience in Elementary and Secondary School* (pp. 659–681). Dordrecht: Springer.

Brooker R. and McDonald, D. (1999) 'Did we hear you? Issues of student voice in curriculum innovation', *Journal of Curriculum Studies*, 31 (1): 83–97.

Burrows, L., Wright, J. and Jungersen-Smith, J. (2002) '"Measure your belly." New Zealand children's construction of health and fitness', *Journal of Teaching in Physical Education*, 22: 39–48.

Carlson, T.B. (1995) 'We hate gym: student alienation from physical education', *Journal of Teaching in Physical Education*, 14: 467–477.

Chaplain, R. (1996) 'Making a strategic withdrawal: disengagement and self-worth protection in male students', in J. Rudduck, R. Chaplain and G. Wallace (eds) *School Improvement – What Can Students Tell Us?* (pp. 101–115). London: David Fulton Publishers.

Christensen, P. and Prout, A. (2002) 'Working with ethical symmetry in social research with children', *Childhood*, 9 (4): 477–497.

Clarke, G. (2006) 'Sexuality and physical education', in D. Kirk, D. Macdonald and M. O'Sullivan (eds) *Handbook of Physical Education* (pp. 723–740). London: Sage.

Cook-Sather, A. (2002) 'Authorizing students' perspectives: towards trust, dialogue, and change in education', *Educational Researcher*, 31 (4): 3–14.

Cook-Sather, A. (2007) 'Translating researchers: re-imagining the work of investigating students' experiences in school', in D. Thiessen and A. Cook-Sather (eds) *International Handbook of Student Experience in Elementary and Secondary School* (pp. 829–873). Dordrecht: Springer.

Cothran, D.J. and Ennis, C.D. (1999) 'Alone in a crowd: meeting students' needs for relevance and connection in urban high school physical education', *Journal of Teaching in Physical Education*, 18: 234–247.

Devis-Devis, J. (2006) 'Socially critical research perspectives in physical education', in D. Kirk, D. Macdonald and M. O'Sullivan (eds) *Handbook of Physical Education* (pp. 37–59). London: Sage.

Dyson, B. (1995) 'Students' voices in two alternative elementary physical education programs', *Journal of Teaching in Physical Education*, 14: 394–407.

Dyson, B. (2001) 'Cooperative learning in an elementary school physical education program', *Journal of Teaching in Physical Education*, 20: 264–281.

Dyson, B. (2002) 'The implementation of cooperative learning in an elementary school physical education program', *Journal of Teaching in Physical Education*, 22: 69–85.

Ellsworth, E. (1989) 'Why doesn't this feel empowering? Working through the repressive myths of critical pedagogy', *Harvard Educational Review*, 59 (3): 297–324.

Ennis, C. (1999) 'Creating a culturally relevant curriculum for disengaged girls', *Sport Education and Society*, 4 (1): 31–49.

Ennis, C. (2003) 'Using curriculum to enhance student learning', in S.J. Silverman and C.D. Ennis (eds) *Student Learning in Physical Education – Applying Research to Enhance Instruction* (2nd edn) (pp. 109–127). Champaign, IL: Human Kinetics.

Ennis, C.D., Cothran, D.J., Davidson, K.S., Loftus, S.J., Owens, L., Swanson, L. and Hopsicker, P. (1997) 'Implementing a curriculum within a context of fear and disengagement', *Journal of Teaching in Physical Education*, 17 (1): 52–71.

Enright, E. and O'Sullivan, M. (2007) 'Can I do it in my pyjamas? Negotiating a physical education curriculum with teenage girls', paper presented at the British Educational Research Association Annual Conference, London, England.

Enright, E. and O'Sullivan, M. (2008) '"Cos that's what I thought ye wanted to hear": participatory methods and research agendas in physical education research', paper presented at the Researching Children's Worlds Conference, Galway, February.

Erickson, E. and Schultz, J. (1992) 'Students' experience of the curriculum', in P.W. Chickenson (ed.) *Handbook of Research on Curriculum* (pp. 465–485). New York: Macmillan.

Evans, J. (2006) 'Social class and physical education', in D. Kirk, D. Macdonald and M. O'Sullivan (eds) *Handbook of Physical Education* (pp. 796–809). London: Sage.

Fielding, M. (2004) 'Transformative approaches to student voice: theoretical underpinnings, recalcitrant realities', *British Educational Research Journal*, 30 (2): 295–311.

Fine, M. (1992) *Disruptive Voices: The Possibilities of Feminist Research*. Michigan: University of Michigan Press.

Fine, M., Roberts, R., Torre, M. and Upegui, D. (2001) 'Participatory Action Research behind bars', *Critical Psychology: The International Journal of Critical Psychology*, 2: 145–157.

Fine, M., Torre, M., Burns, A. and Payne, Y. (2007) 'Youth research/participatory methods for reform', in D. Thiessen and A. Cook-Sather (eds) *International Handbook of Student Experience in Elementary and Secondary School* (pp. 805–828). Dordrecht: Springer.

Fisette, J. (2008) 'A mind/body exploration of adolescent girls' strategies and barriers to their success or survival in physical education', unpublished doctoral dissertation, University of Massachusetts, Amherst.

Fitzgerald, H. (2006) 'Disability and physical education', in D. Kirk, D. Macdonald and M. O'Sullivan (eds) *Handbook of Physical Education* (pp. 752–767). London: Sage.

Fletcher, A. (2004) *Meaningful Student Involvement: Research Guide*. Washington: Soundout!/The Freechild Project.

Flintoff, A. and Scraton, S. (2005) 'Gender and PE', in K. Green and K. Hardman (eds) *Essential Issues in Physical Education*. London, Sage.

Flintoff, A. and Scraton, S. (2006) 'Girls and physical education', in D. Kirk, D. Macdonald and M. O'Sullivan (eds) *Handbook of Physical Education* (pp. 767–784). London: Sage.

Flutter, J. (2007) 'Pupil voice and teacher development', *Educational Review*, special edition on Teacher Development, 18 (3): 343–354.

Freire, P. (1994) *Pedagogy of Hope*. New York: Continuum.

Gard, M. (2006) 'More art than science? Boys, masculinities and physical education research', in D. Kirk, D. Macdonald and M. O'Sullivan (eds) *Handbook of Physical Education* (pp. 784–796). London: Sage.

Giroux, H. (1997) *Pedagogy and Politics of Hope: Theory, Culture and Schooling*. Oxford: Westview Press.

Giroux, H. and Simon, R. (1989) *Popular Culture, Schooling and Everyday Life*. South Hadley, MA: Bergin & Garvey Press.

Glasby, T. and Macdonald, D. (2004) 'Negotiating the curriculum: challenging the social relationships in teaching', in J. Wright, D. Macdonald and L. Burrows (eds) *Critical Inquiry and Problem Solving in Physical Education* (pp. 133–145). London/New York: Routledge.

Gore, J. (1992) 'What we can do for you! What can "we" do for "you"? Struggling over empowerment in critical and feminist pedagogy', in C. Luke and J. Gore (eds) *Feminisms and Critical Pedagogy*. New York: Routledge.

Graham, G. (1995) 'Physical education through students' eyes and in students' voices: implications for teachers and researchers', *Journal of Teaching in Physical Education*, 14 (4): 478–482.

Greene, M. (1993) 'Diversity and inclusion: toward a curriculum for human beings', *Teachers College Record*, 95 (2): 211–221.

Greene, M. (1995) *Releasing the Imagination: Essays on Education, the Arts and Social Change*. San Francisco: Jossey-Bass Publishers.

Greene, M. (1997) 'Teaching as possibility: a light in dark times', *Journal of Pedagogy, Pluralism and Practice*, 1: 1–10.

Greene, M. (2000) 'Imagining futures: the public school and possibilities', *Journal of Curriculum Studies*; 32 (2): 267–280.

Hamzeh, M. (2007) 'A deveiling narrative inquiry: entry and agency in body stories of Muslim girls', unpublished PhD thesis.

Hargreaves, A. (1994) *Changing Teachers, Changing Times: Teachers' Work and Culture in the Postmodern Age*. London: Cassell.

Harrison, L. and Belcher, D. (2006) 'Race and ethnicity in physical education', in D. Kirk, D. Macdonald and M. O'Sullivan (eds) *Handbook of Physical Education* (pp. 740–752). London: Sage.

Hastie, P. (1998) 'The participation and perception of girls during a unit of Sport Education', *Journal of Teaching in Physical Education*, 18: 157–71.

Hastie, P. (2000) 'An ecological analysis of a Sport Education season', *Journal of Teaching in Physical Education*, 19: 355–373.

Heilbrun, C.G. (1988) *Writing a Woman's Life* (1st edn). New York: Norton.

Hodgkin, R. (1998) 'Partnership with pupils', *Children UK* (Summer).

Hopple, C. and Graham, G. (1995) 'What children feel, think and know about physical fitness testing', *Journal of Teaching in Physical Education*, 14: 408–417.

Hunter, L. (2002) 'Young people, physical education and transition: understanding practices in the middle years of schooling', unpublished doctoral thesis, School of Human Movement Studies, Brisbane, University of Queensland.

Kincheloe, J. (2007) 'Clarifying the purpose of engaging students as researchers', in D. Thiessen and A. Cook-Sather (eds) *International Handbook of Student Experience in Elementary and Secondary Education* (pp. 745–775). Dordrecht: Springer.

Kinchin, G.D. and O'Sullivan, M. (1999) 'Making high school physical education meaningful for students', *Journal of Physical Education, Recreation, and Dance*, 70 (5): 40–44.

Lalik, R. and Oliver, K. (2005) '"The Beauty Walk" as a social space for messages about the female body: toward transformative collaboration', in P. Bettis and N. Adams (eds) *Geographies of Girlhood: Identity In-between*. Mahwah, NJ: Lawrence Erlbaum Associates, Inc.

Lather, P. (1991) *Getting Smart: Feminist Research and Pedagogy with/in the Postmodern*. New York: Routledge.

Lather, P. (1992) 'Critical frames in educational research: feminist and poststructural perspectives', *Theory into Practice*, 31 (2): 87–99.

Macbeath, J., Demetriou, H., Rudduck, J. and Myers, K. (2003) *Consulting Pupils: a Toolkit for Teachers*. Cambridge: Pearson.

Macdonald, D. (2003) 'Curriculum change and the postmodern world: is the school curriculum-reform movement an anachronism?', *Journal of Curriculum Studies*, 35 (2): 139–149.

McLaren, P.L. (1999) 'A pedagogy of possibility: reflecting upon Paulo Freire's politics of education', *Educational Researcher*, 28 (2): 49–54.

McMahon, E. (2007) '"You don't feel like ants and giants": student involvement in negotiating the physical education curriculum', unpublished master's thesis, University of Limerick.

Mitra, D.L. (2004) 'The significance of students: can increasing "student voice" in schools lead to gains in youth development?', *Teachers College Record*, 106 (4): 651–688.

Mitra, D.L. (2007) 'Student voice in school reform: from listening to leadership', in D. Thiessen and A. Cook-Sather (eds) *International Handbook of Student Experience in Elementary and Secondary School* (pp. 727–745). Dordrecht: Springer.

Morrow, V. and Richards, M. (1996) 'The ethics of social research with children: an overview', *Children and Society*, 10: 90–105.

Newman, F. (1981) 'Reducing student alienation in high schools: implications of theory', *Harvard Educational Review*, 51: 546–564.

Nieuwenhuys, O. (2004) 'Participatory Action Research in the majority world', in S. Fraser, V. Lewis, S. Ding, M. Kellett and S. Robinson (eds) *Doing Research with Children and Young People*. London: Sage.

Nilges, L. (2006) 'Feminist strands, perspectives and methodology for research in physical education', in D. Kirk, D. Macdonald and M. O'Sullivan (eds) *Handbook of Physical Education* (pp. 76–95). London: Sage.

Noddings, N. (1984) *Caring: A Feminine Approach to Ethics and Moral Education*. Berkeley, CA: University of California Press.

Oldfather, P. (1995) 'Songs "come back most to them": students' experiences as researchers', *Theory into Practice*, 34 (2): 131.

Oliver, K.L. and Hamzeh, M. (2010) '"The boys won't let us play": 5th grade *mestizas* challenge physical activity discourse at school', *Research Quarterly for Exercise and Sport*, 81 (1): 39–55.

Oliver, K.L. and Lalik, R. (2000) *Bodily Knowledge: Learning about Equity and Justice with Adolescent Girls*. New York: Peter Lang Publishing.

Oliver, K.L. and Lalik, R. (2001) 'The body as school curriculum: learning with adolescent girls', *Journal of Curriculum Studies*, 33 (3): 303–333.

Oliver, K.L. and Lalik, R. (2004a) 'Critical inquiry on the body in girls' physical education classes: a critical poststructural analysis', *Journal of Teaching in Physical Education*, 23 (2): 162–195.

Oliver, K.L. and Lalik, R. (2004b) '"The Beauty Walk, this ain't my topic": learning about critical inquiry with adolescent girls', *The Journal of Curriculum Studies*, 36 (5): 555–586.

Oliver, K.L., Hamzeh, M. and McCaughtry, N. (2009) '"Girly girls can play games/Las niñas pueden jugar tambien": co-creating a curriculum of possibilities with 5th grade girls', *Journal of Teaching in Physical Education*, 28 (1): 90–110.

Penney, D. (2006) 'Curriculum construction and change', in D. Kirk, D. Macdonald and M. O'Sullivan (eds) *Handbook of Physical Education* (pp. 565–579). London: Sage.

Penney, D. and Evans, J. (1999) *Politics, Policy and Practice in Physical Education*. London: Routledge.

Pope, C.V. and Grant, B.C. (1996) 'Student experiences in Sport Education', *Waikato Journal of Education*, 2: 103–118.

Pres Girls (The), Enright, E. and O'Sullivan, M. (2008) '"It's our club and it's rapid": our experience of designing an after school physical activity club', paper presented at the PE PAYS Research Forum, June.

Reason, P. (1998) 'Three approaches to participative inquiry', in N.K. Denzin and Y.S. Lincoln (eds) *Strategies of Qualitative Inquiry* (pp. 261–291). London: Sage.

Rudduck, J. (2007) 'Student voice, student engagement, and school reform', in D. Thiessen and A. Cook-Sather (eds) *International Handbook of Student Experience in Elementary and Secondary School* (pp. 587–611). Dordrecht: Springer.

Rudduck, J. and Flutter, J. (2000) 'Pupil participation and pupil perspective: "carving a new order of experience"', *Cambridge Journal of Education*, 30 (1): 75–89.

Sandford, R. and Rich, E. (2006) 'Learners and popular culture', in D. Kirk, D. Macdonald and M. O'Sullivan (eds) *The Handbook of Physical Education*. London: Sage.

Shor, I. (1992) *Empowering Education: Critical Teaching for Social Change*. Chicago, IL: University of Chicago Press.

Shor, I. (1996) *When Students Have Power: Negotiating Authority in a Critical Pedagogy*. Chicago, IL: University of Chicago Press.

Smyth, J. (2007) 'Toward the pedagogically engaged school: listening to student voice as a positive response to disengagement and "dropping out"?', in D. Thiessen and A. Cook-Sather (eds) *International Handbook of Student Experience in Elementary and Secondary School* (pp. 635–658). Dordrecht: Springer.

Soo Hoo, S. (1993) 'Students as partners in research and restructuring schools', *Educational Forum*, 57 (Summer): 386–393.

Thiessen, D. (2007) 'Researching student experiences in elementary and secondary school: an evolving field of study', in D. Thiessen and A. Cook-Sather (eds) *International*

Handbook of Student Experience in Elementary and Secondary School (pp. 1–79). Dordrecht: Springer.

Thiessen, D. and Cook-Sather, A. (eds) (2007) *International Handbook of Student Experience in Elementary and Secondary School.* Dordrecht: Springer.

Tinning, R. and Fitzclarence, L. (1992) 'Postmodern youth culture and the crisis in Australian secondary school physical education', *Quest*, 44: 287–303.

Torre, M. and Fine, M. (2006) 'Researching and resisting: democratic policy research by and for youth', in S. Ginwright, P. Noguera and J. Cammarota (eds) *Beyond Resistance! Youth Activism and Community Change: New Democratic Possibilities for Practice and Policy for America's Youth* (pp. 269–285). New York: Routledge.

Udas, K. (1998) 'Participatory Action Research as critical pedagogy', *Systemic Practice and Action Research*, 11 (6).

Wright, J. (1996) 'The construction of complementarity in physical education', *Gender and Education*, 8 (1): 61–79.

Wright, J. (2003) 'Poststructuralist methodologies – the body, schooling and health', in J. Evans, B. Davies and J. Wright (eds) *Body Knowledge and Control: Studies in the Sociology of Physical Education and Health* (pp. 34–59). London: Routledge.

11 Got the picture?

Exploring student sport experiences using photography as voice

Clive C. Pope

This is my favourite. Just beautiful conditions, the nature of racing, and yea the thrill, the exhilaration, when you are sitting up in the blocks you're just waiting to race and yea, getting a high off it. And its always so good, but if you're losing by a lot obviously you are not going to exactly feel too good about it but usually just so high of the fact that you're racing. As long as you have a good race. You are really scared cos sometimes you hear what times other schools are pulling, but then you get down there and just like, they're not actually that flash, it's the numbers that scare you.

It was such beautiful conditions. The water was really cold and that was when our boys won their bronze. And they're good quite close friends of mine. We got in the van and started driving along and shouting out the window and

Figure 11.1 Nicola's first choice

cheering them. So its kind of an on the run shot actually. It's a great photo . . .
Just the scenery and all the perspective of racing.

Introduction

The meanings young people ascribe to sport can be positioned within sociological,
psychological, philosophical, historical and educational circles. It is the latter,
however, that frames this chapter. Considerable commentary on the edifying value
of sport portrays it as an educational experience. As a derivative of English public
schools, sport was seen as a vehicle to promote school spirit, foster identity and create student cohesion (Rees, 1990).

But how much have such original motives for the presence of sport in
education changed, especially through the eyes of today's young people? Any
effort to enhance the educational landscape should include paying credence
to the experiences youth have with sport. There is little known about how
young people consciously experience sport. This could be due in part to the way we
have communicated about such issues with young people. To enter into such discussion it is necessary to examine the role of sport within the current value
system of today's youth, using research methods that promote youth voices and
perspectives. More specifically, it is prudent to learn a bit more about the social,
historic and cultural features of youth culture and young people's relationship with
sport.

For researchers seeking to understand young people's experiences of sport and
physical education, visual options address in part the multi-sensory nature of
movement-based activities. Sparkes (2009) recently advocated for an acknowledgement of all the senses by researchers of sport and exercise. Sensual ethnographies that include smell, sound and taste would offer a fuller description of the sport
experience. Sparkes also concedes that 'given the current state of play regarding the
absence of many of the senses in ethnographies of sport and exercise, there may be
a case for "reintroducing" one sense at a time as part of a longer term project'
(p. 31). Any exploration of the sport experiences of young people through the visual
is, therefore, only partial.

While social research has traditionally been a 'word-based' discipline, the recent
arrival of affordable and user-friendly technology has allowed researchers to
employ visual technologies including photography, video, drawings, computer
graphics, scrapbooks, the internet or digital diaries. In the case of visual work there
has been limited attention to the way images hold great potential in helping us to
understand more about our social worlds and creating new credible social knowledge. Ethnography has usually described the sport experience from the outsider's
perspective (Sands, 2002). The ethnographer has documented what they have seen
and relayed their interpretation to the reader (Pope, 2009). What has been missing is
what was seen and subsequently communicated by the researched, the participants.
In essence there is a need to give participants a visual voice (Piper and Frankham,
2007).

Exploring the lived experience of something like rowing presents numerous challenges – what is experience in this sense? Can narrative alone do justice to the excitement, complexity and depth of such an activity as experienced by these young people? Will the juxtaposition of images to narrative enhance our understanding of such sport experiences? Such a multi-sensory phenomenon would seem elusive to any written description alone. Returning to Sparkes (2009):

> Even though it is necessary and desirable to engage senses other than the visual during the process of research and in the reporting of ethnographic studies, it is important to recognize the difficulties encountered when faced with deficient notational systems and limited linguistic descriptors for what we hear, taste, touch, and smell. It remains incredibly difficult to communicate what we experience through these senses to others.

The intention will therefore be to move beyond traditional notation and employ photography as a representation for voice.

Contextual background

Recent estimates indicate that 141,000 of 273,000, or 52 per cent, of New Zealand secondary school students participated in high school sport at a competitive level (New Zealand Secondary Schools Sports Council, 2007). Sport remains captive for many young people in Aotearoa New Zealand. The diversity of choice, organizational structure and the adult support, particularly from teachers, has collectively ensured that many young people in New Zealand receive positive sport experiences (Grant and Pope, 2007). In the past seven years there has been a significant increase in the number of top-level events on the secondary school sports calendar. As of 2007, 55 inter-school sports were offered at either North Island, South Island or nationally.

While many new sports have appeared on the sporting radar, some of the more traditional events have continued to thrive and expand. One such example is rowing. In 2007 approximately 3000 students competed competitively for their school. The culmination of the school rowing calendar is an annual week-long national inter-school regatta, known as the Maadi Cup. This event alternates between two world-class venues: Lake Karapiro in the North Island, home of New Zealand Rowing, and Lake Ruataniwha in the South Island. In 2007 a total of 106 of the 340 secondary schools competed in 394 races, culminating in 80 finals over the seven days. The event has evolved in its present form during the last 60 years and, as a result of the marked increase in numbers of students who have taken up rowing as a sport, organizers have had to cap the programme to retain the seven-day structure. Participants attend the Maadi regatta in the last week of March, but training and preparation often commence in late September of the previous year for many schools. Several lead-up events are available on both islands to allow schools to gauge their progress.

The purpose of this chapter is therefore two-fold. First, it sets out to explore the sport experiences of young people – in this case, in the sport of rowing. Second, it examines the process and potential of using photographs as representations of such experiences through the eyes of the participants.

Three senior secondary school rowers were each given a disposable camera with 24 frames available. Nicola Post, Dom Newton-Theunissen and Sam Jones have all rowed for at least two seasons for their school. Nicola rows in fours and eights, Sam rows single sculls, and Dom has rowed in doubles, fours and quadruple sculls. Their school, Hauraki Plains College, is a rural secondary school that services a large farming community in the central North Island of New Zealand. The college has a proud and distinguished history in rowing and, in particular, in the Maadi Cup (Irvine, 2008). These three students volunteered to participate in the project after consultation with Ngaire Harris, the school principal, and Mark Davies, the rowing coach. It should be noted that while this project was conducted under rigid ethics protocol, the students expressly asked for their true identities to be provided. Their preference was supported by the school principal and coach, whose real names and that of their school have also been included. I wish to acknowledge the contribution and support of the Hauraki Plains College participants.

Each rower was asked to document their experiences by photographing places, people or events that seemed significant to them. The overarching question they were asked to address was 'What does Maadi mean to me?' All three senior students attended a meeting prior to their regatta, where ideas and issues were explored, personal details were collected and ethical guidelines were stipulated. Prior consent was gained from the School Board of Trustees, the school principal and head rowing coach. The students were also encouraged to discuss their task with their parents. They were then asked to travel to a national secondary school rowing regatta armed with cameras, information sheets and ethics forms.

One week after their return to their school the rowers were asked to return the cameras for development and digitization. A full set of prints was returned, with a request to each student to reflect on all their photos before selecting and ranking their top five. Three one-to-one photo-elicitation discussions followed. All meetings I conducted were autodriven – a version of photo-elicitation where the conversation about selected images is led by the students (see Clark, 1999). Each chosen photo was discussed around the significance of the image, what it meant to the photographer, why it deserved its ranking, what memories it evoked and anything that the image reveals for them that may not be immediately obvious to other people viewing the picture.

Articulating youth experiences of sport

Youth are arguably active receivers and mediators of sporting experiences (Brettschneider and Heim, 1997). The developmental changes during youth can reveal disagreement between possibilities and responsibilities, between self-examination and social experimentation (Kleiber, 1983). The opportunity must also exist for individuals to learn about themselves, and this requires the freedom to explore and experiment. Can sport help alleviate the confusion that determines the individual's place in the social world? There is no doubt that their world is changing.

Several of the acknowledged changes are applicable to many countries. Although addressing an Australian and New Zealand perspective, Harris (2006) highlights issues that could be applied to many other countries:

> they are growing up in a time of more education, but fewer jobs; more choices, but less security; greater recognition of their participatory rights, but more complicated requirements of mutual obligation and demonstration of responsibility. (p. 222)

Youth society has become marked by a horizontal state – youth often look more within the peer group for leadership and guidance, role models, idols and answers to technological challenges that can often be addressed in the absence of adults. Patterns of relationships create the form of association between members. How those relationships are articulated portrays the youth culture. The group also has its own organizational structure that provides conditions and constraints. Youth cultures are built on values, beliefs, habits and the ways things are done. So it is vital that adults learn more about those factors to help enhance the lived experiences young people seek and receive.

Learning of the lived experiences of youth sports participants can reveal a great deal, but the pursuit of subjective knowledge has had a hard uphill struggle being accepted in wider research circles (Bain, 1995; Seippel, 2006). Because such reflections and descriptions are very personal, they cannot be generalized to wider populations. However, the richness of such descriptions can shed light on personal experience and on specific contexts.

Experience is that which appears at the junction of human existence and the material world, the terrain at the intersection of consciousness and external reality (Moustakas, 1994). An experience is a description of something we live through. Even more, it is exploring the meaning of the expressions of something we experience – in this case sport. The idea is that, through description and meaning, we can come to know more about what something means to us. A sport experience, like many other life experiences, reveals a clustering of emotions, intentions and thoughts (Csikszentmihalyi, 1997) wrapped together like wires within an electrical cable. The outcomes of such experiences can be enjoyment, learning, control, concentration, harmony, attention or satisfaction, to name a few. Of course, sport experiences can also be quite negative and lasting. Too often young people are subjected to adult agendas, ridicule, rejection, harassment and exclusion (Freeman, 1997; Andrews, 1999; Grenfell and Rinehart, 2003). When these behaviours are in evidence the outcome for participants is often disengagement. For many young people sport has the potential to produce positive outcomes, the challenge is through what means and in which contexts could or should they occur, and who gets to achieve such outcomes? By focusing on the means it is pertinent to revisit the process that is often associated with understanding experience. Learning of sport experiences can mean collaboration between the participant and the researcher, traditionally through words but more recently through the use of images.

The visual turn in qualitative research

Like its quantitative equivalent, qualitative research has traditionally featured numbers and words. Howard Becker, a long-time advocate for visual representation, argues that the social sciences have lagged behind the natural sciences in the use of visual materials. The natural sciences have embraced visual derivations like X-ray magnetic resonance imaging and three-dimensional computer modelling, as well as using visual tools to advance forensics. He has presented several arguments for the inclusion of visual elements in ethnography. Becker's argument (2000) is founded on the claim that 'photographs, more aptly than words, display social phenomena in context' (p. 333). Advocacy for visual exploration as a means for research has been offset by a reluctance of many researchers to move from the relatively structured and refined characteristics of scientific research methods to the more intuitive, subjective and arguably disordered visual options (Prosser, 1998; Pole, 2004; Stanczak, 2007).

There has also been an associated suspicion of images (Banks, 2001). For many researchers, visual research is just too messy. For example, Emmison (2004) laments 'it is not putting too fine a point on it to state that the field of visual research stands as one of the most disorganized and theoretically inchoate in the social science academy' (p. 249). Jon Wagner (2007) reminds us that image-based research has a pretty ragged edge, an uncertain centre, and a bit more complexity and ambiguity than many disciplinary scholars would like. Such reluctance is disappointing as scholarship is diminished when we overlook the power of seeing in its many guises when trying to understand culture and social life.

However, despite the inertia demonstrated by many social researchers, there is a growing and renewed interest in the adoption of visual methods within the social sciences. The ubiquity of images in people's everyday lives heightens the potential of images as an alternative orientation to how we communicate. This is not surprising because 'when we plan, analyze, imagine, think, or critique, our thoughts are associated with and largely constituted by images' (Bruner, 1984, p. 41). The visual medium is experiencing something of a renaissance due in part to the advances in technology, digitization and the internet. The potential of visual research methods is increasingly being realized as a means to fill the gaps that scientific research have revealed. This awakening addresses a more holistic approach to research as pictures 'fuel our sociological and anthropological imaginations, providing another way to capture, translate, and render the synthetic totality that is social life and culture' (Margolis, 1990, p. 374).

The earlier work of Rob Walker advocated the adoption of photographic method because it 'touches on the limitations of language, especially language used for descriptive purposes. In using photographs the potential exists, however elusive the achievement, to find ways of thinking about social life that escape the traps set by language' (Walker, 1993, p. 72). Walker became a strong advocate for visual research, arguing that images 'are not just adjuncts to print, but carry heavy cultural traffic on their own' (p. 91).

Pink (2003) proposes that, irrespective of the discipline or sub-discipline, four key areas require attention from visual researchers. The first is the context in which the image was produced. The second relates to the content of the image, and connected directly to this is the third area, the contexts in and subjectivities through which images are viewed. The materiality and agency of images is the final area. Collectively these four areas should help the researcher to understand the meanings associated with the image either in combination or in total but not individually.

The increasing use of visual social research can be partly attributed to the affordability and improved reproduction of digital options, along with a growing interest in visual culture (Jenkings, Woodward and Winter, 2008). Moreover, there has been a repositioning of the image from a realist form of reality to a more subjective version that is marked by ambiguity and promiscuity (McQuire, 1998). The fluidity and subjective nature of images can create challenges for any researcher working in the visual domain (Brace-Govan, 2007). The ambiguity of the image can be a valuable learning tool as multiple meanings often associated with images can be utilized, as Walker and Weidel (1985) explain:

> Ambiguity [of the photograph] can be turned to a strength when it is used to elicit responses or communicate complex messages . . . to get [interviewees] thinking and talking reflectively . . . what is important about the picture is determined, in part at least, by what people say about it. (p. 143)

Over the past decade numerous texts have emerged exploring visual theory and practice methods of social science research (Emmison and Smith, 2000; Pink, 2007; Rose, 2007; Stanczak, 2007) and more specifically within education (Coles and Nixon, 1998; Prosser, 2007; Deppeler, Moss and Agbenyega, 2008; Moss, 2008; Thomson, 2008b).

One of the first photographic studies in education research was conducted by Jon Prosser (Prosser, 1992). In his ethnographic study of a British comprehensive school Prosser followed the amalgamation of three schools into one institution. Prosser offers his experiences to 'establish a primitive benchmark of practice' (p. 397), in the hope that successive projects would lead to the derivation of appropriate guidelines for the use of photography in such forms of qualitative research. While his experiences led to a three-phase heuristic for such work, there has been no real evolution of process. A rare exception to the dearth of photographic projects about schools and education is Coles and Nixon's (1998) collaborative exploration of life in school. This revealing study of the microcosm of schools in Boston is an isolated example of how images can inform. In fact the presence of images such as photographs and their subsequent analysis have suffered from academic conservatism within education circles. Such a status is not only attributed to education. Many of the wider social sciences, including anthropology and sociology (which have traditionally employed images), have failed to fully embrace the potentialities of visual options.

Photo-elicitation

Visual ethnography has evolved from a documentary style of reporting research towards the polysemic (or having multiple meanings) properties of the image with its many and varied interpretations (Schwartz, 1989; Harper, 2002, 2003). Because of its polysemic nature, photo-elicitation has enjoyed a rise in popularity among researchers as the voice of the subject has not only been included in the research process but also accorded authority. Curry (1986) advocates that photo-elicitation can be a useful tool to examine 'the techniques, norms and values found in sport subcultures' (p. 204). To understand the culture of rowing, its participants and, more specifically, the experiences they seek and accrue, such a research technique holds great potential.

Photo-elicitation interviews (PEIs) have involved 'using photographs to invoke comments, memory, and discussion in the course of semi-structured interviews' (Banks, 2001, p. 87). As a method it can be tracked back to the groundbreaking work of the Colliers (Collier and Collier, 1986), and in particular John Colliers' earlier work on mental health in the 1950s. Collier discovered that the adoption and inclusion of photographs extracted significantly more information than interviews based solely on dialogue.

> In the photo-elicitation interview the informant and the interviewer discuss photographs the researcher has made in the setting, giving the interview a concrete point of reference. A phenomenological sense is gained as the informant explains what the objects in the photograph mean, where they have come from, and what might be missing. This method provides a way in which the interview can move from the concrete (as represented by the literal objects in the image) to the socially abstract (what the objects in the photograph mean to the individual being interviewed). (Harper, 1984, p. 21)

As Grady (2008) observes, the interpretation of photographs requires a greater degree of inference 'because the analytic frame that is present in the interview schedule, or the chronological account of the ethnographer's observations, or the storytelling strategy of the person being interviewed, is not found in pictures' (p. 12). The exchange of meaning and experience is at the heart of photo-elicitation. While the creator of the photograph may have a specific interpretation of the image, dialogue and further interpretation with the researcher can take the image and its meaning to new places that were previously unexplored.

Rather than presenting photographs to interviewees for interpretation and discussion (as introduced by the Colliers) a more recent method has evolved where the photos that inform the discussion are taken by the interviewees. This version of photo-elicitation is termed *autodriving*, whereby the interview is driven by the interviewees who are seeing and reflecting on their own experiences and behaviours. Autodriving has become a popular method to work with young people (Clark, 1999). The outcome of such an interview can be a negotiated interpretation as researcher and photographer reflect and exchange their impressions of the images. The technique of autodriving was selected as a preferred strategy for this investigation as it offered the chance for selected young people to actively participate in this quest to understand their experiences of rowing based on their choices and presented through their eyes.

Young people as researchers

A recent recognition of young people's social agency and active participation as researchers has occurred in the social sciences, thereby challenging many taken-for-granted assumptions found in more conventional adult-dominated research (Christensen, 2004; Greene and Hill, 2006). As Pat Thomson (2008a) attests, 'the perspectives of children and young people are of interest to contemporary social scientists precisely because they offer specific insights – about their everyday lives at home and school' (p. 1). How young people communicate with/to adults has traditionally been seen as a diminutive and developing set of adult competencies rather than attempting to explore more rigorously how they communicate and what they are saying.

Although today's young people are living in a visually rich world, we know very little about how they adapt and respond to such environments. France (2004) argues that 'little has been written that deals directly with how we might engage with and encourage the voice of young people' (p. 178). The production of information about children has until recently been couched as proxy reports by researchers or associated professionals reluctant to embrace the emic perspective. Photography reduces the imbalance often associated with traditional literacy forms as many young people can produce images with the same if not more technical skill than adults (Burke, 2007).

Photo-elicitation has been acknowledged as a successful research tool when working with young people (Epstein *et al.*, 2006). Adopting photo-elicitation promotes empowerment of the respondent while at the same time encouraging a 'bridge' between the researcher and respondent (Pink, 2007). During the bridging process, any ambiguity about how selected images should be interpreted can be resolved between photographer and interviewer. This coming together can result in 'deep and interesting talk' (Harper, 2002, p. 23).

There is a claim that young people's photographic practices remain largely unexplored (Tinkler, 2008). Photo-elicitation is classified by Tinkler as a *photo-methods approach*. The more traditional form of this method involves giving young people disposable cameras to record pre-defined projects that are in turn used as a basis for interviews. The rapidly growing use of camera phones and text messaging over the last five years illustrates the increasing interest in the second approach: *cultures of photographic technologies* and young people's responses to new innovations. The third approach is the *photo-making approach*, which is more concerned with young people as photographers from their perspective. The methods approach is basically a communicative tool to enrich their articulation skills. Collectively these three approaches, outlined by Tinkler (2008), 'contribute valuable insights into young people's photographic practices, but these insights are partial and fragmented' (p. 256).

Many of the research methods and processes ascribed to images are still in their infancy. This can be a double-edged sword. On the one hand, a lack of universal conventions means that the collection, analysis and representation of images can lead to a form of visual complacency where results are based on what looks good.

Alternatively, the absence of strict codes of practice allow for the art of image creation to maintain an aesthetic side and thereby support creativity.

Elliot Eisner offers the notion of *epistemic seeing* as a form of knowledge secured through sight (Eisner, 1991). While acknowledging the importance of other senses (see Sparkes, 2009), Eisner uses sight as an exemplar for how, through the visual, individuals can *see* at more than one level. Eisner's contention is that 'primary epistemic seeing depends upon awareness of the particular. Secondary epistemic seeing refers to seeing the particular as a member of a larger set' (p. 68). A photo taken of a rowing crew may make us aware of the particular – such as what they wear or body type – but can also highlight the wider culture of rowing such as the synchronicity of the rowers' movement both within the boat and beyond.

While photographic methods in general and photo-elicitation more specifically are comparatively young, a small but steady line of research is evolving, some of which includes young people as the focus of projects. Orellana (1999) revealed how children's urban experiences were shaped by social class, gender, ethnicity, immigration and racialization. Of most significance was the importance of social relationships in shaping the meanings young people attached to their urban landscapes. In his examination of monastic culture Samuels (2004) conducted or facilitated PEI using participants' (most of whom were young people) photos because 'their own photographs are more likely to reflect the participants' world and thus, better suitable to bridging the culturally distinct worlds of the researcher and the researched' (p. 1530).

Cunningham and Jones (1996) asked children to use cameras to document their after-school activities, choices and spaces, to gauge an understanding of how they used their spare after-school leisure time for independent play. Their study revealed a way of seeing play environments through the eyes of children. The photos revealed children's desire for natural play-spaces and offered some helpful insights for town planners. Burke (2008) explored children's understandings of play. The 'play in focus' project used photo-elicitation to reveal children's needs for safe places, including natural environments and opportunities to meet and cooperatively create intimate and private spaces.

The employment of pictures offers the opportunity to explore the multiple and diverse layers of reality in young people's social worlds. Mizen (2005) argues that photographs taken by young people provide a 'unique, source of evidence' that moves 'beyond this illustrative function, to offer a deeper understanding' (p. 124). Pictures allow connection between contexts, emotions, impressions and associations (Raggl and Schratz, 2004). It is therefore possible to achieve a more holistic portrayal of young people's worlds. Hence, 'photo elicitation may overcome the difficulties posed by in-depth interviewing because it is anchored in an image that is understood at least in part, by both parties' (Harper, 2002, p. 20).

Some of the rowers' selections follow. Each image has been juxtaposed with a brief narrative to accentuate the interplay between image and word, word and image.

These two parents drove the truck with the boats to the regatta. Yea, those are the drivers – it was like three days driving all that way yea, and they were

Figure 11.2 Sam's first choice

looking forward to this race so much, the whole Maadi Cup and before the race
was on they were down there, standing by the big screen as well and they were
watching that there and then they came down, they were on the phone like
commentating to their husbands what's happening and then they started sprint-
ing down to the lakeside with their phones running and smiling and it was like
getting to the end of the racing on to the middle and everyone looks silent and
they jump on the fences and tell them like where the [crew] were going to fin-
ish cos we couldn't see . . . so this is like big stuff at the moment, cos weren't
supposed to be in there [as contenders]. They couldn't help themselves, it was
really good fun and she had her back to me and I am just like yell out to her and
she'd turn around like, just got her in the shot and that was what Maadi's is
about.

Yes, family gets really uptight in every way, yea it's pretty good. But their
boys got the bronze and they were pumped. If you didn't have parents you
couldn't do it, like they can ask what happened but they are only going to last
until it's like me, where I was my first year they actually get up, wake you up
at 6 or [inaudible] parents up at 5.30 bring us in, but like people that live in
[nearby town] they can get up at 5 o'clock, get ready at 5.30 come in and
then they can drop their kids off so they can go back home, they can go back to
bed, I mean that's huge for the parents as well. They're always up at 4.30
getting up at Lake Karapiro so they're over 6.30 for racing at 7.30. There's a
huge commitment on the parents' part of it. And it's not just time . . . it's
the money it's like $2,000 to row, and if you like over four, four years which I

am going to afford that's $8,000 plus you have got so many other things, I'd spend over $1,000 on drinks a year, like really, it's a way of protein I think tell that is like $100, that's for protein, that's for muscle, so you don't get like muscle cramps. Yea, after races and like salts and stuff as well that's $30 I figured out in the last few months, so it's what it's 60 bucks there and then you have got your food like it's heaps of just your own stuff or the regatta food so. It's pretty hard . . . That's on top of your like Maadi food which costs 120, 130 dollars. Then there's all the clothing, polos . . . you have to fork out for . . . well I don't my parents do, if you didn't have parents like doing this nah I couldn't afford to row he [coach] wouldn't have any rowers. But my parents say if me and my mates row and you're on the river . . . they say if you are doing rowing you are off the street so you are not causing trouble so they support us.

Yea this is the place where we watched the finals. Cos I didn't get through to the final, we pulled up a big sign and we painted a symbol of that it might have been down a bit further it was a good like 25x5 metre sign, it was just huge like so everyone can read it and the whole idea was that when they were racing down that they'd get a nice shot of it. We brought it back and our tent was somewhere in line about there and we laid it across there. We were about in front of 4/10ths line when you have a course that's two kilometres long from start to as far as the course goes like caravans and tents and that's really fun all along the bank. Its so amazing and the water's so cold from the mountains . . . yea amazing scenery like I wouldn't have even known that it was like the rest

Figure 11.3 Sam's second choice

of New Zealand but when we did the road trip all the way down to Twizel and we stopped off everywhere, Pukaki, Tekapo – just so big and the colours . . . Oh it's so cool, and like the dams and like you've got your water and it goes right up into the horizon.

This was at 4 o'clock in the morning we were leaving to drive up to get the flight before heading south for Maadi – And all the parents I mean in slippers, pyjamas, saying their last goodbyes, you can't see it because it is too dark but on that side of the bus over there is all these parents along there and all waving goodbye to their kids. We got up at 2 and then we didn't get to bed till about

Figure 11.4 Sam's third choice

10/11 o'clock that night so it was a long day. We had the bus ride for three hours then go to the airport, then fly south for two hours then into mini-buses with trailers and gear for three hours! And we've had racing not the day after that we had this light train and the day after that we had our first races so . . . And this mother came on to say goodbye and then she came down a bit later on. The bus was full there is two coaches but they're like marking and organising so it didn't really matter for them but . . . Yea, sure and then another guy he rowed for NZ as well, so yea took up to four adults like 38 kids, or something like that. (Sam)

That's my crew, I think that was just after our Maadi 8's race, and we're just going down to watch the boys quad? Just all the crews they hang out together, you're with your own crew all the time, get used to everything with them. You are together all week, no moment to yourself. Sometimes you just put the head-phones in but we always just had speakers, and we're into the same music . . . pretty much just about anything. You share . . . You share everything together except on the plane we sat by randomly chosen people, in alphabetical order so it wasn't quite like that but as soon as you got off plane we went our different ways, but I just gave one of my girls from crew my number and we're still talk-ing generally talk and we never now we are just good friends. I hope it will stay like that. Otherwise we've already, two of our girls that are older have already decided that when they leave they are going to come down and stay at Maadi and watch it just because they're part of the crew, they're going to road trip. We stick together in your novie year, if you don't like rowing then you just quit

Figure 11.5 Nicola's second choice

there but after your second year you can't stop like, pretty much no one . . .
hmmm unexplainable I don't know why – you love rowing it's fun and your
friends are all there.

She's our stroke . . . He's from the boys crew and that's our coach with our
Maadi shirt – he used to row for us, not way back he's the same age as my
brother so he's 21 this year I think. We thought the shirts would be hot [as a tro-
phy] but it wasn't as much as we hoped. But we didn't really get time to swap
our shirts because we had to be in them once and you can't really like people
would like to see what shirts they are, like you can't just hold it up, we're at the
same time as you are swapping them and cause we are in our numbers ones
[formal school uniform] it's too hard. This was afternoon tea and we'd just
finished doing our homework and we'd just come and get some food and
Patrick just eats cereal all day . . . I think the camp ground had got some fridges
just for them, cause we had to set up our own kitchen cause kitchen was taken
over by the other people, other schools. Our coach, he tells us what we're not
allowed to eat. So this is obviously some of the food, you have your own junk
as well, in the cabins. They tell us we are not supposed to bring any junk food
obviously but, we're allowed a few lollies after a race, to get our sugar levels
back up. But I ended up bringing some noodles just to snack on and like some
muesli bars we are allowed to have but that's all. Yea but soon as our last
race, we'd go and bought chocolate from the shop cause we're allowed to after
that. All our meals are eaten together, just like everybody – the whole club.
(Nicola)

Figure 11.6 Nicola's third choice

Figure 11.7 Dom's first choice

My favourite, he's one of my mates. Oh, it is just showing how happy he was after getting his medal and knowing that we were the best in NZ and stuff like that it was just a good feeling. We got third in our quad. His name's Brent Walker and everyone calls him Sherman, and because he looks like Sherman from American Pie, and he's pretty cool sometimes but then he does get annoying . . . We're all in the same year level and stuff so we all know each other. He's in his number one's cos he's just been to the medal presentation . . . he's not my best mate – we are all probably about the same like we have our ups and downs just like most people. We talk quite a lot out of rowing and stuff, but we're not, we don't hang out all the time and stuff, we just like we say hi, yea, it's not a major, he's not like one of my main friends at the school. I chose this just to show the happiness that comes through, even if we hadn't have got our medal, last year at Maadi we didn't make an A final, this year we made two. So that was what we wanted and that improvement was great for us.

My second one I picked this food one, It was time for packing up and we were going back to Christchurch so we all got every group like there was us and the seniors, and every group made up, had a box full of food and like if you look at how its bigger than everyone else's and we were like, those would be eights and stuff, and just like the amount we were eating and stuff, I wouldn't usually eat that much and yea. So we got his one and we were pumped because I wanted the energy back and cause rowing takes a lot out of your body. The parents usually would go shopping and stuff through the week so there was always

Figure 11.8 Dom's second choice

heaps of food. So on the day of Maadi they did a big buy up of supplies and that was when we got dropped off at the mall and we went and bought all this fun stuff.

Last Maadi us under 16s knew what we were getting, and the food was great and basically there's pink icing buns, and we always asked for them cause everyone likes them, and we always had heaps. It's pretty good, the food and stuff, like how much we get, there's usually a bowl of fruit or something sitting around so we can just go there and grab it. Lots of food – it takes them like a few hours to peel some potatoes and they go, crockpots, [slow cookers] and they cook in those so they get it all ready like the night before, and then they get it cooked and they've got like the whole menu and stuff laid out, so they know what they're making and stuff. Well usually there's a choice, like with lunch we get all the stuff laid out on the table, and you go along with a bun and choose what you want. And with dinner you help yourself and if your coach wants you to have something else you eat that, and yea, it's just like they don't make, there's nothing yuk that they cook or anything, it's all pretty good. If we didn't eat so much I don't reckon we would have done as well.

That's another person in our quad, Patrick. He's not a morning person. That's why I took it because he just got up or something, and we all woke him up I think that morning. That was our sleep in morning I think, so cause we didn't have any races on our repecharge day, somehow we had a whole day free, so they let us sleep in and get all rested up and then it was like, I don't know,

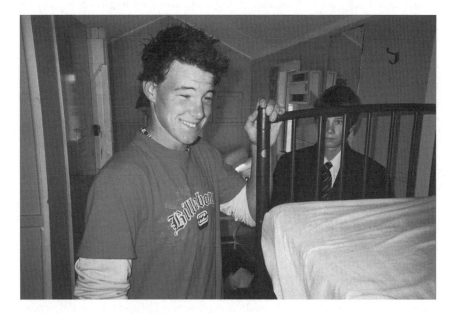

Figure 11.9 Dom's third choice

about sevenish, so we all got him up, cause we thought it was time for him to wake up and yea, then I got a photo of him, cause just to show how tired he was and stuff. There were six of us in the room and if one woke everybody did – It was a tiny cabin in the camping ground but we had everything really, music, next year when it's in Karapiro we'll take down TV, Playstation, and yea, just like whatever anyone takes we really use. We all like rock just like Nickelback and stuff like that. (Dom)

Learning about youth sport from the photographic voice

Sport is an extremely complex social institution, but its multifarious nature should not become a deterrent to exploring it with alternative ways of investigation. There can be little doubt that sport plays a significant role in the lives of many youth. The challenge for educators and providers is to offer an environment and a (co)curriculum that will arouse and support the interests of youth. Schools need to demonstrate innovative and progressive examples of how sport can be more meaningful to our students as well as to the wider educational setting. The invitation is for teachers and coaches to find appropriate solutions to the requirements of adolescent development. At a time when many adolescents are searching for something to identify with, sport should be utilized better,

> because sport has the elements that produce, for many individuals, the stimulus necessary to extend themselves further than they do in many other aspects

of their lives, surely if we understand more about these great moments we would be able to help athletes experience more of them and get more out of them. (McInman and Grove, 1991, p. 348)

Such personal reflection holds huge potential to learn about oneself. Surely if experience and reflection (as evidenced through this photographic activity) are part of participation, a more detailed and complete understanding of that activity is formed? And perhaps more importantly that same participant is able to ascribe genuine, personal and informed values towards their future decisions about sport and physical activity. As Peter Arnold so eloquently suggests:

> For the person in search of self and authenticity sport is a possible answer. It offers a form of freedom in which meanings and values stem from the choices and decisions that are made and lived out in real and committed terms. Once found these meanings and values become motivations for participating in the continuing quest for authenticity. (Arnold, 1979, p. 41)

Young people who are presented with options for participation must view them as viable, attractive, appropriate and enjoyable. If teachers and coaches are to help students delve more deeply into the underlying meanings of sport, they will need to engage the young people (Morgan, Meier and Schneider, 2001) of this world in discussion and expression of how they experience sport, the personal meanings they attach to things like pleasure, success, delight or joy, rather than merely emphasizing and driving performance. In any educational context sport should emphasize its playfulness, its opportunity for experimentation, its presence as a non-serious option, its potential for self-exploration, to encounter the raft of emotions, to learn of their feelings related to success or defeat, the numerous and often vibrant opportunities for personal expression as well as collective tendencies. If participants and providers work to create activities that are inherently pleasurable and intrinsically satisfying then there is a possible future for sport (Morgan, 2006). Sport should not be something that is prescribed or predictable but rather something that is unpredictable, personal, complex and uncertain. And if adults want to understand what youth need from sport it is necessary to understand the youth community and to utilize channels of communication that promote understanding. There is potential for such understanding to be communicated through visual means.

Viewing the collage of images in this chapter reveals a multiplicity of behaviours, practices and insights into the social landscape of sport and activity contexts. For me it revealed the extent and degree Maadi is valued by these student photographers, particularly for its socialness. Despite its highly competitive nature this regatta is important to young people as an opportunity to socialize and explore individual identities. For many of these students Maadi is both gruelling and gregarious. If youth are to be presented with options for participation then the options must be viewed as viable, attractive, appropriate and enjoyable. This could mean that sport is offered in educational settings in a way that equality and excellence are both recognized. The two must be complementary and mutually enhancing.

This project reveals the importance of visual research methods to help understand the nuances of young people's lives, life beyond the school gates, life within other contexts that provide the conjoint to school culture. The challenge for all forms of ethnography this century will be to explore the many sites of social practice that connect and reveal the multiple arenas that our students inhabit: schools, homes, extra-curricular activities, malls, and so on. Each of these contexts invites detailed and prolonged attention so we may learn more of the pace, diversity and complexity of our students' lives. The images these young people have shared hold huge power and potential in helping us to communicate with and understand both the young people we work with as well as how the world is interpreted through their eyes.

If researchers and educationists are to come to know of any real educational value of sport the answer does not necessarily lie within the arguments of those who are supportive or opposed to the historical or contemporary viewpoints. Rather it may be more pertinent to seek authentic interpretations of sport experiences through the voices and depictions of the direct receivers, the students. By engaging with students through appropriate means it may be possible to discover what and how they gain educational benefits from their sport participation. Any dialogue, however, must be empowering and relevant for students. What counts as educational may be a good place to start. Images help to make contact with the lives of strangers through the constant creation of image and conversation, conversation and image. While there is huge scope and promise for this research medium, it remains to be seen whether researchers within our field will realize that potential. Visual depictions reveal the emotion, the tensions, the intensity, the release, the friendships associated with sporting settings and participants, yet each and every one of us will take different interpretations from such depictions. Interpretations will be constantly shifting and changing, keeping in line with a society that is never static, always reinventing itself. Weber has recently argued:

> Whether they are visual or imagined; symbolic or literal; one-, two-, or three-dimensional; analog or digital; material or virtual; drawn with words or with lines; captured by the lens, the brush, the pen, or the poetic eye, images are constantly subject to reconstructions and reinterpretations. (Weber, 2008, p. 42)

Photo-elicitation, photo-voice or any form of visual research offers an alternative kind of data that allows us to reposition the questions we ask – questions that perhaps verbal information may not address (Stewart and Floyd, 2004). Technology now allows us to slow down and even revisit our observations, and arguably enhance the opportunity for reflexivity towards the interpretation process. The more we look, the more we see; the more we see, the more we learn; the more we learn, the more we understand. However, seizing the opportunities that technology now offers for representing research and its findings is no easy task. For visual researchers, representation is compounded by a reluctance of the wider research community to look beyond the privileged word. Andrew Sparkes (2008) recently highlighted the risk of working on the fringes of representation, warning:

Despite the many potential benefits for researchers in [sport and physical education] using new forms of representation, particularly in terms of communicating their findings to a diverse range of audiences, those who attempt to do so feel like artistic intruders. Their work tends to be greeted with suspicion, even hostility, and questions are raised as to whether it constitutes legitimate or 'proper' research. (p. 661)

Nevertheless, the potential that visual research holds for helping us to understand the ways, needs and experiences of our students exists. If we delay such inquiry we delay a fuller understanding.

Like Weber (2008), I am optimistic that the reporting of research and the representation of findings in the humanities and social sciences (including sport and physical education) will see an increasing utilization of images. Like any research method, photographs can provide only a partial and imperfect interpretation of human experience, but the full potential of photography and its visual cousins is still unrealized. In particular, I hope that visual methods will be seen as a viable and effective way to empower and explore the voices of young people to further our understanding of the meanings they ascribe to their sporting and wider school experiences.

References

Andrews, J.C. (1999) 'From school sport to sporting excellence: respecting the rights of minors', *Facta Universitis*, 1 (6): 59–69.

Arnold, P.J. (1979) *Meaning in Movement, Sport and Physical Education*. London: Heinemann.

Bain, L. (1995) 'Mindfulness and subjective knowledge', *Quest*, 47: 238–253.

Banks, M. (2001) *Visual Methods in Social Research*. London: Sage.

Becker, H.S. (2000) 'What should sociology look like in the (near) future?', *Contemporary Sociology*, 29 (2): 333–336.

Brace-Govan, J. (2007) 'Participant photography in visual ethnography', *International Journal of Market Research*, 49 (6): 735–750.

Brettschneider, W.D. and Heim, H. (1997) 'Identity, sport, and youth development', in K.R. Fox (ed.) *The Physical Self: From Motivation to Well-being* (pp. 205–228). Champaign, IL: Human Kinetics.

Bruner, E.M. (ed.) (1984) *Text, Play and Story: The Construction and Reconstruction of Self and Society*. Washington, DC: American Ethnological Society.

Burke, C. (2007) 'The view of the child: releasing "visual voices" in the design of learning environments', *Discourse: Studies in the Cultural Politics of Education*, 28 (3): 359–372.

Burke, C. (2008) 'Play in focus: children's visual voice in participative research', in P. Thomson (ed.) *Doing Visual Research with Children and Young People* (pp. 23–35). London: Routledge.

Christensen, P.H. (2004) 'Children's participation in ethnographic research: issues of power and representation', *Children & Society*, 18: 165–176.

Clark, C.D. (1999) 'The autodriven interview: a photographic viewfinder into children's experience', *Visual Sociology*, 14: 39–50.

Coles, R. and Nixon, N. (1998) *School*. Toronto: Little, Brown & Company.

Collier, J. and Collier, M. (1986) *Visual Anthropology: Photography as a Research Method*. Albuquerque: University of New Mexico Press.

Csikszentmihalyi, M. (1997) *Living Well: The Psychology of Everyday Life*. London: Phoenix Publishing.

Cunningham, C. and Jones, M. (1996) 'Play through the eyes of children: use of cameras to study after-school use of leisure time and leisure space by pre-adolescent children', *Society and Leisure*, 19: 341–361.

Curry, T.J. (1986) 'A visual method of studying sports: the photo-elicitation interview', *Sociology of Sport Journal*, 3: 204–216.

Deppeler, J., Moss, J. and Agbenyega, J. (2008) 'The ethical dilemmas of working the visual and digital across space', in J. Moss (ed.) *Researching Education Visually, Digitally, Spatially* (pp. 229–242). Rotterdam: Sense Publishing.

Eisner, E. (1991) *The Enlightened Eye: Qualitative Inquiry and the Enhancement of Educational Practice*. New York: Macmillan Publishing Co.

Emmison, M. (2004) 'The conceptualization and analysis of visual data', in D. Silverman (ed.) *Qualitative Research: Theory, Method and Practice*. London: Sage.

Emmison, M. and Smith, P. (2000) *Researching the Visual: Images, Objects, Contexts and Interactions in Social and Cultural Inquiry*. London: Sage.

Epstein, I., Stevens, B., McKeever, P. and Baruchel, S. (2006) 'Photo elicitation interview (PEI): using photos to elicit children's perspectives', *International Journal of Qualitative Methods*, 5 (3): 1–9.

France, A. (2004) 'Young people', in S. Fraser, V. Lewis, S. Ding, M. Kellett and C. Robinson (eds) *Doing Research with Young People* (pp. 175–190). London: Sage.

Freeman, M. (ed.) (1997) *The Moral Status of Children: Essays on the Rights of a Child*. London: Martinus Nijhoff Publishers.

Grady, J. (2008) 'Visual research at the crossroads' [electronic version], *Forum: Qualitative Social Research*, 9. Online. Available at: http://www.qualitative-research.net/fqs/.

Grant, B. and Pope, C. (2007) 'Sport in secondary school: sport for all or sport for some', in C. Collins and S. Jackson (eds) *Sport in New Zealand Society* (pp. 246–262). Palmerston North: Dunmore Press.

Greene, S. and Hill, M. (2006) 'Researching children's experience: methods and methodological issues', in S. Greene and D. Hogan (eds) *Researching Children's Experience: Approaches and Methods* (pp. 1–21). London: Sage.

Grenfell, C.C. and Rinehart, R. (2003) 'Skating on thin ice: human rights in youth figure skating', *International Review for Sociology of Sport*, 38: 79–97.

Harper, D. (1984) 'Meaning and work: a study in photo elicitation', *International Journal of Visual Sociology*, 2: 20–43.

Harper, D. (2002) 'Talking about pictures: a case for photo elicitation', *Visual Studies*, 17 (1): 13–26.

Harper, D. (2003) 'Framing photographic ethnography', *Ethnography*, 4 (2): 241–266.

Harris, A. (2006) 'Introduction: critical perspectives on child and youth participation in Australia and New Zealand', *Children, Youth and Environments*, 16 (2): 220–230.

Irvine, P. (2008) *The Maadi Cup Story*. Wanganui: Peter Irvine.

Jenkings, K.N., Woodward, R. and Winter, T. (2008) 'The emergent production of analysis in photo elicitation: pictures of military identity', *Forum: Qualitative Social Research*, 9 (3): Art 30.

Kleiber, D.A. (1983) 'Sport and human development: a dialectical interpretation', *Journal of Humanistic Psychology*, 23 (4): 76–95.

Margolis, E. (1990) 'Visual ethnography: tools for mapping the AIDS epidemic', *Journal of Contemporary Ethnography*, 19: 370–391.

McInman, A.D. and Grove, J.R. (1991) 'Peak moments in sport: a literature review', *Quest*, 43: 333–351.

McQuire, S. (1998) *Visions of Modernity: Representations. Memory. Time and Space in the Age of the Camera*. London: Sage.

Mizen, P. (2005) 'A little "light work"? Children's images of their labour', *Visual Studies*, 20: 124–139.

Morgan, W. (2006) 'Philosophy and physical education', in D. Kirk, D. Macdonald and M. O'Sullivan (eds) *Handbook of Physical Education* (pp. 97–108). London: Sage.

Morgan, W., Meier, K.V. and Schneider, A.J. (eds) (2001) *Ethics in Sport*. Champaign, IL: Human Kinetics.

Moss, J. (ed.) (2008) *Researching Education Visually, Digitally, Spatially*. Rotterdam: Sense Publishing.

Moustakas, C. (1994) *Phenomenological Research Methods*. Thousand Oaks, CA: Sage.

New Zealand Secondary Schools Sports Council (2007) Census of sport participation, unpublished document. Christchurch: New Zealand Secondary Schools Sports Council.

Orellana, M.F. (1999) 'Space and place in an urban landscape. Learning from children's views of their social worlds', *Visual Sociology*, 14: 73–89.

Pink, S. (2003) 'Interdisciplinary agendas in visual research: re-situating visual anthropology', *Visual Studies*, 18 (2): 179–192.

Pink, S. (2007) *Doing Visual Ethnography* (2nd edn). London: Sage.

Piper, D. and Frankham, J. (2007) 'Seeing voices and hearing pictures: image as discourse and the framing of image-based research', *Discourse: Studies in the Cultural Politics of Education*, 28 (3): 373–387.

Pole, C.J. (2004) 'Visual research: potential and overview', in C.J. Pole (ed.) *Seeing is Believing? Approaches to Visual Research. Studies in Qualitative Methodology* (Vol. 7, pp. 1–7). Amsterdam: Elsevier.

Pope, C.C. (2009) 'Sport pedagogy through a wide-angled lens', in L. Housner, M. Metzler, P. Schempp and T. Templin (eds) *Historic Traditions and Future Directions in Research on Teaching and Teacher Education in Physical Education* (pp. 227–236). Morgantown: FIT Publishing.

Prosser, J. (1992) 'Personal reflections on the use of photography in an ethnographic case study', *British Educational Research Journal*, 18 (4): 397–413.

Prosser, J. (1998) *Image-Based Research: A Sourcebook for Qualitative Researchers*. London: Falmer Press.

Prosser, J. (2007) 'Visual methods and the visual culture of schools', *Visual Studies*, 22 (1): 13–30.

Raggl, A. and Schratz, M. (2004) 'Using visuals to release pupils' voices: emotional pathways into enhancing thinking and reflecting on learning', in C.J. Pole (ed.) *Seeing is Believing? Approaches to Visual Research. Studies in Qualitative Methodology* (Vol. 7, pp. 147–162). Amsterdam: Elsevier.

Rees, C.R. (1990) 'What price victory? Myths, rituals, athletics and the dilemma of schooling', in T. Williams, L. Almond and A. Sparkes (eds) *Sport and Physical Activity: Moving Towards Excellence* (pp. 74–79). London: E & FN Spon.

Rose, G. (2007) *Visual Methodologies: An Introduction to the Interpretation of Visual Materials* (2nd edn). London: Sage.

Samuels, J. (2004) 'Breaking the ethnographer's frame', *American Behavioral Scientist*, 47 (12): 1528–1550.

Sands, R.R. (2002) *Sport Ethnography*. Champaign, IL: Human Kinetics.

Schwartz, D. (1989) 'Visual ethnography: using photography in qualitative research', *Qualitative Sociology*, 12 (2): 119–154.

Seippel, O. (2006) 'The meanings of sport: fun, health, beauty or community?', *Sport in Society*, 9 (1): 51–70.

Sparkes, A. (2008) 'Sport and physical education: embracing new forms of representation', in J.G. Knowles and A.L. Cole (eds) *Handbook of the Arts in Qualitative Research* (pp. 653–664). Los Angeles: Sage.

Sparkes, A. (2009) 'Ethnography and the senses: challenges and possibilities', *Qualitative Research in Sport and Exercise*, 1 (1): 21–35.

Stanczak, G.C. (2007) 'Introduction: Images, methodologies, and generating social knowledge', in G.C. Stanczak (ed.) *Visual Research Methods: Image, Society And Representation* (pp. 1–22). Los Angeles: Sage.

Stewart, W.P. and Floyd, M.F. (2004) 'Visualizing leisure', *Journal of Leisure Research*, 36 (4): 445–460.

Thomson, P. (2008a) 'Children and young people: voices in visual research', in P. Thomson (ed.) *Doing Visual Research with Children and Young People* (pp. 1–20). London: Routledge.

Thomson, P. (ed.) (2008b) *Doing Visual Research with Children and Young People*. London: Routledge.

Tinkler, P. (2008) 'A fragmented picture: reflections on the photographic practices of young people', *Visual Studies*, 23 (3): 255–266.

Wagner, J. (2007) 'Observing culture and social life: documentary photography, fieldwork, and social research', in G.C. Stanczak (ed.) *Visual Research Methods: Image, Society and Representation* (pp. 23–60). Los Angeles: Sage.

Walker, R. (1993) 'Finding a silent voice for the researcher: using photographs in evaluation and research', in M. Schratz (ed.) *Qualitative Voices in Educational Research* (pp. 72–92). London: Falmer.

Walker, R.W. and Weidel, J. (1985) 'Using pictures in a discipline of words', in R. Burgess (ed.) *Field Methods in the Study of Education*. Lewes: Falmer Press.

Weber, S. (2008) 'Visual images in research', in J.G. Knowles and A.L. Cole (eds) *Handbook of the Arts in Qualitative Research* (pp. 41–53). Los Angeles: Sage.

Epilogue

12 Hearing, listening and acting

Jonathan Long and David Carless

We both did all right in physical education and sport while at school; if not the very best, at least more likely to be picked than picked on. (Well, DC was a bit better than that, as we suspect were the other authors in this collection.) Like the other contributors we might be seen as establishment insiders from the perspective of the young people in these research projects, though not perhaps by the teachers/deliverers. It is interesting that it is us – and 'people like us' – who take on the task of understanding and making sense of the experiences of young people who are perhaps not having a similarly positive experience in physical education or sport.

We might also add that we are white males. We say this not as some authorial device, but because we believe it important to understand what shapes our own perspectives because that underpins our interpretations of the accounts of others. Just as we have come to appreciate how the ability of respondents to 'enact some identities or realities rather than others is highly contingent on the power-laden space in and through which our experiences are lived' (Valentine and Sporton, 2009, p. 748), so too must we recognize the same for ourselves. That same principle applies to others too, so that in order to understand the formulation of policy and practice in physical education and sport we need to recognize the social and political forces that have shaped those who devise them.

In this closing contribution we reflect on how what *we do and think* – as researchers and insiders – might shape the knowledge we produce through our research. We try to structure our reflections along the lines of some key issues and themes we detect across the chapters that raise important epistemological issues about how we can know the lives of others. In doing so, we want to engage with the implications of these themes and issues in terms of accessing, listening to, responding to and acting upon young people's voices. In the spirit of improving *our* practice as researchers, we hope to identify some ways through which future studies may enhance our understanding of young people's needs and experiences in physical education and youth sport settings.

Engagement with the research process

There is a good argument that research has an ethical responsibility to engage those who are normally seen as non-compliant. Yet non-compliance may well extend to rejection of research and researchers. We contend that approaches that manage to convey the value attached to the experiences, views and stories of young people are more likely to elicit their participation. Asking for their help tends to reverse the typical adult–child authoritative relationship (Erdman and Lampe, 1996) and gives credence to young people's experiences of 'reality'.

Purely observational techniques aside, the success of research requires participants to 'buy in' to the process. In an earlier piece of work (Long and Dart, 2001) with young people 'at risk' we used the inducement of a music voucher to try to encourage their involvement in the research process, only to be rebuffed by one youngster, who retorted, 'I can easily go out and nick it if I want one'. Several of the chapters in this edited collection report projects where securing that commitment has been recognized as a vital part of the study, such as Meegan, Enright and O'Sullivan, and Pope (Chapters 6, 10 and 11, respectively).

One starting point for researchers embarking on the kinds of approach we advocate here is to consider what potential participants might gain from the research process: why *should* they participate? After all, if done well, this kind of research is intense and demanding for participants – they are being asked to 'expose themselves'. There are likely to be limits to how much they are willing to divulge. This will be a function of the interplay between what people are prepared to tell us and what they think we want to hear, which re-emphasizes the relationship between researcher and participant around the question of 'matching' (Long and Wray, 2003). Consider the implications of the researcher being, for example, older, middle-class, non-local and an academic from a different ethnic group.

One of us (JL) has previously suggested that when researching experiences of racism in sport, interviews revealed far more than would have been the case with questionnaires. Perhaps because of the sensitivity of the topic, when it was first raised sportspeople denied that racism happened, or else downplayed it. Only later did they confide: 'It was only because we were talking to them for some time that they became sufficiently confident to discuss such experiences' (Long, 2008, p. 244). In this collection Oliver (Chapter 3) argues for the need to go further, especially when working with young people, believing that deeper knowledge comes from less direct approaches developed over time in repeated encounters. Without detailed exploration, rationalizations and excuses may be too readily accepted and act as a barrier to understanding.

The collection contained in these pages uses a range of different research techniques. We are wary of privileged truth claims for any particular model of research, but like the other authors in this collection want to encourage the use of imaginative techniques that have to struggle to overcome the label of 'alternative'. Cothran in this volume (Chapter 4) contends that there is another value hierarchy that is not addressed by conventional scorings and rankings in questionnaires. Using techniques like those proposed by these authors involves starting from the position that students are varied and that different people take different things from the 'same' experience. The kind of knowledge subsequently produced allows a more nuanced understanding of the student experience. The challenge then, of course, is to devise programmes that will maximize engagement and positive outcomes. For that to work it is not just young people, but practitioners (who may also be young) as well who need to embrace the research. If good relations are not established between researchers, practitioners and young people it can be easy to read research findings as implied criticism. However, it is precisely because we do not underestimate the challenges associated with delivering good practice that we feel it important that research provides practitioners with the best insights possible.

Issues of voice and hearing untellable stories

An important task for us to this end – as researchers and as practitioners – is to reflect on which of the many voices in sport and physical education we listen to and privilege. There is pressure on practitioners and researchers (and, perhaps, managers and politicians?) to listen to the most strident. A challenge for researchers, however, is to make sure that less strident voices are not overlooked. Each contributor in this volume has presented an account of research that offered young people – often young people who are typically 'silenced' – the opportunity to *speak* about their lives. As Gilligan (1993) observes, the opportunity to speak is essential if individuals are to engage with – and, perhaps, subvert – social and cultural processes that shape or constrain their lives. Oliver, for example, has highlighted the importance of this by suggesting that a preparedness to hear what young people have to say via research channels may encourage them to engage more fully in physical education and sport.

Opportunities to create and share stories of one's life (in some form or another) are important at the personal level too because, as Crossley (2000) suggests, through storying our lives we have the opportunity to construct and claim an identity. Sharing stories of our lives helps us 'make sense' of our experiences in relation to the sociocultural context in which we are each immersed because, in McLeod's (1997, p. 40) terms, stories offer 'a means of contextualising or locating feelings and emotions within a broader framework of meaning'. These points reinforce the importance of supporting young people in telling their stories and the need for us (as researchers and practitioners) to take seriously the stories that arise.

While telling one's story can be a positive experience for a participant, the process can also, as the preceding chapters show, provide researchers with theoretical and practical insights regarding an individual's circumstances. But what of those individuals whose stories remain silent? What of those who are unwilling or unable to tell their stories? Do these individuals' experiences matter? Might their stories have something new to offer, something qualitatively different from stories already told?

There are good reasons why some young people may be disinclined to voice their stories – one of which, as Hickey notes in this volume (Chapter 7), involves power relations. To what extent – in light of this power differential – are young people *able* to voice stories that deviate substantially from 'expected' and 'sanctioned' stories? Or, to take a different perspective, to what extent might individuals feel the need to tell stories of bravura or deception as a way to subvert or challenge any power differential? What might *this* strategy tell us about a participant's engagement with the research process and the researcher? Just as people from different classes and ethnicities react to physical education in different ways, so they may respond to particular research methods in different ways (see Lee in this volume, Chapter 2).

A further reason why a story is not voiced might be an individual's *inability* to tell his or her story through issues to do with communication. In this regard, Booth and Booth (1996, p. 56) describe *inarticulateness* among participants who had a learning disability as an 'inability to communicate fluently in words ... generally overlaid by other factors including a lack of self-esteem, learned habits of compliance, social isolation or loneliness, and the experience of oppression'. For these authors, developing a narrative account of the experiences of a person who is 'inarticulate' is particularly challenging – though not impossible – and requires alternative approaches. It should be pointed out that the ability to engage with the prescribed techniques, language and expression of the researcher is something that should be considered in any study and not just restricted to the kind of work considered here.

There are other approaches to data collection that may offer ways round this kind of difficulty. Creatively employing photography as Pope has done in this volume (Chapter 11) offers an alternative way to explore how young people 'experience sport, the personal meanings they attach to things like pleasure, success, delight or joy' (p. 204). Meegan in this volume (Chapter 6) demonstrates another approach by including within the text records of her own observations of interactions in a physical education setting. Elsewhere, Sparkes (2009) provides further food for thought by challenging ethnographers to attend to multiple senses – smell, touch, hearing and vision – in order to develop forms of 'carnal knowing' (Mellor and Shilling, 1997) that focus on participants' embodied ways of knowing, through connecting with the senses. By finding ways to access these kinds of 'data', we have the chance to include the experiences – and therefore 'voices' – of individuals who might otherwise fail to be represented within more traditional interview methods. These kinds of data are likely to call for alternative approaches to analysis and representation if they are to make their way into our research reports; we consider some possible strategies below.

A third possible reason for silence relates to the difficulty of putting certain kinds of experiences into story form. This problem is – in part at least – sociocultural because, as McLeod (1997, p. 94) notes, 'Even when a teller is recounting a unique set of individual, personal events, he or she can only do so by drawing upon story structures and genres drawn from the narrative resources of a culture'. In this regard, Frank (1995, p. 3) points out that:

> From their families and friends, from the popular culture that surrounds them, and from the stories of other . . . people, storytellers have learned the formal structures of narrative, conventional metaphors and imagery, and standards of what is and is not appropriate to tell.

Smith and Sparkes (2008, p. 218) observe that, as a result, some stories are more 'tellable' than others, depending on the situation and the audience. In this regard, tellability 'is something negotiated by the teller and listener in particular local contexts'. 'Untellable' stories have been explored in subjects as diverse as trauma (e.g. Etherington, 2003), physical illness (e.g. Frank, 1995), disability (e.g. Smith and Sparkes, 2008), mental illness (e.g. Stone, 2006), sexuality (e.g. Carless, in press), drug or substance misuse (e.g. Etherington, 2007) and sexual abuse (e.g. Douglas and Carless, 2009a). All of these might be intimately bound to the subject matter of this book. Both Sandford, Armour and Duncombe, and Sykes, in their respective chapters in this volume (Chapters 5 and 8), for example, explore young people's experiences that are likely to be difficult for them to portray in story form.

Stories can be experienced as untellable, McLeod (1997) suggests, through an absence of accessible narrative templates within a particular culture upon which an individual may 'scaffold' her or his personal story. Frank (1995), for example, identifies an absence of alternatives to the dominant medical narrative in western culture to guide the life stories of people who are experiencing cancer. He shows how a *restitution* narrative – which, he suggests, tends to dominate exchanges between ill people and health professionals, family, friends and the media – fails to provide a usable template for those individuals who are unable to achieve restitution or 'cure'. Frank (1995) identifies two alternative narrative types – *chaos* and *quest* narratives – which offer alternative scripts that may better 'fit' some people's experience of illness.

In sport contexts, Douglas and Carless (2006) describe a dominant *performance* narrative (where performance outcomes override all other areas of life), which can act to shape and constrain the stories and experiences of people in sport, silencing alternative stories and inhibiting alternative 'ways of being'. They show how other story types – such as *discovery* (Carless and Douglas, 2009) and *relational* (Douglas, 2009; Douglas and Carless, 2009b) narratives – tend to be silenced or suppressed within elite sport contexts where a performance story is *expected*. In other words, the plot of many stories in sport revolves around winning, or striving to win. While athletes may talk about relationships with others, it is often within the context of a performance story. For example, an athlete might say: 'I couldn't have done it without my father/coach/partner'. This is not a relational story – it is an excerpt of a typical performance story because the plot remains focused on the performance as opposed to the relationship. In this sense, relationships (if they are storied at all) tend to be storied as important on the basis of how they support or facilitate performance.

Awareness of alternative narratives (such as relational or discovery narratives) has the potential to support others in telling *their* stories, particularly when their stories contravene expectations of tellability. Alternative narrative scripts support the personal stories that do not align with the contours of a dominant narrative. On this basis, circulating alternative stories can help to affirm an individual's life, voices and experiences as being worth telling, and thus worth living and claiming (Smith and Sparkes, 2008).

A fourth (and related) reason why certain stories may fail to be 'voiced' concerns *our* ability (as researchers, coaches, teachers) to *hear* threatening or anxiety-provoking stories that stray beyond our own preconceptions or expectations.

Douglas and Carless (2008a) document how sports coaches often failed to accept alternative stories from professional tournament golfers on the basis of their expectation that the life story of any successful athlete *must* conform to a performance narrative. In terms of the performance narrative, Douglas and Carless (2008a: 39) write:

> coaches are highly familiar with this type of story and are likely to accept it as 'the way things are' rather than challenge the socially constructed nature of this discourse. In contrast, relationally-oriented stories are generally *not* widely told or heard . . . In this light, relational stories can be understood as contravening what people generally expect to hear in a story about life in elite sport. As a result, the listener is challenged and has to work hard to make sense of the story precisely because it is at odds with the dominant narrative.

When it comes to alternative stories, there is a danger that the *listener* – researcher, teacher, coach – inadvertently 'steers' the storyteller towards a more 'acceptable' story. By doing so, Frank (1995) notes, we deny not only the person telling the story but also the world in all its possibilities. It is on this basis that Smith and Sparkes (2008, p. 234) suggest that difficult-to-hear stories 'have much to teach us, if only we listen, look long enough, and stay with them'.

To 'stay with' and support this kind of story entails a different orientation towards stories than is often found in academic contexts, one that moves away from 'thinking about' a story – i.e. reducing it to content and then analysing that content – towards 'thinking with' a story. Ellis and Bochner (2000, p. 753) characterize thinking with a story as 'allowing yourself to resonate with the story, reflect on it, become part of it'. Through this process, Douglas and Carless (2009a, p. 317) suggest, 'the boundaries between self (listener or reader) and other (story character) begin to be bridged in a way that can facilitate a deeper level of understanding and empathy'. This orientation is an important first step, we suggest, in opening up other ways to *represent* stories that, subsequently, have the potential to influence or educate others (be they practitioners, researchers, students, or policy makers) through evocative, emotional and embodied ways of knowing. It is to this possibility that we now turn.

Representation and ethics

Promoting alternative voices is only part of the story. Whatever the claims may be to 'let voices speak for themselves', multiple interpretations are always possible. In a joint autobiographical project at the Carnegie Research Institute, challenges to the authors' interpretations came from fellow researchers who shared a similar research agenda and who thought themselves quite close to each other. We emphasize again the point that Burrows (Chapter 9 in this volume) chooses to make through a reading of Foucault that power/knowledge influences the way data are read. Variations in interpretation are not just because of the make-up of the interpreter, but because, as Tsang (2000, p. 45) explains, certain kinds of accounts 'allow for ambiguities to surface and for contradictions to co-exist'. We take the view that this is strength, not a weakness.

As qualitative researchers we often find ourselves, having gathered stories or accounts from our participants, facing the question of how to *represent* these stories effectively to assist others' learning, to contribute to a disciplinary knowledge base, to incite action or to influence policy. The contributors in this book have all done so; they have chosen to tell a particular kind of tale from their research. Sparkes (2002, p. 1) portrays what is perhaps a familiar approach to 'writing up' when he describes writing his doctoral dissertation:

> I was not aware that I was writing any kind of tale at all or that I had any choice of genres. At no point in the process was I asked to reflect on writing as a way of knowing or to reflect on the representational and ethical dilemmas inherent in the act of writing about other people and their lives from my position as a situated author.

In recent years, scholars have begun to question and reflect upon the ways in which we, as researchers, represent those whom we research. Writing itself has become a focus of consideration on the basis that the *way* we write shapes the *kinds* of knowledge we construct and communicate (see Richardson, 2000). Neilsen (2008, p. 386) points out that:

> As language users, we have a range of communication modes available to us. In social science research, we use far fewer than is healthy for the growth of our profession and of our capacity to engage with the world. We have strengthened our muscles for argument, propositional discourse, hortatory expression, categorizing, and creating hierarchies. In social science, and particularly in education, we have let our other muscles languish.

The most common tale in qualitative sport and physical activity research, Sparkes (2002) observes, is the realist tale. This is the tale that has traditionally been 'expected' in academic writing and it is the one the contributors to this book (including ourselves) have all chosen to utilize. Realist tales, according to Sparkes (2002, p. 44):

> are characterized by extensive, closely edited quotations. These are used to convey to the reader that the views expressed are not those of the researcher but are rather the authentic and representative remarks transcribed straight from the mouths of the participants . . . Of course, this is just an illusion . . . a great deal of typographical play, stage-setting ploys, and contextual framing goes into presenting the participant's point of view, and some tricky epistemological stunts are performed on the ethnographic high wire.

This approach to writing – characterized by an analytical orientation of 'thinking about' stories – is, as Sparkes (2002) and Neilsen (2008) note, the traditional mode of academic discourse. As the preceding chapters demonstrate, it holds certain strengths. Key among these, Sparkes (2002, p. 55) suggests, is the way theory and data can be connected in order to create 'spaces for participant voices to be heard in a coherent text, and with specific points in mind. When well constructed, data-rich realist tales can provide compelling, detailed, and complex depictions of the social world'. Realist tales also hold some weakness, however, not least of which is that a reliance on this style of writing means that those 'voices' that are represented are heavily academically mediated: it is the academic's voice that tends to dominate and, ultimately, it is this voice that has the last word. This observation raises questions regarding the degree to which young people's voices can really be heard by those reading the finished text.

So, what are the alternatives to realist forms of writing? One approach that has been used in sport and physical activity contexts is *poetic representation* (e.g. Sparkes *et al.*, 2003; Sparkes and Douglas, 2007). Through poetic approaches, the researcher/participant works to create a meaningful, evocative, distilled representation of the participant's lived experience. The creative processes involved in poetry, according to Richardson (2000), allow us to see, feel and understand the world in new ways. Thus, poetry is 'a practical and powerful method for analyzing social worlds' (Richardson, 2000, p. 933). Leggo (2008) suggests that poetic approaches to analysis and representation can be a powerful way of opening up and exploring otherwise suppressed or silenced stories and experiences. In the context of his own work as an educational researcher:

> Poetry reminds me to challenge the dominant discourses that are typically propagated and supported by school and university curricula and pedagogy. Inspired by poetry, I seek to write in diverse discourses that are alternative, creative, and unconventional. (p. 166)

A second approach that is increasingly used in sport and physical activity research is *storytelling*. Fictional (e.g. Sparkes, 2007; Douglas and Carless, 2008b, 2009a), non-fictional (e.g. Denison, 1996; Carless and Sparkes, 2008) and autoethnographic (e.g. Sparkes, 1996; Tsang, 2000; Douglas, 2009; Carless, in press) approaches that foreground and privilege the story itself – often leaving a story 'intact' for the reader – can complement traditional *story analyst* approaches. Through a storytelling approach, Douglas and Carless (2009a, p. 316) suggest, we are able to 'document, in our minds, the minute details of our characters, their movements and glances, as well as what they feel, hear, see, touch and imagine and then we recreate them in order that others can see'.

Storytellers, according to Frank (2000, p. 361), have an important role to play in research terms because they:

> offer those who do not share their form of life a glimpse of what it means to live informed by such values, meanings, relationships, and commitments. Others can witness what lives within the storyteller's community actually look, feel, and sound like. Storytellers tell stories because the texture of any form of life is so dense that no one can describe this form of life; the storyteller can only invite someone to come inside for the duration of the story.

Thus, as Van Maanen (1988, p. 119) puts it, 'Stories, by their ability to condense, exemplify, and evoke a world, are as valid a device for transmitting cultural under-standings as any other researcher-produced concoction'.

One important strength of storytelling concerns the way this approach to repre-sentation can encourage and support readers in taking an ethical position regarding practice and policy. Both fictional (Douglas and Carless, 2009a) and non-fictional (Douglas and Carless, 2008a) stories have been shown to have pedagogical poten-tial in this regard, stimulating listeners (students and coaches) to take – during sub-sequent discussion – an ethical stand in relation to moral issues raised by the story. Frank (2000, p. 363) identifies this as a priority area in research terms in current times, when he writes that:

> more knowledge may be less important than a clearer sense of value . . . Deciding what to do about what we know requires having an ethical stand-point. The challenge for intellectuals is to help people make policy, clinical, corporate, and personal decisions in a milieu of profound dislocation.

We share Frank's belief that a key task for researchers is to provide the materials through which others may engage with the ethical dilemmas that underlie and pre-empt action concerning contemporary issues in education and social science. While social scientists may not bear the responsibility of formulating emergent ethics, researchers can, as Frank (2000, p. 363) suggests, 'facilitate this emergence by circulating stories, finding commonalities in those stories, and confronting peo-ple with the "inconvenient truth" of stories that have been unheard'.

Relationships with physical education and youth sport

In the midst of debates about national curricula, these approaches cry out for local initiative. In the midst of a moral panic about an obesity epidemic there is a danger of adopting a reductionist view of physical education and youth sport. In the midst of talk of physical education and sport promoting social inclusion we must consider what it is people are being invited to be included in.

Following the current interest in discourse suggests that it is through the telling and retelling of accounts that phenomena like physical education and sport are both experienced and shaped. If some voices go unheard they can have no part in con-structing experience. Observing that educational research so often seems to priori-tize middle-class students (and, we might add, white, non-disabled, male students), Burrows is concerned that we must ensure our research privileges no particular kind of student in shaping what is delivered. More than that, though, given the imbalance in the voices that have shaped practice to date, research has a corrective role to play, and not an easy one.

Sporting institutions might be lauded as culturally resilient or derided for resist-ing cultural change. Further, critical literature typically portrays physical education and sport as reinforcing forms of racism and sexism, but here Oliver, like Ratna (2008), demonstrates how sport can offer the chance to contest these repressive discourses. The challenge then becomes one of identifying what conditions are necessary to facilitate this rather than simply asserting to managers and policy makers that it happens.

The view that sport and physical education should be used to promote inclusion is common in policy circles, with the presumption that everyone should be included irrespective of their assessment of what it is they are being included in, or whether it is something they want for themselves. Recognizing the disjuncture there might be between students' images of themselves and their images of physical education is an important step in devising strategies that might allow young people to be physically active. If students cannot associate their image with that of physical education (we need to remind ourselves that for students this may be seen as an authoritarian field of practice, for example), then in Cothran's American vernacular, they will not 'dress'. It is difficult to arbitrate on whether those individuals who practitioners see as having chosen to disengage have instead been excluded. That is why, for genuine inclusion to occur, it is important that people should be able to contribute to deciding what form participation should take (Long and Bramham, 2006).

Professionals here face a classic dilemma of redistribution: how to meet the needs of the alienated without denying the fulfilment others currently derive from their involvement. If sessions become an exercise in keeping potential troublemakers happy others may be frustrated. The ideal is not to deliver to the lowest common denominator of interest but to use research to identify how more people can develop their physical skills effectively. Cothran is seeking a curriculum that allows multiple goals to be met simultaneously.

So what are physical education and sport about, or rather what should they be about? Surely it is something more than just a tool to counter obesity. Many of the contributions here seek a corrective to the disciplinarian caricature with greater emphasis on fun. Burrows, for example, calls for us to 'foreground the pleasure of movement rather than the need to monitor it'. Fun, yes, and also skill acquisition and physical literacy such that competence allows control and builds confidence. One of the surprises of Oliver's work was that even the 'girly girls' whose value systems seemed at odds with physical education, when invited to design their own activities produced something that addressed many of the teachers' goals.

Given the responsibility for addressing the kind of social dilemmas alluded to at the beginning of this section it is important for those operating in the world of physical education and sport to recognize that it is not independent of more general, and more powerful, social processes. What physical education and sport might contribute to health has been affirmed. However, although the dominant health messages may be about diet and activity, those are not the most insistent voices we hear in a world dominated by consumption. Advertising exhorts us to buy cars and games consoles, to kick back and relax, to eat and watch. And fears for safety frustrate independent activity.

Future directions

In playground culture someone who tells stories makes things up to advance their own position at the expense of someone else. We want to reclaim the label of storytelling for something that gives expression to 'truths' otherwise unheard. If the task of confronting people with stories that have previously tended to be unheard is deemed important – and we believe that it is – then an important future direction for physical education and sport researchers working with young people entails a more thorough and sustained immersion in the questions and challenges of representation: how and why to recount (for others) the stories our participants share (with us). Creative approaches to representation (such as poetic representation, ethnodrama, confessional tales, storytelling), we suggest, have much to offer in terms of the extent to which the emotion of memory can be represented such that others will listen to the 'voices' of young people in sport and physical activity.

In the world of physical education and sport, the approaches represented by the contributions to this collection might be considered 'alternative' to the mainstream, not in a value-free sense, but with an implied inferiority to established routes that can be relied on to deliver 'valid' and 'reliable' findings. What we have tried to suggest here is that those concerned with this field of study might wish to explore fresh approaches, following those who have embraced the narrative turn. This requires us not just to refine research techniques, but to re-learn how to listen, how to experience, empathize and understand. If successful, that might develop a research practice capable of transcending the status quo through an orientation to *what might be*.

The contributions in this volume have sought not just to give voice to the marginalized (Bloor, 1991) but to move the voices of young people from the margin to the centre (Harding, 1991). This involves not just hearing, but actively listening to the stories, with a view to facilitating change. Somewhere along the line someone has to take the step from understanding individual experiences to formulating policy and devising practice. To facilitate this important step we might wish to develop and extend the kind of work described by Enright and O'Sullivan in this volume, where young people are encouraged to become co-researchers or active partners in new research agendas. We might also wish to take seriously the challenge of conducting and representing our research in ways that strive to *engage* and *affect* its audience in an immediate and embodied manner.

References

Bloor, D. (1983) *Wittgenstein: A Social Theory of Knowledge*. New York: Columbia University Press.

Bloor, M. (1991) *Knowledge and Social Imagery*. Chicago, IL: Chicago University Press.

Booth, T. and Booth, W. (1996) 'Sounds of silence: narrative research with inarticulate subjects', *Disability and Society*, 11 (1): 55–69.

Carless, D. (in press) 'Who the hell was *that*? Stories, bodies and actions in the world', *Qualitative Research in Psychology*.

Carless, D. and Douglas, K. (2009) '"We haven't got a seat on the bus for you" or "All the seats are mine": narratives and career transition in professional golf', *Qualitative Research in Sport and Exercise*, 1 (1): 51–66.

Carless, D. and Sparkes, A.C. (2008) 'The physical activity experiences of men with serious mental illness: three short stories', *Psychology of Sport and Exercise*, 9 (2): 191–210.

Crossley, M.L. (2000) *Introducing Narrative Psychology: Self, Trauma and the Construction Of Meaning*. Buckingham: Open University Press.

Denison, J. (1996) 'Sport narratives', *Qualitative Inquiry*, 2 (3): 351–362.

Douglas, K. (2009) 'Storying myself: negotiating a relational self in professional sport', *Qualitative Research in Sport and Exercise*, 1 (2): 176–190.

Douglas, K. and Carless, D. (2006) 'Performance, discovery, and relational narratives among women professional tournament golfers', *Women in Sport and Physical Activity Journal*, 15 (2): 14–27.

Douglas, K. and Carless, D. (2008a) 'Using stories in coach education', *International Journal of Sports Science and Coaching*, 3 (1): 33–49.

Douglas, K. and Carless, D. (2008b) 'The team are off: getting inside women's experiences in professional sport', *Aethlon: The Journal of Sport Literature*, XXV (I): 241–251.

Douglas, K. and Carless, D. (2009a) 'Exploring taboo issues in professional sport through a fictional approach', *Reflective Practice*, 10 (3): 311–323.

Douglas, K. and Carless, D. (2009b) 'Abandoning the performance narrative: two women's stories of transition from professional golf', *Journal of Applied Sport Psychology*, 21 (2): 213–230.

Ellis, C. and Bochner, A. (2000) 'Autoethnography, personal narrative and reflexivity', in N. Denzin and Y. Lincoln (eds) *The Handbook of Qualitative Research* (2nd edn) (pp. 733–768). Thousand Oaks, CA: Sage.

Erdman, P. and Lampe, R. (1996) 'Adapting basic skills to counsel children', *Journal of Counselling and Development*, March/April: 374–378.

Etherington, K. (ed.) (2003) *Trauma, the Body and Transformation: A Narrative Inquiry*. London: Jessica Kingsley Publishers.

Etherington, K. (2007) *Trauma, Drug Misuse and Transforming Identities: A Life Story Approach*. London: Jessica Kingsley Publishers.

Frank, A. (1995) *The Wounded Storyteller*. Chicago, IL: University of Chicago Press.

Frank, A. (2000) 'The standpoint of storyteller', *Qualitative Health Research*, 10 (3): 354–365.

Gilligan, C. (1993) *In a Different Voice: Psychological Theory and Women's Development*. Cambridge, MA: Harvard University Press.

Harding, L. (1991) *Perspectives in Child Care Policy*. London: Longman.

Leggo, C. (2008) 'Astonishing silence: knowing in poetry', in J. Knowles and A. Cole (eds) *Handbook of the Arts in Qualitative Research* (pp. 165–174). Thousand Oaks, CA: Sage.

Long, J. (2008) 'Researching and evaluating sports development', in K. Hylton and P. Bramham (eds) *Sports Development: Policy, Process and Practice* (pp. 236–257). London: Routledge.

Long, J. and Bramham, P. (2006) 'Joining-up policy discourses and fragmented practices: the precarious contribution of cultural projects to social inclusion', *Policy & Politics*, 34 (1): 133–151.

Long, J. and Dart, J. (2001) 'Opening-up: encouraging people to evaluate', *International Journal of Social Research Methodology*, 4 (1): 71–78.

Long, J. and Wray, S. (2003) 'It depends who you are: on asking difficult questions in leisure research', *Loisir et Societé*, 26 (1): 169–182.

McLeod, J. (1997) *Narrative and Psychotherapy*. London: Sage.

Mellor, P. and Shilling, C. (1997) *Re-forming the Body*. London: Sage.

Neilsen, L. (2008) 'Literacy genres: housecleaning – a work with theoretical notes', in J. Knowles and A. Cole (eds) *Handbook of the Arts in Qualitative Research* (pp. 385–395). Thousand Oaks, CA: Sage.

Ratna, A. (2008) 'British Asian females' racialised and gendered experiences of identity and women's football', unpublished PhD thesis, University of Brighton.

Richardson, L. (2000) 'Writing: a method of inquiry', in N. Denzin and Y. Lincoln, (eds) *The Handbook of Qualitative Research* (2nd edn) (pp. 923–948). Thousand Oaks, CA: Sage.

Smith, B. and Sparkes, A.C. (2008) 'Changing bodies, changing narratives and the consequences of tellability: a case study of becoming disabled through sport', *Sociology of Health and Illness*, 30 (2): 217–236.

Sparkes, A.C. (1996) 'The fatal flaw', *Qualitative Inquiry*, 2 (4): 463–494.

Sparkes, A.C. (2002) *Telling Tales in Sport and Physical Activity*. Champaign, IL: Human Kinetics.

Sparkes, A.C. (2007) 'Embodiment, academics, and the audit culture: a story seeking consideration', *Qualitative Research*, 7 (4): 521–550.

Sparkes, A.C. (2009) 'Ethnography and the senses: challenges and possibilities', *Qualitative Research in Sport and Exercise*, 1 (1): 21–35.

Sparkes, A.C. and Douglas, K. (2007) 'Making the case for poetic representations: an example in action', *The Sport Psychologist*, 21 (2): 170–189.

Sparkes, A.C., Nilges, L., Swan, P. and Dowling, F. (2003) 'Poetic representations in sport and physical activity: insider perspectives', *Sport, Education and Society*, 8 (2): 153–177.

Stone, B. (2006) 'Diaries, self–talk, and psychosis: writing as a place to live', *Auto/Biography*, 14: 41–58.

Tsang, T. (2000) 'Let me tell you a story', *Sociology of Sport Journal*, 17 (10): 44–59.

Valentine, G. and Sporton, D. (2009) 'How other people see you, it's like nothing that's inside: the impact of processes of disidentification and disavowal on young people's identities', *Sociology*, 43 (4): 735–751.

Van Maanen, J. (1988) *Tales of the Field*. Chicago, IL: University of Chicago Press.

Index

eBooks – at www.eBookstore.tandf.co.uk

A library at your fingertips!

eBooks are electronic versions of printed books. You can store them on your PC/laptop or browse them online.

They have advantages for anyone needing rapid access to a wide variety of published, copyright information.

eBooks can help your research by enabling you to bookmark chapters, annotate text and use instant searches to find specific words or phrases. Several eBook files would fit on even a small laptop or PDA.

NEW: Save money by eSubscribing: cheap, online access to any eBook for as long as you need it.

Annual subscription packages

We now offer special low-cost bulk subscriptions to packages of eBooks in certain subject areas. These are available to libraries or to individuals.

For more information please contact webmaster.ebooks@tandf.co.uk

We're continually developing the eBook concept, so keep up to date by visiting the website.

www.eBookstore.tandf.co.uk